PARADISO

THE DIVINE COMEDY
PARADISO

DANTE ALIGHIERI

THE JOHN CIARDI
TRANSLATION

THE MODERN LIBRARY
NEW YORK

Acknowledgment is made to *Venture, The Italian Quarterly,*
The Saturday Review, Between Worlds, The Massachusetts Review,
New World Writing, and *Arbor,* in which excerpts
from the present work first appeared.

Canto I was first published in *Italian Quarterly,* 1965.
Canto VIII was first published in *Arbor,* 1961
Canto XXI was first published in *Hartwick Review,* 1967.
Canto XXXIII was first published in *The Rarer Action: Essays in Honor of
Francis Fergusson,* ed. Alan Cheuse and Richard Koffer, 1970.

This edition published by arrangement with
W. W. Norton & Company, Inc., New York.

Jacket illustration: Dante, illumination from an early fifteenth century Italian
manuscript of *The Inferno,* courtesy of The Granger Collection, N.Y.

Library of Congress Cataloging-in-Publication Data is available
ISBN 0-679-60211-9

Random House website address: http://www.randomhouse.com/

Printed in the United States of America on acid-free paper ♾

2   4   6   8   9   7   5   3   1

DANTE ALIGHIERI

Dante Alighieri, the Italian poet whose great allegory *The Divine Comedy* has exerted a profound effect on Western literature and thought, was born in Florence in May 1265. He came from a noble though impoverished family, descendants of the city's Roman founders. Relatively little is known with certainty about Dante's early life, but it is noteworthy that he grew up during the restless period that followed decades of bloody rivalry between two opposing Florentine political groups, the Guelphs and the Ghibellines. His childhood was doubtless colored by stories of this partisan strife from which, as Machiavelli later wrote, "there resulted more murders, banishments and destruction of families than ever in any city known to history."

Dante probably received his early schooling from the Franciscans and the Dominicans; later, he studied rhetoric with the Guelph statesman and scholar Brunetto Latini. Another significant mentor was the aristocratic poet Guido Cavalcanti, who strongly influenced his early work. For the young Dante, writing poetry became an important expression of his passion for art and learning, and of his abiding concern with the nature of love and spiritual fulfillment. A Florentine woman of exceptional beauty, Beatrice Portinari, provided a powerful stimulus to the poet's artistic development. Dante idealized her as the "bringer of blessings," a beatific guide capable of pointing him toward the inner perfection sought by every noble mind. Following her untimely death in 1290, Dante, overcome with grief, celebrated her grace and virtue in *La vita nuova* (1292–1294), a small "book of memory" written in verse and prose. He then sought renewal in an extensive study of theology and philosophy.

In 1295 Dante entered public life and within a few years emerged as a prominent figure in Florentine politics. By then he had entered into an arranged marriage with Gemma Donati, a gentlewoman by whom he had several children. In the summer of 1300 Dante was named one of the six governing magistrates of Florence. During this time he was involved in the clash between two hostile factions of the Guelph party, the Whites and the Blacks. Aligning himself with the White Guelphs, Dante campaigned to preserve the independence of Florence and repeatedly opposed the machinations of Pope Boniface VIII, who was attempting to place all of Tuscany under papal control. In 1301, however, the Black Guelphs seized power, and Dante was banished at once on trumped-up charges of graft, embezzlement, and other transgressions. Later sentenced to death by fire if he returned to Florence, Dante never entered his native city again.

Dante's remaining years were spent with a series of patrons in various courts of Italy. Two uncompleted works date from his early period of exile. *De vulgari eloquentia* (1303–1304), a scholarly tract in Latin on the eloquence of the Italian vernacular, is generally acknowledged to be the key to Dante's artistic inquiries. *Il convivio* (1304–1307), a glorification of moral philosophy, is viewed as the cornerstone of his investigations into knowledge and wisdom. Perhaps as early as 1306, Dante began to compose *The Divine Comedy*, the greatest poem of the Middle Ages and the first masterpiece of world literature written in a modern European language. The Latin treatise *De monarchia* (1312–1313), a practical guide calling for the restoration of peace in Europe under a secular ruler in Rome, is a statement of the poet's political theories. In his final years Dante was given asylum in Ravenna, where he completed *The Divine Comedy* shortly before his death in September 1321.

PARADISO

CANTO I

The Earthly Paradise—The Invocation

*Ascent to Heaven—The Sphere of Fire · The Music of the
Spheres*

Dante states his supreme theme as Paradise itself and invokes the
aid not only of the Muses but of Apollo.

Dante and Beatrice are in *The Earthly Paradise,* the Sun is at
the Vernal Equinox, it is noon at Purgatory and midnight at
Jerusalem when Dante sees Beatrice turn her eyes to stare
straight into the sun and reflexively imitates her gesture. At
once it is as if a second sun had been created, its light dazzling
his senses, and Dante feels the ineffable change of his mortal soul
into Godliness.

These phenomena are more than his senses can grasp, and
Beatrice must explain to him what he himself has not realized:
that he and Beatrice are soaring toward the height of Heaven at
an incalculable speed.

Thus Dante climaxes the master metaphor in which purifica-
tion is equated to weightlessness. Having purged all dross from
his soul he mounts effortlessly, without even being aware of it at
first, to his natural goal in the Godhead. So they pass through *The
Sphere of Fire,* and so Dante first hears *The Music of the Spheres.*

The glory of Him who moves all things rays forth
   through all the universe, and is reflected
   from each thing in proportion to its worth.   3

I have been in that Heaven of His most light,
   and what I saw, those who descend from there
   lack both the knowledge and the power to write.   6

For as our intellect draws near its goal
   it opens to such depths of understanding
   as memory cannot plumb within the soul.   9

Nevertheless, whatever portion time
  still leaves me of the treasure of that kingdom
  shall now become the subject of my rhyme.   12

O good Apollo, for this last task, I pray
  you make me such a vessel of your powers
  as you deem worthy to be crowned with bay.   15

One peak of cleft Parnassus heretofore
  has served my need, now must I summon both
  on entering the arena one time more.   18

Enter my breast, I pray you, and there breathe
  as high a strain as conquered Marsyas
  that time you drew his body from its sheath.   21

O power divine, but lend to my high strain
  so much as will make clear even the shadow
  of that High Kingdom stamped upon my brain,   24

and you shall see me come to your dear grove
  to crown myself with those green leaves which you
  and my high theme shall make me worthy of.   27

So seldom are they gathered, Holy Sire,
  to crown an emperor's or a poet's triumph
  (oh fault and shame of mortal man's desire!)   30

that the glad Delphic god must surely find
  increase of joy in the Peneian frond
  when any man thirsts for it in his mind.   33

Great flames are kindled where the small sparks fly.
  So after me, perhaps, a better voice
  shall raise such prayers that Cyrrha will reply.   36

The lamp of the world rises to mortal view
  from various stations, but that point which joins
  four circles with three crosses, it soars through   39

to a happier course in happier conjunction
  wherein it warms and seals the wax of the world
  closer to its own nature and high function.   42

That glad conjunction had made it evening here
  and morning there; the south was all alight,
  while darkness rode the northern hemisphere;   45

when I saw Beatrice had turned left to raise
  her eyes up to the sun; no eagle ever
  stared at its shining with so fixed a gaze.   48

And as a ray descending from the sky
  gives rise to another, which climbs back again,
  as a pilgrim yearns for home; so through my eye   51

her action, like a ray into my mind,
  gave rise to mine: I stared into the sun
  so hard that here it would have left me blind;   54

but much is granted to our senses there,
  in that garden made to be man's proper place,
  that is not granted us when we are here.   57

I had to look away soon, and yet not
  so soon but what I saw him spark and blaze
  like new-tapped iron when it pours white-hot.   60

And suddenly, as it appeared to me,
  day was added to day, as if He who can
  had added a new sun to Heaven's glory.   63

Beatrice stared at the eternal spheres
　　entranced, unmoving; and I looked away
　　from the sun's height to fix my eyes on hers.　　　66

And as I looked, I felt begin within me
　　what Glaucus felt eating the herb that made him
　　a god among the others in the sea.　　　69

How speak trans-human change to human sense?
　　Let the example speak until God's grace
　　grants the pure spirit the experience.　　　72

Whether I rose in only the last created
　　part of my being, O Love that rulest Heaven
　　Thou knowest, by whose lamp I was translated.　　　75

When the Great Wheel that spins eternally
　　in longing for Thee, captured my attention
　　by that harmony attuned and heard by Thee,　　　78

I saw ablaze with sun from side to side
　　a reach of Heaven: not all the rains and rivers
　　of all of time could make a sea so wide.　　　81

That radiance and that new-heard melody
　　fired me with such a yearning for their Cause
　　as I had never felt before. And she　　　84

who saw my every thought as well as I,
　　saw my perplexity; before I asked
　　my question she had started her reply.　　　87

Thus she began: "You dull your own perceptions
　　with false imaginings and do not grasp
　　what would be clear but for your preconceptions.　　　90

You think you are still on earth: the lightning's spear
　never fled downward from its natural place
　as rapidly as you are rising there."　　　　　　93

I grasped her brief and smiling words and shed
　my first perplexity, but found myself
　entangled in another, and I said:　　　　　　96

"My mind, already recovered from the surprise
　of the great marvel you have just explained,
　is now amazed anew: how can I rise　　　　　99

in my gross body through such aery substance?"
　She sighed in pity and turned as might a mother
　to a delirious child. "The elements　　　　　102

of all things," she began, "whatever their mode,
　observe an inner order. It is this form
　that makes the universe resemble God.　　　105

In this the higher creatures see the hand
　of the Eternal Worth, which is the goal
　to which these norms conduce, being so planned.　108

All Being within this order, by the laws
　of its own nature is impelled to find
　its proper station round its Primal Cause.　　111

Thus every nature moves across the tide
　of the great sea of being to its own port,
　each with its given instinct as its guide.　　114

This instinct draws the fire about the moon.
　It is the mover in the mortal heart.
　It draws the earth together and makes it one.　117

Not only the brute creatures, but all those
  possessed of intellect and love, this instinct
  drives to their mark as a bow shoots forth its arrows. 120

The Providence that makes all hunger here
  satisfies forever with its light
  the heaven within which whirls the fastest sphere. 123

And to it now, as to a place foretold,
  are we two soaring, driven by that bow
  whose every arrow finds a mark of gold. 126

It is true that oftentimes the form of a thing
  does not respond to the intent of the art,
  the matter being deaf to summoning— 129

just so, the creature sometimes travels wide
  of this true course, for even when so driven
  it still retains the power to turn aside 132

(exactly as we may see the heavens' fire
  plunge from a cloud) and its first impulse may
  be twisted earthward by a false desire. 135

You should not, as I see it, marvel more
  at your ascent than at a river's fall
  from a high mountain to the valley floor. 138

If you, free as you are of every dross,
  had settled and had come to rest below,
  that would indeed have been as marvelous 141

as a still flame there in the mortal plain."
  So saying, she turned her eyes to Heaven again.

NOTES

1. *of Him who moves all things:* God as the unmoved mover. Since any change from perfection would have to be toward a lessening, God is changeless in Dante's conception. Himself changeless (unmoved), therefore, he imparts the creating motion to all things.

2–3. *reflected . . . in proportion to its worth:* The more perfect the thing, the more perfectly it will reflect God's perfect shining. The more clouded the glass, so to speak, the less its ability to reflect the light.

4. *that Heaven of His most light:* "That heaven that takes (i.e., "receives" and, by implication, "reflects again") the most of His light." The Empyrean.

5–12. *those who descend . . . lack:* Dante was not a mystic in the pure sense of the word, but all mystics have stressed the ineffability of the mystical experience. How does one convey any rapturous experience once the rapture is over? William James in his *Varieties of Religious Experience* offers a fine introductory discussion of this question. *as our intellect draws near its goal:* The goal of intellect is God.

13–36. THE INVOCATION. Herefore, Dante has invoked the Muses. Now he invokes Apollo himself as the God of Poetry, and as the father of the Muses. Note, too, that Apollo is identified with the Sun and that Dante has consistently used the Sun as a symbol for God.

15. *crowned with bay:* The laurel wreath awarded to poets and conquerors. See also line 29 and XXV, 1–12.

16. *one peak of cleft Parnassus:* Parnassus has two peaks: Nisa, which was sacred to the Muses; and Cyrrha, which was sacred to Apollo. Heretofore Nisa has been enough for Dante's need, but for this last canticle he must summon aid from both peaks (i.e., from all the Muses and from Apollo as well).

20–21. *Marsyas:* The satyr Marsyas challenged Apollo to a singing contest and was defeated. Ovid (*Metamorphoses* VI, 382–400) recounts in gory detail how Apollo thereupon punished him by pulling him out of his skin leaving all the uncovered organs still functioning.

Note that in this godly sport the skin was not pulled off Marsyas but that Marsyas was pulled out of his skin. In citing this incident Dante may be praying that he himself, in a sense, be pulled out of himself (i.e., be made to outdo himself), however painfully. *its sheath:* its skin.

23–27. *make clear even the shadow:* Sense: "Lend me enough power to make clear so much as the shadow of the ineffable light, and your power and my lofty theme will win me a laurel crown." *your dear grove:* The grove in which grows the sacred laurel, or bay.

31. *the glad Delphic god:* Apollo.

32. *Peneian frond:* The laurel or bay, so called for Daphne, daughter of the river god Peneus. Cupid, to avenge a taunt, fired an arrow of love into Apollo and an arrow of aversion into Daphne. Fleeing from the inflamed Apollo, Daphne prayed to her father and was changed into a laurel tree.

36. *Cyrrha will reply:* Cyrrha, Apollo's sacred peak, is here taken for Apollo himself. If Apollo does not heed his prayer, Dante will at least show the way, and perhaps a better poet will come after him and have his prayer answered by Apollo, whereby Paradise will at last be well portrayed.

37–42. THE POSITION OF THE SUN AT THE VERNAL EQUINOX. Short of pages of diagrams, there is no way of explaining Dante's astronomical figure in detail. A quick gloss must do: *the lamp:* The Sun. *various stations:* various points on the celestial horizon from which the sun rises at various times of the year. *four circles with three crosses:* The four circles here intended are: (1) the celestial horizon, (2) the celestial equator, (3) the ecliptic, and (4) equinoxial colure. The equinoxial colure is the great circle drawn through both poles and the two equinoxial points (the solsticial colure, similarly, passes through both poles and the two solsticial points). Since the equinox occurs when the sun crosses the celestial equator, both equinoxial points must lie on the equator and the equinoxial colure must be at right angles to the celestial equator. The celestial equator is the infinite extension of the plane of the earth's equator into the celestial sphere.

When the sun is in the position shown in the diagram the time is sunrise of the vernal equinox and all four circles meet, each of the other three forming a cross with the celestial horizon. Astrologers took this to be a particularly auspicious conjunction. Its *happier course* (line 40) brings the brighter and longer days of summer. Its *happier conjunction* (line 40) with the stars of Aries brings it back to the sign of the first creation (see *Inferno* I, 38–39, note). And certainly the fact that the diagram forms three crosses would weigh it with the good omens of both the cross and trinity. All would once more be in God's shaping hand. So the *wax of the world* (line 41) is warmed and sealed, in a first sense by the warmth of approaching summer, and in a clearly implicit spiritual sense by the favor of God's will upon His creation.

This complicated figure could hardly have failed to suggest, further, some reference to the Four Cardinal Virtues, the Three Theological Virtues, and to the approaching Sun as Divine Illumination, now drawing to the full summer of mankind—for bear in mind that the southern hemisphere, in Dante's geography, was all water: there would be no mankind for the Sun to shine upon in its southern summer.

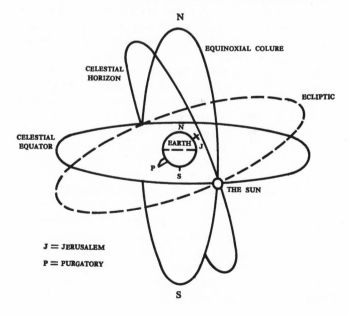

43–44. *evening here and morning there:* At the time Dante returned from drinking the waters of Eunöe. It is now noon, for only at noon could the entire southern hemisphere be alight and the north dark—or so Dante must clearly intend, though I do not understand how that could be.

46. *had turned left:* Beatrice had been facing east with Eunöe before her. She now turns her eyes north to the sun.

47. *no eagle ever:* In the Middle Ages men believed that the eagle was able to stare directly into the sun.

49–54. *and as a ray:* Just as a descending ray of light strikes a reflecting surface and sends a reflected ray back upward, and at the same angle at which it struck the surface, so Beatrice's action in looking at the sun descends upon Dante like a ray from on high that enters through his eyes and strikes upward to his mind giving rise to a "reflected" action.

62. *day was added to day:* Dante perceives the increased brilliance of the light as if God had added a second sun to the sky, and he wonders at it. He does not yet know that the light has grown so much more brilliant because he is soaring through space toward the sun. He believes himself to be still in the Terrestrial Paradise.

Dante's device here, in showing himself as soaring toward God at enormous speed without, at first, realizing that he is soaring, is a superbly conceived climax to the whole theme of Purification as Gradual Weightlessness. In Hell all is gross and heavy. At the start of the Ascent of Purgatory, Dante almost drops from exhaustion. As he mounts and sin is stricken from him, he climbs ever more lightly. Now purified and perfected, he need not even think about mounting on high. His new nature draws effortlessly to God.

68. *Glaucus:* The fisherman Glaucus, noting how his catch revived and leaped into the sea after being laid upon a certain herb, ate some of it and was transformed into a god (Ovid, *Metamorphoses* XIII, 898–968). Staring at Beatrice, Dante feels the beginning inside himself of that change that will make him, too, immortal.

73–75. *the last created part of my being:* The soul, which is created after the body. (See *Purgatorio* XXV, 37–75.) *O Love that rulest Heaven:* God. *whose lamp:* Beatrice as the reflector of God's love.

76–78. *The Great Wheel etc.:* Dante says, literally: "The wheel that Thou, in being desired [i.e., loved] by it, makest eternal." The Great Wheel is the Primum Mobile, its motion deriving from the love of God. *captured my attention:* Indicates that Dante turned his eyes from Beatrice to look up again. *that harmony:* The Music of the Spheres.

80. *ablaze with sun:* Dante believed that the earth's atmosphere extended as high as the Sphere of the Moon. Beyond the Moon is another atmosphere of fire. This sphere of fire was believed to cause lightning. (See also line 115, "the fire about the moon.")

92. *natural place:* The Sphere of Fire. It summons all fire to itself. Conflicting forces of nature force the lightning downward, but the fiery elements dislocated under stress find their way back to their natural place. Dante still has not realized that he and Beatrice are soaring toward Heaven at an incalculable speed.

93. *there:* To the Sphere of Fire.

104. *an inner order:* In relation to one another, and each in its relation to the total and to its final end, as fire to fire (see line 115). The end of man is God; therefore, the purified soul ascends naturally and inevitably to Him.

106. *the higher creatures:* The rational beings of creation: angels, heavenly spirits, and men.

108. *these norms:* The mode and form of lines 103–104.

123–124. *the heaven:* The Empyrean, *the fastest sphere:* The Primum Mobile. The Empyrean does not move and it is beyond space. It is eternal and perfect Love (therefore unchangeable) and holds within its constancy all of space, including the outermost and greatest sphere, the Primum Mobile.

125. *that bow:* The innate impulse of all creatures to seek their place in God.

127–135. The free will of creatures allows them, despite the innate order of all things, to yield to false pleasures and so to resist God's plan as the matter in which the artist works, being base and imperfect, may resist his intent to give it ideal form. One might argue against this figure that the artist in this case, being God, is omnipotent and could, at will, work in perfect matter. But to enter into such an argument would only be to bump heads on the question of fallible free will within an omnipotent creation—a question that has vexed Christian theology for millennia.

141. *that would indeed have been . . . marvelous:* Because then it would be going against the order of the universe. What is purified must ascend to God as inevitably as earthly waters must flow downhill.

CANTO II

Ascent to the Moon—Warning to the Reader

The First Sphere: The Moon—Beatrice Explains the Markings on the Moon

Dante and Beatrice are soaring to *The Sphere of the Moon* at a speed approaching that of light. Dante warns back the shallow reader: only those who have eaten of the knowledge of God may hope to follow him into the last reaches of his infinite voyage, for it will reveal such wonders as only faith can grasp.

His warning concluded, he and Beatrice enter the Sphere of the Moon and pass into the substances of the moon as light into water, as God incarnated himself into man, or as the saved soul reenters God, without disruption of the substance thus entered.

Still unenlightened by the ultimate revelation, Dante does not understand how there can appear on the diamond-smooth surface on the moon (as he conceived it) those markings we know as *The Man in the Moon,* and which the Italians knew as *Cain with His Bush of Thorns.*

Beatrice asks for his explanation, refutes it, and proceeds to explain the truth of the moon's markings.

O you who in your wish to hear these things
  have followed thus far in your little skiffs
  the wake of my great ship that sails and sings,   3

turn back and make your way to your own coast.
  Do not commit yourself to the main deep,
  for, losing me, all may perhaps be lost.   6

My course is set for an uncharted sea.
  Minerva fills my sail. Apollo steers.
  And nine new Muses point the Pole for me.   9

You other few who have set yourselves to eat
  the bread of angels, by which we live on earth,
  but of which no man ever grew replete;   12

you may well trust your keel to the salt track
  and follow in the furrow of my wake
  ahead of the parted waters that close back.   15

Those heroes who sailed to Colchis, there to see
  their glorious Jason turned into a plowman,
  were not as filled with wonder as you will be.   18

The connate and perpetual thirst we feel
  for the God-like realm, bore us almost as swiftly
  as the sight soars to see the heavens wheel.   21

Beatrice was looking upward and I at her
  when—in the time it takes a bolt to strike,
  fly, and be resting in the bowstring's blur—   24

I found myself in a place where a wondrous thing
  drew my entire attention; whereat she
  from whom I could not hide my mind's least yearning 27

turned and said, as much in joy as beauty:
  "To God, who has raised us now to the first star
  direct your thoughts in glad and grateful duty."   30

It seemed to me a cloud as luminous
  and dense and smoothly polished as a diamond
  struck by a ray of sun, enveloped us.   33

We were received into the elements
  of the eternal pearl as water takes
  light to itself, with no change in its substance.   36

If I were a body (nor need we in this case
   conceive how one dimension can bear another,
   which must be if two bodies fill one space)   39

the more should my desire burn like the sun
   to see that Essence in which one may see
   how human nature and God blend into one.   42

There we shall witness what we hold in faith,
   not told by reason but self-evident;
   as men perceive an axiom here on earth.   45

"My lady," I replied, "in every way
   my being can, I offer up my thanks
   to Him who raised me from the world of clay.   48

But tell me what dark traces in the grain
   of this bright body show themselves below
   and cause men to tell fables about Cain?"   51

She smiled a moment and then answered me:
   "If the reckoning of mortals fails to turn
   the lock to which your senses hold no key,   54

the arrows of wonder should not run you through:
   even when led by the evidence of the senses
   the wings of reason often do not fly true.   57

But what do *you* believe the cause to be?"
   And I: "That these variations we observe
   are caused by bodies of varying density."   60

And she: "You will certainly come to know your view
   is steeped in falsehood. If you listen well
   to the counter-arguments I shall offer you.   63

The eighth sphere shines with many lamps, and these
  may be observed to shine with various aspects,
  both in their qualities and quantities.   66

If rare or dense alone could have produced
  all this, one power would have to be in all,
  whether equally or variously diffused.   69

Diversity of powers can only spring
  from formal principles, and all but one
  would be excluded by your reasoning.   72

Now if rarity produced the marks you mention,
  then the matter of this planet must be transparent
  at certain points, due to its rarefaction;   75

or it must be arranged like fat and lean
  within a body, as, so to speak, a book
  alternates pages. But it may be seen   78

in an eclipse that the first cannot be true,
  for then the sun's light, as it does in striking
  rare matter of any sort, would pass right through.   81

Since it does not, we may then pass along
  to the second case, and if I prove it false,
  I shall have shown that your whole thought is wrong.   84

If this rare matter is not spread throughout
  the planet's mass, then there must be a limit
  at which the denser matter will turn about   87

the sun's rays, which, not being allowed to pass,
  will be reflected as light and color are
  from the leaded back of a clear looking glass.   90

Now you may argue, in Avicenna's track,
   that the ray seems darker in one place than in others
   since it is being reflected from further back.   93

From such an *instance* (if you will do your part)
   you may escape by experiment (that being
   the spring that feeds the rivers of man's art).   96

Take three clear mirrors. Let two be set out
   at an equal distance from you, and a third
   between them, but further back. Now turn about   99

to face them, and let someone set a light
   behind your back so that it strikes all three
   and is reflected from them to your sight.   102

Although the image from the greater distance
   is smaller than the others, you must note
   that all three shine back with an equal brilliance.   105

Now, as the power of the sun's rays will strip
   the wintry ground on which the snow has lain
   of the cold and color that held it in their grip,   108

so you, with mind stripped clean, shall I delight
   with such a radiance of the living truth
   that it will leap and tremble in your sight.   111

Within the heaven of peace beyond the sky
   there whirls a body from whose power arises
   the being of all things that within it lie.   114

The next sphere, that which is so richly lit,
   distributes this power to many essences
   distinct from itself, yet all contained within it.   117

The other spheres, in various degrees,
  dispose the special powers they have within
  to their own causes and effects. All these   120

great universal organs, as you now know,
  proceed from grade to grade. Each in its order
  takes power from above and does its work below.   123

Now then, note carefully how I move on
  through this pass to the truth you seek, for thus
  you shall learn how to hold the ford alone.   126

The motion and the power of the sacred gyres—
  as the hammer's art is from the smith—must flow
  from the Blessèd Movers. It is their power inspires.   129

And thus that Heaven made loveliest in its wheel
  by many lamps, from the deep mind that turns it
  takes the image and makes itself the seal.   132

And as the soul within your mortal clay
  is spread through different organs, each of which
  is shaped to its own end; in the same way   135

the high angelic Intelligence spreads its goodness
  diversified through all the many stars
  while yet revolving ever in its Oneness.   138

This varying power is variously infused
  throughout the precious body that it quickens,
  in which, like life in you, it is diffused.   141

Because of the glad nature from which it flows,
  this many-faceted power shines through that body
  as through the living eye the glad soul glows.   144

From this source only, not from rare and dense,
  comes that by which one light and another differs—
  the formal principle whose excellence,   147

conforming to its own purposes, makes appear
  those markings you observe as dark and clear.

NOTES

3. *of my great ship:* See *Purgatorio* I, 1–2. There Dante refers to
"the little bark of my indwelling powers." For the present voyage
nothing less than a great (God-inspired) ship will do.

7–9. No poet has ever undertaken any such subject as Dante
now sings. Poetically, therefore, he is embarking on waters no man
has ever sailed. Apollo will guide his helm by the rules of poetry,
but it is Minerva, goddess of wisdom, who must fill his sails, and the
Muses who must be his navigators. *nine new Muses:* Dante says, sim-
ply, *"nove Muse."* But *"nove"* may mean either "nine" or "new." *the
Pole:* Dante says "the Bears" (Ursa Major and Ursa Minor. The North
Star is in Ursa Minor but its position in the sky is usually located by
first identifying Ursa Major, the stars of Ursa Minor being dim).

11. *the bread of angels:* The knowledge of God. It is by that, Dante
says, that we are able to live, but no mortal man can grasp enough of
it to become satisfied, the Divine Mystery being veiled from man.

13–15. The few who have sought the knowledge of God are de-
scribed as having keels. Hence they sail in something more seawor-
thy than the little skiffs of the others. Those few may dare the voyage,
but note how closely they must follow Dante—they must stay in the
very furrow of his wake, ahead of the waters that flow back to close
it. Clearly, Dante means that he must be followed with the most
scrupulous attention if the truth of his poem is to be grasped.

16–17. *Those heroes:* The Argonauts. Jason led them to Colchis to get
the Golden Fleece. The Colchian King offered to give Jason the fleece
if he would subdue two fire-breathing brass-hooved bulls, yoke them,
plow the field of Ares with them, sow the field with dragon's teeth, and
then defeat the army of warriors that would spring up from the teeth.

19. *connate:* Dante says *"concreata."* The thirst for God is born in the instant the soul is formed.

20–21. *almost as swiftly as the eye:* Dante and Beatrice soar upward at almost the speed of light.

23–24. The bolt of a crossbow would leave the bowstring so rapidly that human sense could not measure the rate of change. Hence, the figure means "instantly." But Dante has deliberately reversed the motion, a daring hysteron-proteron. Prof. John Freccero cites it, in the best interpretation known to me, as an example of Dante's "retrospective technique." Bear in mind that Dante is looking backward at the world and sees earthly actions in reverse. See XXII, 109, for another such usage.

27. *drew my entire attention:* As noted in line 22, Dante's attention had been fixed on Beatrice.

29. *to the first star:* The "first star" is the Moon. Dante has reached the first sphere of the Ptolemaic system.

32. *dense and smoothly polished as a diamond:* Dante finds the surface of the Moon to be diamond-smooth and highly polished (the telescope that was to reveal the jagged surface had not yet been invented).

35. *the eternal pearl:* The Moon.

37–42. THE UNITY OF GOD AND MAN. Dante is dealing here in the mysteries of faith. On Earth two bodies, being conceived as solids, cannot occupy the same space ("one dimension cannot bear another"). Yet, as light is received by water with no change in its self-unity, so Dante enters into the substance of the Moon, and this miraculous unity with which he enters the Moon-substance without disrupting it sends his mind soaring to the mystery of the incarnation of God, and to the ultimate reception of the good man into the ineffable Logos. *that Essence:* Christ as the Man-God.

44. *not told by reason:* Reason is only the handmaiden of faith. With his final purification in the Earthly Paradise, Dante passed beyond reason to the greater way of knowing. Virgil's last words to Dante were: "Lord of yourself I crown and miter you." With his subsequent purification Dante achieves the state in which every effort of the will and of the intellect cease. Yet the understanding

grows, for now the soul perceives as self-evident what had seemed incomprehensible to mere reason.

49–51. *dark traces . . . Cain?:* In Dante's Italy what we call the Man in the Moon was fabled to be Cain with a Bush of Thorns. Recall that Dante has just described the lunar surface as being diamond-smooth and polished: such a surface would not show dark traces.

52–57. Sense: No wonder men fable falsely when they have no sensory evidence on which to base their reasoning. Even in matters about which firm sensory evidence is available to them they do not always reason correctly.

64–66. *The eighth sphere:* The Sphere of the Fixed Stars. *lamps:* Stars. *qualities and quantities:* Coloration and intensity. The phrasing of Beatrice's disquisition is characteristically Scholastic: one can only repeat the admonition of the first six lines of the present Canto and hope the willing reader will accept the invitation of lines 10–18.

68. *power:* The influence of the stars upon the earth and upon the lives of men.

71. *formal principle:* Scholastic teaching distinguishes two principles in all bodies: the *material,* which is to say, the first matter, which is the same in all; and the *formal,* which is to say the substantial form that produces the various species and innate abilities of living forms. The *formal principle* is active; the *material principle,* passive. Dante's reasoning is false in that it would reduce all to a single principle.

73 ff. BEATRICE'S EXPLANATION OF THE MARKINGS OF THE MOON. In *Il Convivio* II, 14, Dante had attributed these traces to differences in the density of the lunar matter, whereby the body reflected the light unequally. In this he followed Avicenna. (The reference to Avicenna in line 91 is not explicitly in the original text, but it is clearly implied.) Now, with Beatrice as his revelation, he refutes his earlier belief, having her first show that such a belief leads to impossible conclusions, and then having her assign the true cause to the special power diffused by the Primum Mobile. That power, though itself indivisible, dispenses itself with varying intensity according to the different bodies it permeates—as the soul, for example, permeates some parts of the body more intensely than it does others.

Beatrice's argument is a curious one, Scholastic, pragmatic, and mystical by turn. She begins by demonstrating that Dante's belief involves, a true dilemma (an either/or) and proceeds to reduce either term to an absurdity, offering in evidence practical observations of an eclipse and an experiment she suggests to Dante. As noted above, she then explains the phenomenon by the mystic nature of the Primum Mobile.

93. *reflected:* Dante says *"rifratto"* (refracted). The physics of his time did not distinguish between reflection and refraction.

94. *instance:* A technical term *("instanza")* of Aristotelian and Scholastic logic signifying "counter-proposition." Dante's figure treats the *instance* as a trap from which one must escape with the aid of experiment.

96. *art:* Learning. See *Inferno* XI, 97–105. In Dante "art" signifies the skills, the crafts, and all the methods by which man understands and wins control over nature. It is always distinct from the higher knowledge of faith.

97–105. THE EXPERIMENT. Dante assumes in this experiment that the heavenly bodies are highly reflective surfaces. Thus by shining a light into three mirrors, two equidistant from him and one further back, and noting (though the size of the remoter image is smaller) that the brightness of all three is equal, he seems to argue that light of equal intensity is equally brilliant from whatever distance it is reflected. The argument is ingenious but any reader interested in the rudiments of science will be able to offer his own refutation of the experiment when its conclusions are applied to heavenly bodies at astronomic distances as seen at varying angles through a varying atmosphere.

108–109. *cold and color:* Both the cold and the whiteness are removed from the ground, *so you, stripped in your mind:* So Dante, the cold and color of error stripped from his mind, will be flooded with the living light (like the fructifying light and heat of returning Spring) of the truth.

112. *the heaven of peace beyond the sky:* The Empyrean. I have had to take liberties here. A literal rendering would be: "within the heaven of the divine peace."

113. *a body:* The Primum Mobile. Since the Empyrean (which lies beyond) is beyond space, the sphere of the Primum Mobile contains all of the universe. Taking its power from the all-encompassing Godhead (The Empyrean), it gives rise to all being.

115. *the next sphere:* Of the Fixed Stars.

120. *to their own causes and effects:* Each sphere to those causes and effects influenced by its particular powers.

123. *takes power from above:* From God. *and does its work below:* Ultimately upon man (the influence of the heavens upon mortal lives) but intermediately some of the work of each sphere must be to transmit certain powers (undiminished) to the spheres below.

124–126. Beatrice, as ever, is acting as Dante's teacher. Here, in a military figure, she instructs him to take careful note of how her argument proceeds through the next point, that by her example Dante may learn how to defend the ford (the crossing to the truth) by himself.

127. *gyres:* Circlings.

129. *the Blessed Movers:* The Angels, Powers, Principalities, and Intelligences who influence each sphere.

130. *the Heaven made loveliest by many lamps:* The Sphere of the Fixed Stars.

131–132. *from the deep mind:* Of God. The Sphere of the Fixed Stars receives its power from God (through the Primum Mobile) and taking His image from above, makes itself the seal that impresses that image on the spheres below (as a seal impresses its given image upon wax).

135. *shaped to its own end:* As the eye to sight, the ear to sound, *etc.*

140. *the precious body:* Of the Sphere of the Fixed Stars, here compared to the human body, because its unity comprises so many varied organs.

142. *the glad nature:* Of God.

147. *formal principle:* (See also note to line 71.) The power of the Divine and Angelic Intelligence is the intrinsic and substantial cause which produces the effect of dark and clear according to the various ways in which it enters into conjunction with the stars.

CANTO III

The First Sphere: The Moon—The Inconstant · Piccarda,
Constance

As Dante is about to speak to Beatrice he sees the dim traceries
of human faces and taking them to be reflections, he turns to see
what souls are being so reflected. Beatrice, as ever, explains that
these pallid images are the souls themselves. They are *The Incon-*
stant, the souls of those who registered holy vows in Heaven, but
who broke or scanted them.

Among them *Piccarda Donati* identifies herself, and then iden-
tifies *The Empress Constance.* Both, according to Dante's beliefs,
had taken vows as nuns but were forced to break them in order
to contract a political marriage. Not all the souls about them
need have failed in the same vows, however. Any failure to fulfill
a holy vow (of holy orders, to go on a pilgrimage, to offer special
services to God) might place the soul in this lowest class of the
blessed.

Piccarda explains that every soul in Heaven rejoices in the en-
tire will of God and cannot wish for a higher place, for to do so
would be to come into conflict with the will of God. In the per-
fect harmony of bliss, everywhere in Heaven is Paradise.

That sun that breathed love's fire into my youth
  had thus resolved for me, feature by feature—
  proving, disproving—the sweet face of truth.   3

I, raising my eyes to her eyes to announce
  myself resolved of error, and well assured,
  was about to speak; but before I could pronounce   6

my first word, there appeared to me a vision.
  It seized and held me so that I forgot
  to offer her my thanks and my confession.   9

As in clear glass when it is polished bright,
  or in a still and limpid pool whose waters
  are not so deep that the bottom is lost from sight,   12

a footnote of our lineaments will show,
  so pallid that our pupils could as soon
  make out a pearl upon a milk-white brow—   15

so I saw many faces eager to speak,
  and fell to the error opposite the one
  that kindled love for a pool in the smitten Greek.   18

And thinking the pale traces I saw there
  were reflected images, I turned around
  to face the source—but my eyes met empty air.   21

I turned around again like one beguiled,
  and took my line of sight from my sweet guide
  whose sacred eyes grew radiant as she smiled.   24

"Are you surprised that I smile at this childish act
  of reasoning?" she said, "since even now
  you dare not trust your sense of the true fact,   27

but turn, as usual, back to vacancy?
  These are true substances you see before you.
  They are assigned here for inconstancy   30

to holy vows. Greet them. Heed what they say,
  and so believe; for the True Light that fills them
  permits no soul to wander from its ray."   33

So urged, I spoke to those pale spirits, turning
  to one who seemed most eager, and began
  like one whose mind goes almost blank with yearning. 36

"O well created soul, who in the sun
  of the eternal life drinks in the sweetness
  which, until tasted, is beyond conception;   39

great would be my joy would you confide
  to my eager mind your earthly name and fate."
  That soul with smiling eyes, at once replied: 42

"The love that fills us will no more permit
  hindrance to a just wish than does that Love
  that wills all of Its court to be like It.   45

I was a virgin sister there below,
  and if you search your memory with care,
  despite my greater beauty, you will know   48

I am Piccarda, and I am placed here
  among these other souls of blessedness
  to find my blessedness in the slowest sphere.   51

Our wishes, which can have no wish to be
  but in the pleasure of the Holy Ghost,
  rejoice in being formed to His decree.   54

And this low-seeming post which we are given
  is ours because we broke, or, in some part,
  slighted the vows we offered up to Heaven."   57

And I then: "Something inexpressibly
  divine shines in your face, subliming you
  beyond your image in my memory: 60

therefore I found you difficult to place;
  but now, with the assistance of your words,
  I find the memory easier to retrace.   63

But tell me, please: do you who are happy here
    have any wish to rise to higher station,
    to see more, or to make yourselves more dear?"   66

She smiled, as did the spirits at her side;
    then, turning to me with such joy she seemed
    to burn with the first fire of love, replied: 69

"Brother, the power of love, which is our bliss,
    calms all our will. What we desire, we have.
    There is in us no other thirst than this.   72

Were we to wish for any higher sphere,
    then our desires would not be in accord
    with the high will of Him who wills us here;   75

and if love is our whole being, and if you weigh
    love's nature well, then you will see that discord
    can have no place among these circles. Nay,   78

the essence of this blessèd state of being
    is to hold all our will within His will,
    whereby our wills are one and all-agreeing.   81

And so the posts we stand from sill to sill
    throughout this realm, please all the realm as much
    as they please Him who wills us to His will.   84

In His will is our peace. It is that sea
    to which all moves, all that Itself creates
    and Nature bears through all Eternity."   87

Then was it clear to me that everywhere
    in Heaven is Paradise, though the Perfect Grace
    does not rain down alike on all souls there.   90

But as at times when we have had our fill
  of one food and still hunger for another,
  we put this by with gratitude, while still   93

asking for that—just so I begged to know,
  by word and sign, through what warp she had not
  entirely passed the shuttle of her vow.   96

"The perfection of her life and her great worth
  enshrine a lady hereabove," she said
  "in whose rule some go cloaked and veiled on earth, 99

that till their death they may live day and night
  with that sweet Bridegroom who accepts of love
  all vows it makes that add to His delight.   102

As a girl, I fled the world to walk the way
  she walked, and closed myself into her habit,
  pledge to her sisterhood till my last day.   105

Then men came, men more used to hate than love.
  They tore me away by force from the sweet cloister.
  What my life then became is known above.   108

This other splendor who lets herself appear
  here to my right to please you, shining full
  of every blessedness that lights this sphere,   111

understands in herself all that I say.
  She, too, was a nun. From her head as from mine
  the shadow of the veil was ripped away.   114

Against her will and all propriety
  she was forced back to the world. Yet even there
  her heart was ever veiled in sanctity.   117

She is the radiance of the Empress Constance
  who by the second blast of Swabia
  conceived and bore its third and final puissance."   120

She finished, and at once began to sing
  Ave Maria, and singing, sank from view
  like a weight into deep water, plummeting   123

out of my sight, which followed while it could,
  and then, having lost her, turned about once more
  to the target of its greater wish and good,   126

and wholly gave itself to the delight
  of the sweet vision of Beatrice. But she
  flashed so radiantly upon my sight   129

that I, at first, was blinded, and thus was slow
  to ask of her what I most wished to know.

NOTES

1. *That sun:* Beatrice. It was she who first breathed love's fire into Dante's youth. (See also *Purgatorio* XXX, 40–42, and *Paradiso* XXX, 75.)

3. *proving:* Her views, the truth, *and disapproving:* My views, error.

9. *my confession:* Of the error Dante now recognizes (concerning the markings of the moon).

13. *a footnote of our lineaments:* The figure seems oddly out of context but its intent is clear: Dante is suggesting that the image is related to the face as a footnote is related to the text.

15. *a pearl upon a milk-white brow:* The brow would have to be death-pale as marble, but perhaps Dante intends these spirits to be chalky-white.

16. THE INCONSTANT. All these spirits registered vows in Heaven and then either broke or slighted them. Both of those cited

took vows as nuns and were then forced to break them against their own wishes. One must assume, however, that the same category would include not only monks and priests who similarly gave up holy orders, but all who offered up a vow of any sort and then failed to observe it strictly.

They are "assigned here" (line 30), which is to say they appear on the moon (the inconstant planet), but each has his throne in the Empyrean (see IV, 23). All the souls of the blessed, whatever their rank in Heaven, experience as much bliss as they are capable of and cannot wish for more. Within the divine order each seeks and finds its proper place.

18. *the smitten Greek:* Narcissus. His error was in taking a reflection (his own) to be a real face. Dante's opposite error is in taking real faces to be reflections.

32. *the True Light:* God.

33. *permits no soul to wander:* So Dante's phrasing, but it should be understood that filled as these souls are by the True Light, their inability to stray from its ray (contrast Dante's situation in line 27) is not a prohibition but a choice of their own perfected volition. They are not capable of error.

44. *that Love:* God, as the essence of *Caritas.*

46. *virgin sister:* A nun.

49. *Piccarda:* Piccarda Donati was the daughter of Simone Donati (*Inferno* XXV, 32) and sister of Forese (*Purgatorio* XXIII, 48) and of the war-leader, Corso (*Purgatorio* XXIV, 82 ff.). Forese was Dante's friend. Dante was married to Gemma Donati, who also had a brother named Forese, but Piccarda's family was grander than Dante's in-laws.

Piccarda was already a nun and living in her convent when her brother Corso, needing to establish a political alliance, forced her to marry Rossellino della Tossa of Florence. Various commentators report that Piccarda sickened and soon died as a consequence of having been so forced against her will and vows.

52–54. THE BLISS OF THE BLESSED. Every soul in Heaven, whatever its station, is entirely happy because it is entirely identified with God's plan and has no joy but in being formed to His will. The essence of God is love, i.e., *caritas,* the love of others. With *caritas* as the essential mood of the *Paradiso,* no soul can help but rejoice in the joy of all about it. Contrast the state of things in the *Inferno:* the infernal souls have all refused to accept and to identify themselves with the Divine Love; each, therefore, is closed into itself, and no soul in Hell can derive any comfort from any other (see *Inferno* V, note to line 102). Joy finds its increase exactly in being freely given to others. As Piccarda soon makes clear to Dante, that joy is expressed in Heaven in no way but in the complete identification with God's love.

63. *easier to retrace:* A desperate simplification of Dante's untranslatable *"m'è più latino"* (literally: "it is more Latin to me"). Learned men of Dante's time used Latin naturally and gracefully. Thus to make a thing "more Latin" was to facilitate it. An opposite form of a similar idiom is our still current "It's Greek to me."

66. *to make yourselves more dear:* To God.

69. *the first fire of love:* Could variously be taken to mean God, the Moon (the first lit sphere of the Universe, which is Love), or the bliss mortals feel in the fire of newly awakened love. On the narrative level the last seems most likely, but the other meanings could function along with it.

95–96. *warp . . . shuttle:* The vertical strings of a loom are the warp. Across them the shuttle draws the woof. Not to draw the shuttle entirely through is to leave the weaving unfinished, hence her vow unfulfilled.

98. *a lady:* Saint Clara of Assisi (1194–1253). Born Chiara Sciffi, she became a disciple of St. Francis and, under his influence, founded in 1212 an order of nuns. *hereabove:* Higher in Heaven. Probably in the Empyrean, but Dante does not mention her again.

101. *that sweet Bridegroom:* Christ. He is so called several times in the New Testament.

102. *all vows . . . that add to His delight:* Only those vows that conform to His love are acceptable. A vow to perform a trivial or an evil action would have no standing.

109. *This other splendor:* The Empress Constance (1154–1198). As the last of the line of Norman kings who took southern Italy in

the eighth century, she was Empress of the Two Sicilies (Sicily and Naples). She married the Emperor Henry VI in 1185 and became the mother of Frederick II. Dante follows a legend, for which there was no basis in fact, that she had become a nun and was forced to leave her convent to marry Henry.

109. *lets herself appear:* Dante says, "who shows herself to you." Clearly, the souls in Paradise can make themselves visible or invisible at will (i.e., Heaven reveals itself of its own love). At the end of the conversation the whole company withdraws from sight.

119. THE THREE BLASTS OF SWABIA. These are the three great princes whose origins were in Swabia (in Germany). Frederick Barbarossa was the first. His son, Henry VI, was the second. To Henry, Constance bore the third, Frederick II.

CANTO IV

The First Sphere: The Moon—Beatrice Discourses:
The True Seat of the Blessed · Plato's Error · Free Will ·
Recompense for Broken Vows

Piccarda has told Dante that she inhabits the sphere of the inconstant Moon because she broke her vows against her will. Dante is torn by doubts that could lead to heresy. Was Plato right in saying souls come from their various stars preformed, and then return to them? If so, what of *Free Will*? And if Heaven is Justice, how have these souls sinned in being forced against their wills? And if Heaven is truth, what of the contradiction between Piccarda's statements and Beatrice's?

Beatrice resolves all of Dante's doubts. When she has finished Dante asks if men may offer *Other Recompense for Broken Vows.*

A man given free choice would starve to death
  between two equal equidistant foods,
  unable to get either to his teeth.   3

So would a lamb, in counterbalanced fear,
  tremble between two she-wolves and stand frozen.
  So would a hound stand still between two deer.   6

If I stood mute, then, tugged to either side,
  I neither blame myself, nor take my doubt—
  it being necessary—as cause for pride.   9

I did not speak, but on my face, at once,
  were written all my questions and my yearnings,
  far more distinctly than I could pronounce.   12

And Beatrice did as Daniel once had done
  when he raised Nebuchadnezzar from the wrath
  that made him act unjustly in Babylon.   15

"I see full well how equal wish and doubt
  tear you two ways," she said, "so that your zeal
  tangles upon itself and cannot breathe out.   18

You reason: 'If the will that vowed stays true,
  how can another's violence take away
  from the full measure of bliss that is my due?'   21

And I see a second doubt perplex that thought
  because the souls you see seem to return
  to the stars from which they came, as Plato taught. 24

These are the questions that bear down your will
  with equal force. Therefore, I shall treat first
  the one whose venom has more power to kill.   27

Choose the most God-like of the Seraphim—
  take Moses, or Samuel, or take either John,
  or even Mary—not one is nearer Him,   30

nor holds his seat atop the blessèd spheres
  in any heaven apart from those you saw;
  nor has his being more or fewer years.   33

All add their beauty to the Highest Wheel,
  share the sweet life, and vary in it only
  by how much of the Eternal Breath they feel.   36

They showed themselves here not because this post
  has been assigned them, but to symbolize
  that they stand lowest in the Heavenly host.   39

So must one speak to mortal imperfection,
  which only from the *sensible* apprehends
  whatever it then makes fit for intellection.   42

Scripture in like manner condescends,
  describing God as having hands and feet
  as signs to men of what more it portends.   45

So Holy Church shows you in mortal guise
  the images of Gabriel and of Michael,
  and of the other who gave back Tobit's eyes.   48

For if Timaeus—as seems rather clear—
  spoke literally, what he says about souls
  is nothing like the truth shown to us here.   51

He says the soul finds its own star again,
  from which, as he imagines, nature chose it
  to give form to the flesh and live with men.   54

But it may be the words he uses hide
  a second meaning, which, if understood,
  reveals a principle no man may deride.   57

If he means that the blame or honor due
  the influence of each sphere returns to it,
  his arrow does hit something partly true.   60

This principle, misunderstood, once drove
  almost the whole world to attach to planets
  such names as Mars and Mercury and Jove.   63

The other doubt that agitates your mind
  is not as venemous, for not all its malice
  could drive you from my side to wander blind.   66

For mortal men to argue that they see
  injustice in our justice is in itself
  a proof of faith, not poisonous heresy.   69

But since the truth of this lies well within
   the reach of your own powers, I shall explain it,
   just as you wish.—If violence, to begin,   72

occurs when those who suffer its abuse
   contribute nothing to what forces them,
   then these souls have no claim to that excuse.   75

For the will, if it will not, cannot be spent,
   but does as nature does within a flame
   a thousand or ten thousand winds have bent.   78

If it yield of itself, even in the least,
   then it assists the violence—as did these
   who could have gone back to their holy feast.   81

If their whole will had joined in their desire—
   as whole will upheld Lawrence on the grill,
   and Mucius with his hand thrust in the fire—   84

just so, it would have forced them to return
   to their true way the instant they were free.
   But such pure will is too rare, we must learn!   87

If you have gleaned them diligently, then
   these words forever destroy the argument
   that would have plagued your mind time and again.   90

But now another pass opens before you,
   so strait and tortuous that without my help
   you would tire along the way and not win through.   93

I made you understand beyond all doubt
   that these souls cannot lie, for they exist
   in the First Truth and cannot wander out.   96

Later you heard Piccarda say that she
  who stood beside her kept her love of the veil;
  and it seems that what she said contradicts me.   99

Time and again, my brother, men have run
  from danger by a path they would not choose,
  and on it done what ought not to be done.   102

So, bending to his father's prayer, did he
  who took his mother's life. Alcmaeon I mean,
  who sought his piety in impiety.   105

Now weigh within your own intelligence
  how will and violence interact, so joining
  that no excuse can wipe out the offense.   108

Absolute will does not will its own harm,
  but fearing worse may come if it resists,
  consents the more, the greater its alarm.   111

Thus when Piccarda spoke as she did to you,
  she meant the absolute will; and I, the other.
  So both of us spoke only what was true."   114

—Such was the flowing of that stream so blest
  it flows down from the Fountain of All Truth.
  Such was the power that laid my doubts to rest.   117

"Beloved of the First Love! O holy soul!"
  I said then, "You whose words flow over me,
  and with their warmth quicken and make me whole,   120

There is not depth enough within my love
  to offer you due thanks, but may the One
  who sees and can, answer for me above.   123

Man's mind, I know, cannot win through the mist
  unless it is illumined by that Truth
  beyond which truth has nowhere to exist.   126

In That, once it has reached it, it can rest
  like a beast within its den. And reach it can;
  else were all longing vain, and vain the test.   129

Like a new tendril yearning from man's will
  doubt sprouts to the foot of truth. It is that in us
  that drives us to the summit from hill to hill.   132

By this am I encouraged, by this bidden,
  my lady, in all reverence, to ask
  your guidance to a truth that still lies hidden: 135

can such as these who put away their veils
  so compensate by other good works done
  that they be not found wanting on your scales?"   138

Beatrice looked at me, and her glad eyes,
  afire with their divinity, shot forth
  such sparks of love that my poor faculties   141

gave up the reins. And with my eyes cast down
  I stood entranced, my senses all but flown.

NOTES

1–9. DANTE'S DOUBT. The phrasing of this passage is difficult.
Nor am I sure I have found the right rendering of all the grammatical ambiguities. The intent, on the other hand, is clear. Piccarda's account of herself has raised questions that, as we shall see, tear Dante's understanding in two directions at once. Beatrice, as usual, senses his self-division and resolves all in the conversation that follows.

The difficulty of the phrasing is caused by the interplay of the ideas "free choice" and "necessity." Dante follows Aquinas in this: if the choices offered to a man are entirely equal, no choice can be made and the man cannot act. Thus Dante takes neither blame nor praise for his indecisive doubts since he was unable to choose between them.

13. *as Daniel had done:* Nebuchadnezzar, King of Babylon, condemned all his diviners to death because they could not interpret a dream he had forgotten. Daniel first divined the dream and then interpreted it, calming the fury of the king (*Daniel* ii, 1–45).

19. *if the will that vowed stays true:* Dante is thinking of what Piccarda said. If her will to keep her vows never faltered, how can the fact that her brother's violence forced her to act against her will alter her just reward for the purity of her intentions (which, seemingly, should have earned her a higher place in Heaven)?

24. *as Plato taught:* As Dante rendered the *Timaeus,* Plato taught that souls existed in the stars before they entered human bodies (Wordsworth's "Ode on the Intimations of Immortality" is a well-known treatment of this theme) and returned, at the body's death, to the same stars from which they had come. Such a doctrine, however, denies free will, the soul being pre-created to a fixed place in Heaven's order. And yet the souls of the Inconstant seem to return to the inconstant Moon. Thus one thought negates the other, leaving Dante's mind ensnared between the two.

27. *whose venom has more power to kill:* The doctrine within which lurks the greater danger of self-destroying heresy.

28–63. THE PLACE IN HEAVEN OF THE BLEST. Every soul in heaven is equally a part of God. As Beatrice goes on to explain, all have their seats in the Empyrean. The various spheres in which *they appear to Dante* only symbolize the degree of their beatitude. It is necessary to use such symbols because the limited comprehension of mankind could not begin to grasp the truth in any other way. Thus, the Bible speaks of God as if he had a manlike body when he is in fact Essence. Beatrice's point is that every elect soul is equally in God. All have their place in one Heaven, all are eternal. They vary only in the degree of their beatitude, which is determined by their own ability to absorb the infinity of God's bliss.

36. *the Eternal Breath:* Recall from *Genesis* that it was God's breath that quickened the dust to life. The Eternal Breath, therefore, is the gift of life, and the difference in the beatitude of the blessed must be in the degree to which they are quickened to their Eternal life. The pallor of those moon-souls, as contrasted to the blinding radiance of those who appear higher, may also, perhaps, be taken as a measure of how much of the Eternal Breath is in them.

48. *the other:* Raphael, the third archangel. He cured Tobit of blindness (*Tobit* xi, 2–17).

54. *to give form:* (The rest of this line, though implicit in Dante, is my own rhyme-forced addition.) The soul, in Scholastic teaching, is the *formative power* (see *Purgatorio* XXV, 40–42, note). The body is simply the matter upon which it works to impress its form.

61–63. *this principle:* That souls come down from the stars (or spheres, or planets) and return to them. *almost the whole world:* The exception was the Jews. All others imagined multiple gods (Mars, Mercury, and Jove, for example) whose names they attached to the planets. *Jove:* For Jupiter.

64–69. *the other doubt:* Of the justice of placing Piccarda and Constance among the Inconstant when they were forced to break their vows against their will. This doubt is not as venomous because it does not lead to heresy. The Council of Constantinople (540 A.D.) had denounced the doctrine of the *Timaeus* as heretical. But the church had not pronounced infallibly on the matter of Dante's second doubt. That second doubt, therefore, might lead Dante into error but not into heresy. It could not, therefore, drive him from Beatrice (Revealed Truth) to wander blind outside the church. *proof of faith:* To doubt a particular manifestation of divine justice implies a belief in its existence.

77. *as nature does within a flame:* The flame, that is to say, rises again.

81. *their holy feast:* Their convents and their vows.

83. *Lawrence:* In 258, during the reign of Valerius, St. Lawrence, then deacon of Rome, was ordered by the Roman Prefect to send him the treasure of the church. Lawrence sent him the poor and the oppressed, declaring that they were the one treasure. He was there-

upon martyred. After many other tortures, he was roasted on a grill, but remained steadfast under torture. Jacobus de Voragine *(The Golden Legend)* reports him as saying to his torturer: "Thou hast roasted the one side, tyrant, now turn the other and eat."

84. *Mucius:* Mucius Scaevola, a young man of ancient Rome. He vowed to kill Porsenna and let his right hand be consumed by fire when its thrust missed the mark. Note that, as in the Whips and Reins of the Purgatory, Dante presents both a sacred and a classical example.

94. *I made you understand:* See III, 31–33.

96. *the First Truth:* God.

97–98. *she who stood beside her:* Constance.

105. *his piety:* To his father. *impiety:* To his mother. For Alcmaeon see *Purgatorio* XII, 49–51 and note.

106–114. The central idea of this passage is the difference between the Absolute and Conditioned Will. The Absolute Will is incapable of willing evil. The Conditioned Will, when coerced by violence, interacts with it and consents to a lesser harm in order to escape a greater. All that Piccarda said was true of the Absolute Will, but all that Beatrice has said is true of the Conditioned Will.

113–115. *that stream:* Stands for both Beatrice and her discourse, *the Fountain of All Truth:* God. Dante's figure also expounds Beatrice's allegorical function as Revealed Truth (which flows from God, the Fountain of All Truth, and calms all doubt from the souls of those to whom it descends).

127. *In That:* In the truth of God, within which the soul may rest as instinctively as does a beast within its den.

CANTO V

Ascent to the Second Sphere—Beatrice Discourses

*The Second Sphere: Mercury—The Seekers of Honor · The
Emperor Justinian*

Beatrice explains the *Sanctity of the Vow, its Relation to Free Will,
The Limited Range Within Which Vows May Be Altered,* and the
Dangers of Evil Vows.

When she has finished, she and Dante soar to the *Second
Sphere.* There a host of radiant souls gathers to dance homage
around Beatrice and Dante. These are the *Seekers of Honor,* souls
who were active in their pursuit of the good, but who were mo-
tivated in their pursuit by a desire for personal honor, a good
enough motive, but the least of all good motives.

One soul among them addresses Dante with particular joy. In
Canto VI this soul identifies itself as the radiance that in mortal
life was the *Emperor Justinian.*

"If, in the warmth of love, I manifest
  more of my radiance than the world can see,
  rendering your eyes unequal to the test,   3

do not be amazed. These are the radiancies
  of the perfected vision that sees the good
  and step by step moves nearer what it sees.   6

Well do I see how the Eternal Ray,
  which, once seen, kindles love forevermore,
  already shines on you. If on your way   9

some other thing seduce your love, my brother,
  it can only be a trace, misunderstood,
  of this, which you see shining through the other.   12

You ask if there is any compensation
  the soul may offer for its unkept vows
  that will secure it against litigation."   15

So Beatrice, alight from Heaven's Source,
  began this canto; and without a pause,
  continued thus her heavenly discourse: 18

"Of all creation's bounty realized,
  God's greatest gift, the gift in which mankind
  is most like Him, the gift by Him most prized,   21

is the freedom he bestowed upon the will.
  All his intelligent creatures, and they alone,
  were so endowed, and so endowed are still.   24

From this your reasoning should make evident
  the value of a vow that is so joined
  that God gives His consent when you consent.   27

When, therefore, God and man have sealed the pact,
  the man divests himself of that great treasure
  of which I speak—and by his own free act.   30

What can you offer, then, to make amends?
  How can you make good use of what is His?
  Would you employ extortion to good ends?   33

This much will make the main point clear to you.
  But since the church grants dispensations in this,
  whereby what I have said may seem untrue,   36

you must yet sit at table, for the food
  you have just taken is crusty; without help
  you will not soon digest it to your good.   39

Open your mind to what I shall explain,
  then close around it, for it is no learning
  to understand what one does not retain.   42

The essence of this sacrificial act
  lies, first, in *what* one does, and, second, in *how*—
  the *matter* and the *manner* of the pact.   45

This second part cannot be set aside
  except by full performance; on this point
  what I said earlier stands unqualified.   48

Thus it was mandatory to sacrifice
  among the Jews, though the offering itself
  might vary, or a substitute might suffice.   51

The other—what I have called the *matter*—may
  be of the sort for which a substitution
  will serve without offending in any way.   54

But let no man by his own judgment or whim
  take on himself that burden unless the keys
  of gold and silver have been turned for him.   57

And let him think no change a worthy one
  unless what he takes up contains in it,
  at least as six does four, what he puts down.   60

There are, however, things whose weight and worth
  tip every scale, and for these there can be
  no recompense by anything on earth.   63

Let no man make his vow a sporting thing.
  Be true and do not make a squint-eyed choice
  as Jephthah did in his first offering.   66

He had better have cried, 'I had no right to speak!'
  than, keeping his vow, do worse. And in like case
  will you find that chief war leader, the great Greek   69

whose Iphigenia wept her loveliness,
  and made both fools and wise men share her tears
  hearing of such dark rites and her distress.   72

Be slower to move, Christians, be grave, serene.
  Do not be like a feather in the wind,
  nor think that every water washes clean.   75

You have the Testaments, both old and new,
  and the shepherd of the church to be your guide;
  and this is all you need to lead you true.   78

If cunning greed comes promising remission,
  be men, not mad sheep, lest the Jew among you
  find cause to point his finger in derision.   81

Do not be like the lamb that strays away
  from its mother's milk and, simple and capricious,
  fights battles with itself in silly play!"   84

—Thus Beatrice to me, just as I write.
  Then she turned, full of yearning, to that part
  where the world is quickened most by the True Light.   87

Her silence, her transfigured face ablaze
  made me fall still although my eager mind
  was teeming with new questions I wished to raise.   90

And like an arrow driven with such might
  it strikes its mark before the string is still,
  we soared to the second kingdom of the light.   93

My lady glowed with such a joyous essence
  giving herself to the light of that new sky
  that the planet shone more brightly with her presence. 96

And if the star changed then and laughed with bliss,
  what did I do, who in my very nature
  was made to be transformed through all that is?   99

As in a fish pond that is calm and clear
  fish swim to what falls in from the outside,
  believing it to be their food, so, here,   102

I saw at least a thousand splendors move
  toward us, and from each one I heard the cry:
  "Here is what gives increase to our love!"   105

And as those glories came to where we were
  each shade made visible in the radiance
  that each gave off, the joy that filled it there.   108

Imagine, reader, that I had started so
  and not gone on—think what an anguished famine
  would then oppress your hungry will to know.   111

So may you, of yourself, be able to see
  how much I longed to know their names and nature
  the instant they had shown themselves to me.   114

—"O well born soul, permitted by God's grace
  to see the thrones of the Eternal Triumph
  while still embattled in the mortal trace,   117

the lamp that shines through all the vaults of Heaven
  is lit in us; if, therefore, you seek light
  on any point, ask and it shall be given."   120

—So spoke one of those pious entities.
  And my lady said: "Speak. Speak with full assurance.
  And credit them as you would deities!"   123

"I do indeed see that you make your nest
  in your own light, and beam it through your eyes
  that dazzles when you smile, o spirit blest.   126

But I know not who you are, nor why you are
  assigned here, to this sphere that hides itself
  from men's eyes in the rays of another star."   129

These were my words, my face turned to the light
  that had just spoken; at which it made itself
  far more resplendent yet upon my sight.   132

Just as the sun, when its rays have broken through
  a screen of heavy vapors, will itself
  conceal itself in too much light—just so,   135

in its excess of joy that sacred soul
  hid itself from my sight in its own ray,
  and so concealed within its aureole,   138

it answered me, unfolding many things,
  the manner of which the following canto sings.

NOTES

9–12. *some other thing:* The light of God, once seen, kindles eternal love and no soul so kindled can stray from it. Since Dante's soul has already been so kindled, the only possible error remaining to him is that he could mistakenly believe he sees the light of God in some lesser object and so be seduced by that lesser thing, not because his love is lacking, but because his understanding is.

15. *litigation:* At the bar of judgment.

16–18. An odd tercet. In it Dante pauses only to say Beatrice did not pause but spoke and went on speaking. A literal rendering (I have had to take liberties) would be: "So Beatrice began this canto; and, like a man who does not interrupt his discourse, continued her sacred process [of reasoning and explication] as follows:"

19–33. THE SANCTITY OF HOLY VOWS. Dante has asked if a man may not, by other good works, made amends for an unfulfilled vow. Beatrice replies that God's greatest gift to man is his free will, and that a vow is a direct compact with God wherein man, of his free will, offers that freedom back to God. Once God accepts, the man's will is no longer free for it has been given to God. How then is man free to will what is good, his will and freedom now belonging to God? To assert a free will that is no longer his is to seek to embezzle his way to the good.

23. *All his intelligent creatures:* Angels and men.

43. *this sacrificial act:* It need not, of course, be restricted to the vows taken for religious orders. One might, for example, vow to fast, or to go on a pilgrimage, or to give some or all of his goods to the poor, or to live in a specified way.

49–57. *Thus it was mandatory:* The law of the Jews absolutely required them to offer sacrifices to the Lord (the *substance* of the covenant) but allowed them some latitude in what might be sacrificed (the *manner*). The manner of the vow may be changed if its substance is kept, but the change must not be arbitrary (for man, having given away his will, may not choose at his own pleasure), and no man should make such a change without having submitted his case to church authority (whereby the gold and silver keys of papal authority are turned for him).

58–60. Sense of this tercet: Let no man think it worthy (even with church authority) to change the substance of his vow to a lesser thing. Rather, the new substance should be greater than the former at least as six is to four. It is always well to look for a special significance in Dante's use of numbers, but I know of none here. He seems to be using six-to-four simply as a reasonable ratio of increase.

61–62. *things whose weight and worth tip every scale:* A vow of chastity would involve such a thing, virginity being irreplaceable. A vow of a lifetime of service would, similarly, involve what is irreplaceable. By contrast, a man who vowed to make a gift of money to charity every year of his life, and who then loses all his money, might satisfy his vow by substituting labor, or even, if he grows infirm, prayer. Were he, on the other hand, to steal in order to keep his money vow, that would be an evil thing.

66. *Jephthah:* King of Israel. He fought the Ammonites and vowed that if he were victorious he would offer up to God the first thing he saw coming out of the door of his house. The first thing he saw was his daughter and he sacrificed her (*Judges* xi).

67. *have cried, 'I had no right to speak!':* No right to speak such a vow. In so crying he would have renounced the vow, and better so, says Dante, than to do worse in the act of keeping it.

69–70. *the great Greek whose Iphigenia:* Agamemnon. Iphigenia was his daughter. Dante follows the legend in which Agamemnon vowed before the birth of Iphigenia that he would sacrifice to Artemis the loveliest creature the year brought forth. Rather than sacrifice Iphigenia, he did not keep his vow. Years later, however, when the Greek ships were becalmed at Aulis, the other Greek leaders, especially Menelaus, blamed their distress on the unkept vow and Agamemnon was finally persuaded to send for Iphigenia and to sacrifice her.

79. *cunning greed:* The greed of those who offer dispensations and other holy offices for money. To Dante such practices were damnable simony.

80. *lest the Jew among you:* The Jew could then point his finger in derision because his law was incorruptible in the matter of sacrifices.

86–87. To avoid a volume of scholarly disputation, let these lines be taken to mean that Beatrice turned to both the Sun (it was at the equator) and the Empyrean (thus toward the "True Light" in both senses) and that she and Dante ascended in the same way as before. In an instant, then, they soar to Mercury, their arrival signified by the increase in Beatrice's radiance.

94. *glowed with such a joyous essence:* Both the joy and the light are greater because she is now nearer God and has more of His essence breathed into her.

97–99. *the star:* Mercury. Dante regularly refers to planets as stars. Sense of these lines: "If the star could be so changed (being material), how could I not change, who was created with soul as my essence, hence born to be transformed through all there is, from dust to Godliness."

100 ff. THOSE WHO SOUGHT HONOR VISIBLY (THE PERSONALLY AMBITIOUS). The souls in the sphere of Mercury worked, in their earthly lives, for honor and glory. On seeing the newcomers they burst into joyous revels (as in their heart's wish they had sought themselves to be honored by such revels? each giving what is most nearly of himself?). These souls sought the good actively and for good reason, but, in a sense, *for the least of all good reasons.* The light they give forth is so bright that they are often lost to Dante's sight in their own radiance—a double felicity, first, as it describes the essence of their natures, and, second, because Mercury is so near the Sun that it is often hard to see because it is swallowed into the Sun's glow.

107–108. *each shade made visible, in the radiance:* The counterplay of "shade" and "radiance" seems to imply that the lineaments of these souls were traced upon the radiance that enclosed them.

114. *the instant they had shown themselves to me:* Note here and hereafter how regularly Dante speaks of the Paradisal souls as showing themselves rather than as being seen by him (cf. III, 109). It is the nature of what belongs to Heaven to reveal itself of its own love and volition rather than to be apprehended by mortal means. There is also, of course, the fact that these souls are here only as symbolic manifestations, their real seat being in the Empyrean (IV, 28–63 and note).

117. *while still embattled:* Dante says, literally, "before your time in the militia is left behind." The essential point is that Heaven is the Eternal Triumph of which mortal life (for man) is the battle. Cf. the common phrase, "the church militant."

128–129. *this sphere that hides itself from men's eyes in the rays of another star:* The other star is the Sun. As noted above (note to 100 ff.) Mercury is often lost in the Sun's aura.

CANTO VI

The Second Sphere: Mercury—Seekers of Honor:
Justinian · The Roman Eagle

The Spirit Identifies Itself as the soul of *The Emperor Justinian* and
proceeds to recount its life on earth, its conversion by *Agapetus,*
and its subsequent dedication to *The Codification of the Law.*

It proceeds next to a *Discourse on the History of the Roman
Eagle.* It concludes by identifying the spirit of *Romeo da Villanova*
as one among the souls of the Second Heaven.

"Once Constantine had turned the eagle's wing
  against the course of Heaven, which it had followed
  behind the new son of the Latian king,   3

two hundred years and more, as mankind knows,
  God's bird stayed on at Europe's furthest edge,
  close to the mountains out of which it rose.   6

And there, his wings spread over land and sea,
  he ruled the world, passing from hand to hand;
  and so, through many changes, came to me.   9

Caesar I was, Justinian I am.
  By the will of the First Love, which I now feel,
  I pruned the law of waste, excess, and sham.   12

Before my work absorbed my whole intent
  I knew Christ in one nature only, not two;
  and so believing, I was well content.   15

But Agapetus, blessèd of the Lord,
  he, the supreme shepherd pure in faith,
  showed me the true way by his holy word.   18

Him I believed, and in my present view
  I see the truth as clearly as you see
  how a contradiction is both false and true.   21

As soon as I came to walk in the True Faith's way
  God's grace moved all my heart to my great work;
  and to it I gave myself without delay.   24

To my Belisarius I left my spear
  and God's right hand so moved his that the omen
  for me to rest from war was more than clear.   27

Of the two things you asked about before
  this puts a period to my first reply.
  But this much said impels me to say more   30

that you may see with how much right men go
  against the sacred standard when they plot
  its subornation or its overthrow.   33

You know what heroes bled to consecrate
  its holy destiny from that first hour
  when Pallas died to give it its first state.   36

You know that for two centuries then its home
  was Alba, till the time came when the three
  fought with the three and carried it to Rome.   39

What it did then from the Sabine's day of woe
  to good Lucretia's, under the seven kings
  who plundered the neighboring lands, you also know, 42

and how it led the Chosen Romans forward
  against the powers of Brennus, and of Pyrrhus,
  and of many a rival state and warring lord.   45

Thence the fame of Torquatus, curly Quintius,
　　and the Decii and Fabii. How gladly
　　I bring it myrrh to keep it glorious.　　　　　　48

It dashed to earth the hot Arabian pride
　　that followed Hannibal through the rocky Alps,
　　from which, you, Po, sweet river, rise and glide.　　51

Under it triumphed at an early age
　　Scipio and Pompey. Against the mountain
　　that looked down on your birth it screamed its rage.　54

Then as that age dawned in which Heaven planned
　　the whole world to its harmony, Caesar came,
　　and by the will of Rome, took it in hand.　　　57

What it did then from the Var to the Rhine is known
　　to Isère, Arar, Seine, and every valley
　　from which the waters of the Rhone flow down.　　60

And what it did when it had taken flight
　　from Ravenna and across the Rubicon
　　no tongue may hope to speak nor pen to write.　　63

It turned and led the cohorts into Spain;
　　then to Dyrrachium; and then struck Pharsalus
　　so hard that even the hot Nile felt the pain.　　66

Antandros and the Simoïs, where it first saw light,
　　it saw again, and Hector's grave, and then—
　　woe to Ptolemy—sprang again to flight.　　　69

Like a thunderbolt it struck at Juba next;
　　then turned once more and swooped down on your West
　　and heard again the Pompeian trumpet vexed.　　72

For what it did above its next great chief
  Brutus and Cassius wail in Cocytus;
    and Modena and Perugia came to grief.   75

For that, the tears still choke the wretched wraith
  of Cleopatra, who running to escape it,
    took from the asp her black and sudden death.   78

With him it traveled far as the Red Sea;
  and with him brought the world such peace that Janus
    was sealed up in his temple with lock and key.   81

But what this sign that moves my present theme
  had done before, all it was meant to do
    through the mortal realm it conquered—all must seem 84

dim shadows of poor things, if it be scanned
  with a clear eye and pure and honest heart,
    as it appears in the third Caesar's hand;   87

for the Living Justice whose breath I here breathe in
  gave it the glory, while in that same hand,
    of avenging His just wrath at Adam's sin.   90

Now ponder the double marvel I unfold:
  later, under Titus, it *avenged*
    the vengeance taken for that crime of old!   93

And when the sharp tooth of the Lombard bit
  the Holy Church, victorious Charlemagne,
    under those same wings, came and rescued it.   96

Now are you truly able to judge those
  whom I accused above, and their wrongdoing,
    which is the cause of all your present woes.   99

One speeds the golden lilies on to force
  the public standard; and one seizes it
  for private gain—and who knows which is worse? 102

Let them scheme, the Ghibellines, let them plot and weave
  under some other standard, for all who use
  this bird iniquitously find cause to grieve! 105

Nor let the new Charles think his Guelphs will be
  its overthrow, but let him fear the talons
  that have ripped the mane from fiercer lions than he. 108

Many a father's sinfulness has sealed
  his children's doom: let him not think his lilies
  will take the place of God's bird on his shield. 111

—This little star embellishes its crown
  with the light of those good spirits who were zealous
  in order to win honor and renown; 114

and when desire leans to such things, being bent
  from the true good, the rays of the true Love
  thrust upward with less force for the ascent; 117

but in the balance of our reward and due
  is part of our delight, because we see
  no shade of difference between the two. 120

By this means the True Judge sweetens our will,
  so moving us that in all eternity
  nothing can twist our beings to any ill. 123

Unequal voices make sweet tones down there.
  Just so, in our life, these unequal stations
  make a sweet harmony from sphere to sphere. 126

Within this pearl shines, too, the radiance
  of Romeo, whose good and beautiful works
  were answered by ingratitude and bad chance.   129

But the Provençals who worked his overthrow
  have no last laugh: he walks an evil road
  who finds his loss in the good that others do.   132

Four daughters had Count Raymond, each the wife
  of a Christian king, thanks to this Romeo,
  a humble man, a pilgrim in his life.   135

Envy and calumny so moved Raymond then
  that he demanded accounting of this just soul
  whose management had returned him twelve for ten.   138

For this he wandered, aged, poor, and bent,
  into the world again; and could the world
  know what was in his heart that road he went   141

begging his life by crusts from door to door,
  much as it praises him now, it would praise him more.

NOTES

General Note: THE FIGURE OF JUSTINIAN. The glowing spirit identifies itself as the soul of Justinian (482–565) who became Emperor of Rome in 527.

He emerges, in his own account, as a luminous and magnanimous spirit. A Christian, he subscribed to the Monophysitic Heresy, which accepted the divine nature of Christ but rejected his incarnation in mortal flesh. From this heresy he was converted by Agapetus (Pope from 535–536). As soon as he was converted, God's grace moved him to his great task of codifying the Roman Law, and to that work he gave himself wholly, leaving the conduct of his armies (which he had led with great success) to his general, Belisarius. So Dante sees him.

Another reading of history might have suggested several pits of Hell that might have claimed Justinian. Dante seems not to have known of the tyrannies of Justinian's reign, nor that the Justinian codification was the work of Tribonius, undertaken by him on Imperial command.

Whatever one's reading of history, one should note as part of Dante's structure that in *Inferno* VI he summarizes the condition of Florence, in *Purgatorio* VI, the state of Italy, and here in *Paradiso* VI, the history of the Roman Empire.

1–3. *turned the eagle's wing:* The Imperial Eagle, standard and symbol of Rome. In 330 Constantine moved the seat of Empire to Byzantium. Thus the Roman eagle flew east "against the course of Heaven," which turns from east to west, but also against the will of heaven, for Dante believed God had decreed Rome to be the seat of His church and the Roman Empire to be its earthly arm.

He also believed that Constantine moved the seat of empire to Byzantium in order to give Rome to the church. This gift was the "Donation of Constantine" (see *Inferno* XIX, 109–111, note) whereby the church (as Dante believed) grew rich and corrupt, hence, once more "against the course of Heaven."

The "new son of the Latian king" was Aeneas. He came from Troy (*with* the course of heaven), married Lavinia, daughter of the Latian king, and founded the line of the Roman Empire.

4. *two hundred years and more:* Byzantium became the imperial seat in 330. Justinian became emperor in 527. Thus the eagle had stayed at Europe's furthest edge for 197 years before it came to Justinian's hand. Some commentators argue that Dante meant the period from 330 to Justinian's military conquests in the east in 536. Such a reading brings the period to 206 years, justifying Dante's "two hundred years and more." It seems simpler, however, to assume that Dante made a mistake in his dates.

6. *close to the mountains out of which it rose:* The Trojan mountains. They are not far from Byzantium on a continental scale.

10–12. *Caesar I was:* On earth. But now only the name given him at the baptismal font is valid. *which now I feel:* May be taken to mean "now I am in Heaven" but the primary interpretation must be "now since my conversion."

19–20. *as closely as you see, etc.:* As a first principle of logic, a statement that contradicts itself contains both truth and falsehood. Of two contradictory terms only one can be true and the other must be false. Dante uses it here as an example of what is self-evidently true to human intellect. In Justinian's present state (informed by divine revelation) the duality of Christ's nature is as clear to him as is the nature of a logical contradiction to mortal intellect. (See also II, 45.)

25. *Belisarius:* Justinian's famous general was born 505, died 565. His successful campaigns against the Ostrogoths restored most of the Empire's authority over Italy. Dante seems not to have known that Justinian, in 562, in one of the endless intrigues of the Byzantine court, stripped "his" Belisarius of rank and had him imprisoned—an arrangement that became nearly standard as the Roman soldier's pension plan.

31–33. DENUNCIATION OF GUELPHS AND GHIBELLINES. Dante has asked to know (V, 126–127) the spirit's identity and why he was in the Sphere of Mercury. Lines 1–27 answer Dante's first question, but the nature of that reply moves Justinian to add a denunciation of both the Guelphs and Ghibellines for opposing the true purpose of the Holy Roman Empire, whose history (and divine right) he then recounts. *with how much right:* None at all. *the sacred standard:* The Imperial Eagle. *when they plot its subornation:* The Ghibellines; they sought to suborn imperial authority to their own ends. *or its overthrow:* The Guelphs; they sought to end imperial authority and leave matters in the hands of local lords.

36. *Pallas:* Son of Evander, a Greek who had founded a kingdom on the present site of Rome. Evander joined Aeneas in fighting Turnus, king of the Rutulians. In the fighting Pallas was killed by Turnus. As a result of his victory, Aeneas acquired a kingdom that included the hereditary rights of Pallas. Thus Pallas died to give the eagle its first kingly state. Or so at least runs the Virgilian version followed by Dante.

THE HISTORY OF THE ROMAN EAGLE

37–39. Following his victory over Turnus, Aeneas established his seat at Lavinium. His son, Ascanius, moved it from there to Alba Longa, called the Mother of Rome. There the eagle remained until in the seventh century B.C. the Curiatii (the three heroes of Alba) were vanquished by the three Horatii of Rome.

40–42. Expelled from Alba, Romulus established a base in Rome on the Palatine and recruited a band of raiders who carried out the raid on the Sabines (the often-painted Rape of the Sabine Women) in order to get wives. From this robber settlement grew the kingdom of Rome. Through a succession of seven kings it raided and looted its neighbors until Sextus, son of Tarquinius Superbus (the last of the Roman kings), violated Lucretia. When she died as a result of his attack, the people rose in anger, overthrew the king, and founded the Republic of Rome, in 510 B.C.

43–45. During the Republic, the Eagle was carried to many triumphs by Chosen Romans. Condensing almost three full centuries of history into nine lines, Dante cites the defeat of Brennus and his Gauls (circa 390 B.C.) and of Pyrrhus and his Greek invaders (280 B.C.).

46–48. From the Republican victories was born the fame of Torquatus (Titus Manlius Torquatus) who defeated (among others) the Gauls. In these battles one of the Fabii also distinguished himself. As did Lucius Quintius, called Cincinnatus because of an unruly lock of hair (from Latin *cincinnus,* a curl). The story of how he left the plow to become dictator of Rome and to conquer the Aquians in 485 B.C. is well known to schoolboys. Three generations of the Decii died in battle from 340 to 280 B.C., the last of these engagements being the defeat of the Greeks under Pyrrhus. And in 218 B.C. Quintus Fabius Maximus, the most notable of the Fabii, defeated Hannibal (see below).

Justinian recites these names and says he rejoices in anointing their fame with myrrh. (Myrrh was used by the ancients in embalming, as a means of preserving the body.) Note that Justinian, though on earth he was ambitious for his own glory, now rejoices in citing the glory of others.

49–51. It (the Eagle) defeated Hannibal in 218 B.C. Dante follows the custom of his times in referring to all inhabitants of north Africa as Arabs. The Po, here apostrophized, rises in the Alps.

52–54. Bracketing Scipio and Pompey, Justinian leaps from 218 to 81 B.C. In 218 Scipio Africanus, then seventeen, saved his father's life in battle against Hannibal at Ticinus. At twenty he defeated Hannibal's forces in Spain. And at thirty-three, by his successful invasion of Africa, brought about the destruction of Hannibal and of Carthage.

Pompey's first great victory (over Marius in 81 B.C.) occurred when he was twenty-five.

"The mountain that overlooked your [Dante's] birth" is Fiesole, and at Fiesole, according to Roman legend, the Eagle of the Republic overthrew Catiline.

55–60. These two tercets refer to the coming of Julius Caesar (born 102 or 100 B.C.; assassinated March 15, 44 B.C.) and to the Gallic Wars. In Dante's view of the Empire as the seat God had chosen for His church, Caesar was serving Heaven's plan in laying the foundation of Empire, for the Empire would bring the whole world into the harmony that would arise from unification under a single imperial rule.

Lines 58–60 describe the territory of the Gallic Wars (58–50 B.C.).

61–66. The Rubicon flows between Ravenna and Rimini. In Caesar's time it marked the boundary line between Italy and Gaul. In crossing it (January 11, 49 B.C.), Caesar left his province without permission of the senate, thus precipitating civil war.

64–66. Before the year was out Caesar struck Ilerda in Spain, defeating Pompey's lieutenants. (Note that in this case the eagle is striking against the eagle, for Pompey's cohorts also carried the Roman standard.) In the next year Caesar laid siege to Pompey in Dyrrachium (modern Durres in Albania), broke off, and then engaged Pompey again at Pharsalus in Thessaly (August 9, 48 B.C.), this time winning a great victory. *even the Nile felt the pain:* Because Pompey fled to Egypt and was killed there by Ptolemy.

67–69. Antandros is a coastal town near Troy. The Simoïs is a nearby river. Aeneas sailed from Antandros when he brought the eagle to Italy. After Pompey's death, Caesar visited Troy. Thus the Eagle saw its homeland again. From Troy ("Woe to Ptolemy") Caesar moved to Egypt, defeated Ptolemy, and gave Egypt to Cleopatra.

70–72. Led by Caesar, the Eagle next overthrew Juba, king of Numidia (46 B.C.) under whom fourteen republican legions had formed. In the next year he struck again at Spain ("on your West") where Pompey's two sons had gathered a new army.

73–78. Augustus, Caesar's nephew, was "its next great chief." After Caesar's murder led by Cassius and Brutus, Augustus became the standard-bearer. He defeated Marc Antony at Modena in 43 B.C., then formed an alliance with him, and the two together finished Brutus and Cassius at Philippi in 42 B.C. In 41 B.C. Augustus defeated Marc Antony's brother Lucius at Perugia. And in 31 B.C. Augustus defeated Marc Antony at Actium. Antony committed suicide soon after his defeat, and Cleopatra did the same when she heard the news.

79–81. *him:* Augustus. *far as the Red Sea:* The limit of the Empire. Augustus was now undisputed ruler of all Rome and the Empire was at peace. *Janus:* The gates of his temple were always open in time of war. Now they were closed (as they had been only twice before) to indicate peace throughout the Empire. Thus the serene time was set for the birth of Christ, the Prince of Peace.

85–90. Tiberius was the third Caesar. The great glory given the eagle in his reign was the Crucifixion, for thereby the sin of Adam was wiped clean and the gates of Heaven were opened to redeemed mankind.

91–93. Under Titus, the fourth Caesar, Jerusalem was taken in a bloody conquest which Dante saw as a vengeance taken for a just vengeance. His argument would probably run that it was just to exact vengeance for Adam's sin and that God sent His only begotten son to mankind for that purpose. Yet, in exacting a vengeance upon the man, the Jews also offended the god, and it is just that they be made to suffer for that crime against God. Such would seem to be the basis for the prejudice against the Jew, and many vexed questions are, of course, involved: If God decreed the Crucifixion, had the Jews any choice? Are they more guilty than Pilate who simply washed his hands and let his soldiers drive the nails? What is free will in confrontation with a preordained act of God's will? Such questions must be referred to a quality of revelation unknown to footnotes.

94–96. Justinian now leaps ahead over six centuries. Desiderius, an eighth-century king of the Lombards, rose against the church but was overthrown by Charlemagne in 774 A.D. Charlemagne, as Emperor of the Holy Roman Empire, was still bearing the eagle standard.

97–98. *those whom I accused above:* The Guelphs and Ghibellines. See lines 31 ff.

100–102. *one speeds the golden lilies on to force the public standard:* The Guelphs. They urge the Lilies of France against the Eagle. *one seizes it for private gain:* The Ghibellines. They seek to pervert the Imperial standard to their own ends.

106. *the new Charles:* Charles II (The Lame) of Anjoy, King of Naples and leader of the Guelphs.

109–111. *father's sinfulness . . . children's doom:* Justinian is pronouncing what may be a general sentiment, but he must certainly intend some reference to the woes that befell the house of Anjou, as Charles Martel (son of Charles the Lame) will amplify in VIII, 40–84.

112–114. Justinian has now answered Dante's first question (concerning his identity) and completed his additional remarks. He now addresses the second question (as to why he is in the Sphere of Mercury and what sort of spirits are with him). He identifies this sphere as the manifest realm of the personally ambitious.

115–120. Dante's phrasing is especially dense in these lines and I have had to take more than usual liberties in order to bring it to rhyme. His point here may be stated as follows: "We of this sphere worked for the Good but did so in seeking honor for ourselves rather than for the one true motive, which is the love of God. When desire is so bent from the true good, it follows that the upward thrust toward God is lesser for being bent aside. Therefore we are low in Heaven. Yet part of our joy is in knowing that our station is well chosen, our reward being exactly equal to our merit."

121–123. *By this means:* By letting us recognize how exactly our present state corresponds to the merit we showed in our lives.

124. *down there:* On earth.

128. *Romeo:* Romeo da Villanova. He was born circa 1170 and became prime minister and chamberlain of Raymond Berenger IV, Count of Provence from 1209 to 1245. Dante follows the legend that Romeo, passing through Provence on his way back from a pilgrimage, attached himself to Raymond's court and soon achieved high station by his wise management of Raymond's affairs. Among his triumphs, Romeo negotiated the marriages of Raymond's four daughters, each to a king. Later the local nobles, envious of Romeo's position, accused him of mismanaging the treasury. When Raymond demanded an accounting, Romeo pointed to the increase in the treasury, and picking up his pilgrim's staff once more, left the court to wander as he had come.

131. *have no last laugh:* The nobles of Provence have committed the sin of envy and must suffer for it. They also have no last laugh in that Provence lost a good manager of the realm.

CANTO VII

The Second Sphere: Mercury—Seekers of Honor: Justinian

Ascent to the Third Sphere—Beatrice Discourses

Justinian and his companions break into a *Hymn to the God of Battles* and, dancing, disappear into the distance. Dante, torn by doubt, longs to ask how a just vengeance may justly be avenged, but dares not speak. Beatrice, sensing his confusion, answers his question before he can ask it.

She explains the *Double Nature of the Crucifixion,* and why the Jews, though blameless in the crucifixion of the man, were still guilty of sacrilege against the God. She then explains why God chose this means of redemption, and why that choice was *The Greatest Act of All Eternity.*

She then explains the difference between *Direct and Indirect Creation* and concludes by proving *Why the Resurrection of the Flesh Is Certain.*

"*Osanna sanctus Deus Sabaoth*
  superillustrans claritate tua
  felices ignes horum malachoth!"   3

—So, giving itself to its own harmony,
  the substance of that being, over which
  two lights were joined as one, appeared to me.   6

And all those souls joined in a holy dance,
  and then, like shooting sparks, gone instantly,
  they disappeared behind the veil of distance.   9

I stood, torn by my doubts, "Speak up. Speak up,"
  I said inside myself. "Ask the sweet lady
  who slakes your every thirst from the sweet cup."   12

But the awe that holds my being in its sway
  even at the sound of BEA or of TRICE
  kept my head bent as if I dozed away.   15

But she soon soothed my warring doubt and dread,
  for with a smile whose ray could have rejoiced
  the soul of a man tied to the stake, she said: 18

"I know by my infallible insight
  you do not understand how a just vengeance
  can justly be avenged. To set you right   21

I shall resolve your mind's ambivalence.
  Listen and learn, for what I shall now say
  will be a gift of lofty consequence.   24

Because he would not, for his own good, take
  God's bit and rein, the man who was not born,
  damning himself, damned mankind for his sake. 27

Therefore, for many centuries, men lay
  in their sick error, till the Word of God
  chose to descend into the mortal clay.   30

There, moved by His Eternal Love alone,
  he joined in His own person that other nature
  that had wandered from its Maker and been cast down. 33

Now heed my reasoning: so joined again
  to its First Cause, this nature (as it had been
  at its creation) was good and without stain.   36

But by its own action, when it turned its face
  from the road of truth that was its road of life,
  it was driven from the garden of God's grace.   39

If the agony on the cross, considering this,
  was a punishment of the nature thus assumed,
  no verdict ever bit with greater justice;   42

Just so, no crime to match this can be cited
  when we consider the Person who endured it
  in whom that other nature was united.   45

Thus, various sequels flow from one event:
  God and the Jews concurred in the same death;
  for it the earth shook and the heavens were rent.   48

You should no longer find it hard to see
  what is meant in saying that just vengeance taken
  was afterwards avenged by just decree.   51

I see now that your mind, thought upon thought,
  is all entangled, and that it awaits
  most eagerly the untying of the knot.   54

You think: 'I grasp the truth of what I hear.
  But why God chose this means for our redemption—
  this and no other—I cannot make clear.'   57

No one may grasp the hidden meaning of
  this edict, brother, till his inborn senses
  have been made whole in the sweet fire of love.   60

Truly, therefore, since so many sight,
  and so few hit, this target, I shall now
  explain exactly why this means was right.   63

That Good, which from Itself spurns every trace
  of envy, in Itself sends out such sparks
  as manifest the everlasting grace.   66

Whatever is uttered by Its direct expression
  thereafter is eternal; His seal once stamped,
  nothing can ever wipe out the impression.   69

Whatever is poured directly from Its spring
  is wholly free; so made, it is not subject
  to the power of any secondary thing.   72

The Sacred Fire that rays through all creation
  burns with most joy in what is most like It;
  the more alike, the greater Its elation.   75

All of these attributes endow the nature
  of humankind; and if it fail in one,
  it cannot help but lose its noble stature.   78

Sin is the one power that can take away
  its freedom and its likeness to True Good,
  whereby it shines less brightly in Its ray.   81

Its innate worth, so lost, it can regain
  only by pouring back what guilt has spilled,
  repaying evil pleasure with just pain.   84

Your nature, when it took sin to its seed,
  sinned totally. It lost this innate worth,
  and it lost Paradise by the same deed.   87

Nor could they be regained (if you heed my words
  with scrupulous attention) by any road
  that does not lead to one of these two fords: 90

either that God, by courtesy alone,
  forgive his sin; or that the man himself,
  by his own penitence and pain, atone.   93

Now fix your eye, unmoving, on the abyss
  of the Eternal Wisdom, and your mind
  on every word I say concerning this!   96

Limited man, by subsequent obedience,
  could never make amends; he could not go
  as low in his humility as once,   99

rebellious, he had sought to rise in pride.
  Thus was he shut from every means himself
  to meet God's claim that He be satisfied.   102

Thus it was up to God, to Him alone
  in His own ways—by one or both, I say—
  to give man back his whole life and perfection.   105

But since a deed done is more prized the more
  it manifests within itself the mark
  of the loving heart and goodness of the doer,   108

the Everlasting Love, whose seal is plain
  on all the wax of the world, was pleased to move
  in all His ways to raise you up again.   111

There was not, nor will be, from the first day
  to the last night, an act so glorious
  and so magnificent, on either way.   114

For God, in giving Himself that man might be
  able to raise himself, gave even more
  than if he had forgiven him in mercy.   117

All other means would have been short, I say,
  of perfect justice, but that God's own Son
  humbled Himself to take on mortal clay.   120

And now, that every wish be granted you,
  I turn back to explain a certain passage,
  that you may understand it as I do.   123

You say: 'I see the water, I see the fire,
  the air, the earth; and all their combinations
  last but a little while and then expire.   126

Yet all these were creations! Ought not they—
  if what you said of them before is true—
  to be forever proof against decay?'   129

Of angels and this pure kingdom of the soul
  in which you are, it may be said they sprang
  full-formed from their creation, their beings whole. 132

But the elements, and all things generated
  by their various compoundings, take their form
  from powers that had themselves to be created.   135

Created was the matter they contain.
  Created, too, was the informing power
  of the stars that circle them in Heaven's main.   138

From the given potencies of these elements
  the rays and motions of the sacred lamps
  draw forth the souls of all brutes and all plants.   141

But the Supreme Beneficence inspires
  your life directly, filling it with love
  of what has made it, so that it desires   144

that love forever.—And from this you may
  infer the sure proof of your resurrection,
  if you once more consider in what way   147

man's flesh was given being like no other
  when He made our first father and first mother."

NOTES

1–3. The hymn sung by these spirits as they depart is addressed
to the God of triumphant armies (the God, as Dante believed, who
led the Roman Eagle) and is compounded of Hebrew and Latin, the
two languages of Heaven (though *malachoth*—"kingdoms"—should
properly be *mamlachoth*) and may be rendered: "Hosannah, holy God
of Sabaoth [of the armies], lighting from above with Your luster the
blessed fires of these kingdoms!" The blessed fires *(felices ignes)* are
the souls of heaven.

4–6. *its own harmony:* The harmony of the blessed voices. *two
lights:* May stand, perhaps, for Justinian's double glory as Emperor
and Lawgiver. *appeared to me:* Note, throughout the *Paradiso,* how
Dante's phrasing suggests not that he saw the things of Heaven with
his own senses, but that they were manifested to him by the blessed
spirits as an act of love.

10 ff. DANTE'S DOUBT. Dante is torn between his thirst to
know and his reluctance to ask. The question that fills him is "How
can a just revenge be justly punished?" As usual, Beatrice (and her
action in all such cases is certainly an allegory of her character as Di-
vine Revelation) knows his wish before he can speak it and grants it
before he can ask.

13–15. Intent of these lines: "But, as ever, the awe that overcomes
my being if I hear so much as part of her name, made me unable to
raise my head to speak and I kept it bent down like the head of a
man who is dozing off while in an upright position."

25–51. THE CRUCIFIXION. Beatrice argues that the death of
Christ was just because he had taken upon Himself both the nature
and guilt of mankind. His expiation was just because the sin of His
human nature was great. But since He was also a God, the pain in-
flicted upon His divinity was a sacrilege and demanded punishment.
So ran the Scholastic argument Dante follows here.

26. *the man who was not born:* Adam.

29. *the Word of God:* Christ.

31–33. *Eternal Love:* The Holy Ghost. *His own person:* Christ, the Son. *that other nature:* Man. *Maker:* God the Father.

40. *considering this:* Considering what I have just said of the guilt of human nature and of the fact that Christ willingly assumed that guilt in His own person.

48. *earth shook . . . heavens were rent:* See *Matthew* xxvii, 11–15.

66. *Grace:* Dante says "beauty." The Scartazzini-Vandelli commentary offers the following interpretation of this tercet: "The Divine Goodness, which rejects from Itself every trace of envy, being in Itself a single ardent flame, scintillates so that it shoots forth from Itself, like sparks, part of its Eternal Beauty, and by these (sparks) makes beautiful Its creatures. One must say *part* (of Itself) because a finite creature is not capable of the Infinite."

67–72. Dante is distinguishing here between "direct" (Godly) and "secondary" (angelic and human) creation. What God creates directly is eternal because nothing can wipe out the impression of His seal, and it is free because secondary creations have no power upon it. The point is further made in lines 130–144 below.

76. *all of these attributes:* The three Godly gifts are named above: immortality (lines 67–69), freedom (lines 70–72), and resemblance to God (lines 73–75). It follows that to lose any one these attributes is to fall from the first-created nobility (Adam's original state).

81. *it shines less brightly in Its ray:* Since God's fire rays forth most brightly in that which is most like God, and since sin makes man less like God, sin makes man shine less brightly in God's ray.

85–86. *seed . . . totally:* The seed is Adam. By his sin, all mankind fell from its first innate worth and lost Paradise.

97. *Limited man:* Man is limited by his mortal means. Within them, no depth of humility to which he could descend could be proportionate to the height he had sought in his rebellious sin. For man's sin was in seeking to become God, and there is no equivalent depth to which he could sink in recompense, for in sinning he had already damned himself to Hell.

104–105. *by one* (way): Mercy. *or both:* Mercy and Justice. Since man could not save himself, God could have forgiven him outright as an act of mercy. Or he could have created a man so perfect that he was capable of just expiation (that would have been the way of Justice). But in giving Himself through His own Son, He chose the double way that was both divine mercy and human justice. In the tercets that immediately follow Dante celebrates this choice as the supreme act of all eternity. *his whole life and perfection:* Because through Christ's redemption he could once more be received into Heaven and the whole life from which Adam's sin had excluded him.

114. *on either way:* On the way of mercy or on the way of justice.

122. *explain a certain passage:* Lines 67 ff. There Beatrice had explained that whatever God utters as His direct expression is eternal.

124–125. *water . . . fire . . . air . . . earth:* These were believed to be the four elements of which all things were compounded. Hence, they and their combinations make up all the material creation. These elements (seen as phenomena of the matter they contain, the matter itself being directly created) are the effects of certain directly created powers in nature, not as direct effects of God. As secondary effects, therefore, they are corruptible, whereas the soul of man, a direct creation, is eternal.

135. *powers that had themselves to be created:* Angels. God, of course, is the one power that did not Itself have to be created.

139–141. The four elements that give form to all matter (the matter being itself God-created and eternal but itself formless) derive their potencies from fixed (and first created) principles of nature which are ruled by angels. The stars in their courses then work upon these potencies and draw from them the sensitive and vegetative souls of beasts and plants (but not man's soul, which is God-created).

145–149. THE PROOF OF THE RESURRECTION OF THE FLESH. "From this," says Beatrice—from the principle declared in lines 67–68 that everything directly created by God is eternal, and from the fact that Adam and Eve were directly created by God— "you may infer the sure proof of your resurrection." There seems to be no explanation of Beatrice's reason for saying "your" (rather than "the" or "our") resurrection. As a codescendant of Adam and Eve, she must herself expect the resurrection of her flesh on Judgment Day.

CANTO VIII

The Third Sphere: Venus—The Amorous: Charles Martel

Dante and Beatrice reach the *Sphere of Venus, the Third Heaven*. Instantly, a band of souls that had been dancing in the Empyrean descends to the travelers. These are the souls of the *Amorous*. As we learn in Canto IX, many of them, perhaps all, were so full of the influence of Venus that they were in danger of being lost to carnality. Through the love of God, however, their passion was converted from physical love to true *caritas,* and thus do they rejoice in Heaven.

Their spokesman is *Charles Martel of Anjou*. He identifies himself and prophesies dark days for the Kingdom of Naples because of the meanness of King Robert, his brother. Dante asks how it is that mean sons can be born of great fathers, and Charles answers with a *Discourse on the Diversity of Natural Talents,* a diversity he assigns to the influence of the stars, as God provided them for man's own good as a social being, for only by diversity of gifts can society function. God had planned all these variations to a harmonious end. It is mankind, by forcing men into situations not in harmony with their talents, that strays from God's plan.

The world, to its own jeopardy, once thought
  that Venus, rolling in the third epicycle,
  rayed down love-madness, leaving men distraught.   3

Therefore the ancients, in their ignorance,
  did honor not to her alone, but offered
  the smokes of sacrifice and votive chants   6

to Dione and to Cupid, her mother and son,
  and claimed that he had sat on Dido's lap
  when she was smitten by love's blinding passion.   9

From her with whom my song began just now
  they took the name of the star that woos the Sun,
  now shining at its nape, now at its brow.   12

I reached it unaware of my ascent,
  but my lady made me certain I was there
  because I saw her grow more radiant.   15

And as a spark is visible in the fire,
  and as two voices may be told apart
  if one stays firm and one goes lower and higher;   18

so I saw lights circling within that light
  at various speeds, each, I suppose, proportioned
  to its eternal vision of delight.   21

No blast from cold clouds ever shot below,
  whether visible or not, so rapidly
  but what it would have seemed delayed and slow   24

to one who had seen those holy lights draw nigh
  to where we were, leaving the dance begun
  among the Seraphim in Heaven on high.   27

And from the first who came, in purest strain
  "Hosannah" rang; so pure that, ever since,
  my soul has yearned to hear that sound again.   30

Then one of them came forward and spoke thus:
  "We are ready, all of us, and await your pleasure
  that you may take from us what makes you joyous. 33

In one thirst and one spiraling and one sphere
  we turn with those High Principalities
  to whom you once cried from the world down there: 36

'O you whose intellects turn the third great wheel!'
  So full of love are we that, for your pleasure,
  it will be no less bliss to pause a while."   39

I raised my eyes to the holy radiance
   that was my lady, and only after she
   had given them her comfort and assurance,   42

did I turn to the radiance that had made
   such promises. "Who are you?" were my words,
   my voice filled with the love it left unsaid.   45

Ah, how it swelled and grew even more bright,
   taking increase of bliss from my few words,
   and adding new delight to its delight.   48

So changed, it said: "My life there among men
   was soon concluded; had it lasted longer
   great evils yet to be would not have been.   51

The ecstasy that is my heavenly boon
   conceals me: I am wrapped within its aura
   as a silkworm is enclosed in a cocoon.   54

You loved me much, and you had reason to,
   for had I stayed below, you would have seen
   more than the green leaves of my love for you.   57

The left bank of the land washed by the Rhone
   after its waters mingle with the Sorgue's
   waited, in due course, to become my own;   60

as did that horn of Italy that lies
   south of the Tronto and Verde, within which
   Bari, Gaeta, and Catona rise.   63

Already on my brow there shone the crown
   of the land the Danube bathes when it has left
   its German banks. And though not yet my own,   66

beautiful Sicily, the darkened coast
  between the Capes of Faro and Passero,
    there on the gulf that Eurus lashes most,   69

(not dimmed by Typhoeus, as mythology
  would have men think, but by its rising sulfur)
    would yet have looked to have its kings, through me, 72

from Charles and Rudolph, but that the bitter breath
  of a populace subjected to misrule
    cried out through all Palermo's streets 'Death! Death!' 75

And could Robert have foreseen how tyranny
  will drive men mad, he would have fled in fear
    from Catalonia's greedy poverty.   78

For some provision surely must be made,
  by him or by another, lest on his ship,
    already heavy laden, more be laid.   81

His nature, born to avarice from the loins
  of a liberal sire, would have required lieutenants
    who cared for more than filling chests with coins." 84

—"Sire, I hold dearer this felicity
  that fills me when you speak, believing it
    as visible to you as it is to me,   87

there where every good begins and ends.
  And this, too, I hold dear—that you discern it
    in looking on Him from whom all love descends. 90

You have given me joy. Now it is in your power
  to give me light. For your words leave me in doubt:
    how, if the seed is sweet, may the fruit be sour?" 93

Thus I. And he: "Could I make you recognize
  one truth of what you ask, then what is now
  behind your back, would be before your eyes.   96

The Good by which this kingdom you now climb
  is turned and gladdened, makes its foresight shine
  as powers of these great bodies to all time.   99

Not only does that Perfect Mind provide
  for the diversities of every nature
  but for their good and harmony beside.   102

And thus whatever arrow takes its arc
  from this bow flies to a determined end,
  it being aimed unerringly to its mark.   105

Else would these heavens you now move across
  give rise to their effect in such a way
  that there would be not harmony, but chaos.   108

This cannot be unless the intellects
  that move these stars are flawed, and flawed the first,
  which, having made them, gave them such defects.   111

—Should I expound this further?" he said to me.
  And I: "There is no need, for now I know
  nature cannot fall short of what must be."   114

And he: "Would man be worse off than he is,
  there on earth, without a social order?"
  "Yes!" I replied. "Nor need I proof of this."   117

"And can that be, unless men there below
  lived variously to serve their various functions?
  Your master, if he knows, answers you 'no.' "   120

So point by point that radiant soul disputes.
  Now he concludes: "Your various aptitudes,
  it follows, therefore, must have various roots.   123

So one man is born Xerxes, another Solon;
  one Melchizedek, and another he
  who, flying through the air, lost his own son.   126

That ever-revolving nature whose seal is pressed
  into our mortal wax does its work well,
  but takes no heed of where it comes to rest.   129

So Esau parted from Jacob in the seed;
  and Romulus was born of such humble stock
  that Mars became his father, as men agreed.   132

Begotten and begetter, but for the force
  of overruling providence, the son's nature
  would always follow in the father's course.   135

—And now what was behind shines out before.
  But to make you understand how much you please me,
  I would wrap you in one corollary more: 138

what Nature gives a man Fortune must nourish
  concordantly, or nature, like any seed
  out of its proper climate, cannot flourish.   141

If the world below would learn to heed the plan
  of nature's firm foundation, and build on that,
  it then would have the best from every man.   144

But into holy orders you deflect
  the man born to strap on a sword and shield;
  and make a king of one whose intellect   147

is given to writing sermons. And in this way
  your footprints leave the road and go astray."

NOTES

1. *to its own jeopardy:* Because in so believing it risked the wrath that has often descended upon the idolatrous.

2. *epicycle:* Not to be confused with "sphere." The epicycle of Venus turns around the center line of the Third Sphere. Thus the planet keeps appearing in various positions around the sun, "now shining at its nape" (behind it, hence Venus as evening star), "now at its brow" (before it, hence Venus as morning star) as Dante says in line 12 below. In line 96 this epicyclic motion becomes allegorically significant. In line 135 this image theme is brought to rest. This sweetly managed development is a fine example of Dante's way with imagery.

3. *rayed down love-madness:* The rays of Venus, the pagans believed, drove men and women mad with love.

7. *Dione:* One legend has it that Venus was the daughter of Dione and Zeus. *Cupid:* He has many mythological manifestations. Dante is here taking him as the son of Venus by Mars or, more probably, by Mercury.

8–9. *had sat on Dido's lap:* When she was smitten by love for Aeneas, the passion that led to her death. (See *Inferno* V, 61, 86). Line 9 is my own rhyme-forced addition and does not occur in Dante.

10. *her:* Venus.

11–12. *that woos the Sun:* The apparent motion of Venus is from one side of the Sun to the other. See note to line 2, above.

19 ff. THE AMOROUS. These lights are the souls of the Amorous; not the pagan distortion of love-madness, but the Christian and divine radiance of *caritas*. Like all the souls of Heaven, they manifest themselves (at will) in their appropriate sphere, but they have their true place in the Empyrean among the Seraphim. They have been dancing there in their eternal joy when they become aware of Dante and Beatrice and, in a passion of *caritas*, descend to them at inconceivable speeds, still dancing and singing *Hosannah*.

22–24. *blast from cold clouds, etc.:* Hot dry vapors colliding with cold wet clouds were believed to discharge visible or invisible blasts of wind at great speeds. Lightning was believed to be a blast of wind moving so fast that the friction of its motion caused it to ignite. But even such a rate of descent would have seemed laggard as compared to the descent of these souls when they see Dante and Beatrice. *below:* In earth's atmosphere.

31. *Then one of them:* Charles Martel (see below). He explains that all the souls of this sphere dance in perpetual bliss in the Empyrean, but that they are all so full of love and so eager to give joy to others, that to pause from bliss a while in order to give joy to others will seem no less bliss.

34. *In one thirst:* For God's love. *and one spiraling:* In one eternal circling of God's throne. *and one sphere:* In a round with the angels and powers of this third Heaven.

35–37. *those High Principalities:* The third heaven, we are to understand, is moved by Principalities (angels of a certain rank), or so Dante himself once addressed them in the words here quoted (from the *Convivio*). In IX, 61, however (see note), that function is assigned to Thrones. For the orders of angels see XXVIII.

40–84. CHARLES MARTEL. Born 1271, the first son of Charles II (The Lame) of Anjou. Crowned King of Hungary (though in title only) 1290. Died 1295. His conversation indicates that he and Dante had met on earth, probably when Charles visited Florence in 1294, and that Charles had intended to be Dante's royal patron. This Charles Martel must not be confused with the better known Charles Martel (Charles the Hammer), King of the Franks, who lived circa 688–741. The following dates may offer some useful points of reference in the maze of intrigue that marked the Kingdom of the Two Sicilies:

1268 Charles I of Anjou (French) defeats Conradin German) Tagliacozzo. (See *Inferno* XXVIII, 17.)

1271 Charles Martel (grandson of Charles I) born.

1282 The Sicilian Vespers (Easter Day) in which most of the French (rulers of Sicily) were massacred in a popular uprising. In Octo-

ber of the same year Peter III of Aragon (Spanish) invaded Sicily
and captured Messina, last French strongpoint. The House of
Anjou is not totally driven from Sicily but retains the Kingdom
of Naples (it and Sicily being the "Two Sicilies"). Soon after
Peter's invasion, Pope Martin IV, anxious to defend the temporal
rights of the Church in Sicily, declares a crusade against Aragon.

1284 Charles II (the Lame), father of Charles Martel, is captured in
the Bay of Naples by the forces of Peter III of Aragon, and is
held for ransom in Spain.

1286 Charles I dies while Charles II is still captive, and Charles
Martel becomes regent at age 15.

1288 Charles II is released and takes over the rule of Naples.
(Robert, Lodovico, and John, younger brothers of Charles Mar-
tel . . . are surrendered to Peter of Aragon as hostages for
Charles' ransom, and they remain in Spain until 1295.)

1290 Charles Martel becomes titular King of Hungary.

1295 Charles Martel dies (before his father).

The warfare that followed the Sicilian Vespers continued for thirty
years, spurred constantly by the Vatican, and involved not only the
powers of Anjou and of Aragon, but of Valois and of Sicily, and of
the Papal States, in various shifting alliances.

In lines 50–51, Charles points out that he died young, but de-
clares that had he lived longer he might have averted the great evils
of this long warfare by establishing harmony among the contesting
forces. As becomes heavenly souls, Charles is a bit of an optimist: the
intrigues of the various Popes who ruled from 1282 to 1303, and of
their various seculiar allies, could hardly have been combed smooth
by a stripling, but Charles seems to have had generous intentions to-
ward Dante, and Dante repays him even more generously.

43. *the radiance that had made:* Charles. In line 33 he had promised
to give Dante what would make him joyous.

48. *adding new delight to its delight:* Love of others is the delight
and radiance of these souls. The thought of being able to give plea-
sure to Dante by answering his question makes the light of loving
bliss swell and burn even more brightly.

51. *yet to be:* Charles is talking, of course, as of 1300. There were yet to be more than two years of war before the defeat of Charles of Valois in Sicily and the peace of 1303.

54. The silkworm in its cocoon was a common symbol of transfiguring rebirth. Note that the Sphere of Venus is the last in which the souls suggest any trace of human form or lineaments. The spirits higher up appear only as flames, until, in the Empyrean, something like their human forms reappears but mystically transfigured.

57. *more than the green leaves:* Charles stayed in Florence for three weeks on his visit of 1294, was warmly received by the Florentines, and responded warmly. Dante seems to have struck up a friendship with Charles and seems to have been promised Charles' love and patronage. Had Charles lived, Dante would have seen more than the promise (the green leaves) of Charles' love; he would have seen the fruit of it (active patronage).

58–60. *The left bank, etc.:* The land so marked was Provence. Charles I (King of Naples and brother of the King of France) acquired it by marriage. It thus became attached to the crown of Naples, was passed on to Charles II, and would have passed on to Charles Martel as the firstborn son.

61. *that horn of Italy:* The territory so described was the former Kingdom of Naples, to which Charles was also heir. The Tronto and the Verde (now called the Garigliano) draw a nearly complete line across Italy. Together they were the main boundary between the Papal States to the north and the Kingdom of Naples to the south.

64–66. The Danube rises in Germany and flows east through Hungary. Charles Martel had the glow of the Hungarian crown on his brow, but the throne was occupied by Andreas III of Venice. Charles was King in title only. In 1310 Charles Robert, son of Charles Martel, became King of Hungary in fact as well as in title.

66–75. *And though not yet my own:* The passage is in Dante's denser style and complicated by the strange parenthesis about Typhoeus, a Titan associated with the fires and smokes of the earth's interior. He rose against Zeus, who (in the legend Dante follows) hurled him deep into the earth and piled Aetna upon him. Dante, in his paradisal freedom from the errors of mythology, explains that the smoke shrouds of Sicily are caused not by Typhoeus but by the burning sulfur of volcanoes.

The parenthesis understood, the gist of the rest of the passage is that Charles Martel, but for the overthrow of the French in the Sicilian Vespers, would have ruled Sicily and so continued in his sons the bloodlines of Anjou (on his side) and of Rudolph of Hapsburg (on his wife's side). *Faro:* Cape Faro, the northeast tip of Sicily. *Passero:* Cape Passero, the southeast tip. Dante calls them Pelorus and Pachynus. *Eurus:* The east wind. *the bitter breath . . . Palermo's streets:* The Sicilian Vespers. *misrule:* Of Charles I of Anjou.

76–78. *Robert:* Became King of Naples in 1309. He was one of the younger brothers of Charles Martel who remained in Spain from 1288 to 1295 as hostages for Charles II. In Catalonia, Robert made friends among the Spanish, who later became powerful in his government of Naples and who, in the greed of their poverty, oppressed the people. Charles is prophesying that Robert, a weak man, will reap a bad harvest from the seeds of misrule he has sown.

80. *on his ship:* Charles Martel may mean the "ship" of Robert's soul, already wallowing under the load of Catalonian avarice he has permitted, and which may damn him too; or he may mean the "ship" of state of abused Naples, once destined to be his own kingdom.

85–90. The sense of this difficult passage depends on the reader's awareness of "there where every good begins and ends." I believe "there" is best understood as "the Empyrean" (the true seat of these souls whose manifestations appear in the various heavens). With "there" so understood, the passage may be paraphrased: "Because I believe this felicity I feel is as clear to you up 'there' as it is to me, is it the dearer to me. And it is also dear to me that you discern my felicity (up 'there') by looking directly upon God (to whom my joy is known) rather than by looking merely into my heart."

93 ff. THE VARIATIONS OF PERSONAL ENDOWMENT. Dante asks how sweet seed can bear sour fruit, i.e., how a noble father can beget a mean son. Charles explains the central truth whereby what is now behind Dante's back (hence, unseen) will reveal itself to his eyes.

Obviously it would not be just for one family or bloodline to inherit all the high qualities of mankind, as would be the case if the sons of great fathers always inherited greatness. God does not will it so.

Yet such would be the case were the qualities of the father (the active male principle as discussed in *Purgatorio* XXV, 37 ff.) transmitted to the children without any external force affecting the transmission. That external force is the influence of the stars bearing on the hour of the individual's birth in order to serve God's just and harmonious ends. For God created man as a social being, and since society requires many different talents, God assigns to the spheres the power to generate this necessary diversity.

99. *these great bodies:* The heavenly bodies. Their influences on mankind are powers granted them by God's providence. (Note that Dante uses "providence" always in the sense of "pre-vision," i.e., foresight.)

109–111. The argument here is *reductio ad absurdum*. The heavenly bodies could produce chaos instead of harmony only if the Intelligences that move each sphere were imperfect, and if the First Intelligence (God) were also imperfect, having created defective agents. Since these things cannot be, the argument is false, and one must conclude that only harmony can flow from the order of God's creation, all things interplaying to His ordained ends.

114. *nature cannot fall short of what must be:* The universe, having been created and predestined to God's sure purpose, cannot do less than He predestined it to do.

117. *Nor need I proof of this:* Charles has just presented proofs of reason to support the truth of universal harmony. Dante is saying that on this point of the good of society to mankind he needs no such proofs, his own intellect being sufficient. In *De Monarchia* Dante discussed the nature of man as a civic being.

120. *Your master:* Aristotle. In the *Ethics* and elsewhere he expounds the various offices men in society must serve for the good of all.

120–123. The soul of Charles Martel has carried the disputation forward by deduction. Now it concludes: the various (and necessary) endowments required of social man could not follow from the single genetic source of the active (father) principle (which would reproduce itself without change) but must arise from various roots (the shifting influences of the heavenly bodies).

124–126. *Xerxes:* The Persian King. He is the type of the war-leader. *Solon:* Athenian lawgiver of the seventh century B.C., the type of the legislator. *Melchizedek:* As in *Genesis* xiv, 18, "he was the priest of the most high God," hence, the type of the spiritual leader. *he who, flying . . . lost his own son:* Daedalus, the type of the artisan and mechanic.

127–129. *That ever-revolving nature:* The power of the ever-turning spheres. This nature (this rank of nature) impresses its influence upon mortals as a seal is pressed into wax, thus effecting its generalized purposes (the distribution of various gifts to mankind) but without regard to where its gift lodges.

130–132. *Esau . . . Jacob:* Though twins, they were markedly different in character. "In the seed" is crucial here: Dante seems to imply that their genetic inheritance was identical. If so, only the diverse influence of the stars could have affected their differences. *Romulus:* His father was so humble that men were able to say he was born of Mars (as they could not have said had his father been sufficiently well known to have been remembered).

139–141. If a man's natural abilities (from his genetic inheritance and from the influences of the stars) sort well with the conditions into which he is born (as determined by Fortune, the agent of divine foresight), then the man prospers. But if his abilities and his fortune are not so sorted, then, like a seed planted in an unsuitable climate, his gift cannot achieve its full growth.

145–148. *into holy orders:* Charles' general sense is clear enough here but he probably intends an additional reference to his younger brother Lodovico who became Bishop of Toulouse, *and make a king of one:* Here, in addition to the general sense, Charles certainly intends a reference to his brother Robert, who paid little attention to his duties as King of Naples, and who composed a number of ornate sermons and other discourses.

CANTO IX

The Third Sphere: Venus—The Amorous:
Cunizza, Folquet, Rahab

Cunizza da Romano next appears, lamenting the woes that have befallen her native Venetia and prophesying great grief to her countrymen for pursuing false fame on earth. Cunizza has begun her remarks by pointing out a soul who rejoices beside her in Heaven as one who pursued good ends. When she finishes speaking that soul identifies itself as *Folquet, once Bishop of Marseilles.* Folquet narrates his life and indicates that, like Cunizza, his amorous nature first led him to carnality but later filled him with passion for the True Love of God. Folquet then answers Dante's questions about the *Nature of the Third Heaven,* identifies *Rahab,* the Whore of Jericho, as the first soul to ascend to that sphere, and concludes with a *Denunciation of Boniface VIII* for neglecting the Holy Land and all things spiritual, and a further *Denunciation of Florence* as a corrupt state and as the source of Papal corruption. A just vengeance, he prophesies, will not be long delayed.

Fair Clemence, when your Charles, in speaking thus
  had shone his light into my mind, he told me
  of the schemes and frauds that would attack his house. 3

But he said to me: "Say nothing. Let the years
  turn as they must." And so I can say only
  that they who wrong you shall find cause for tears.   6

Now to the Sun, the all-sufficing good,
  the eternal being of that sacred lamp
  had turned itself again to be renewed.   9

O souls deceived! ill-born impieties
  who turn your hearts away from the True Love
  and fix your eyes on empty vanities!   12

—And lo! another of those splendors now
  draws near me, and his wish to give me pleasure
  shows in the brightening of his outward glow.   15

The eyes of Beatrice, which, as before
  were fixed on me, saw all my wish and gave it
  the assurance of their dear consent once more.   18

"O blessed spirit, be pleased to let me find
  my joy at once," I said. "Make clear to me
  that you are a true mirror of my mind!"   21

Thereat the unknown spirit of that light,
  who had been singing in its depths, now spoke,
  like one whose whole delight is to delight.   24

"In that part of the sinful land men know
  as the Italy which lies between Rialto
  and the springs from which the Brenta and Piave flow, 27

there stands a hill of no imposing height;
  down from it years ago there came a firebrand
  who laid waste all that region like a blight.   30

One root gave birth to both of us. My name
  was Cunizza, of Romano, and I shine here
  because this star conquered me with its flame.   33

Yet gladly I embrace the fate that so
  arranged my lot, and I rejoice in it,
  although it may seem hard to the crowd below.   36

This bright and precious jewel of our sky,
  whose ray shines here beside me, left great fame
  behind him on the earth; nor will it die   39

before this centenary is five times told.
  Now ask yourself if man should seek that good
  that lives in name after the flesh is cold.   42

The rabble that today spills through the land
  bound by the Tagliamento and the Adige
  think little of that, nor, though war's bloody hand   45

rips them, do they repent. But Paduan blood,
  having shunned its duty, shall soon stain the water
  that bathes Vicenza and drains into mud.   48

And there rules one who yet holds high his head,
  there where the Sile and the Cagnano join,
  for whom the net already has been spread.   51

And Feltro shall yet weep the treachery
  of its foul priest; no man yet entered Malta
  for a crime as infamous as his shall be.   54

Great would that ever be that could hold at once
  the blood Ferrara will spill, and tired the man
  who set himself to weigh it ounce by ounce;   57

—all this the generous priest will freely give
  to prove his party loyalty; but then
  such gifts conform to how those people live.   60

On high are mirrors (you say 'Thrones') and these
  reflect God's judgment to us; so enlightened,
  we have thought it well to speak these prophecies."   63

Here she fell still and, turning, made it clear
  she was drawn to other things, joining once more
  the wheel of souls that dance through that third sphere. 66

That other Bliss, he I had heard her say
  was precious to her, now showed himself to me
  like a fine ruby struck by the sun's ray.   69

Up there, joy makes those souls add light to light,
  as here it makes us laugh, while down below
  souls darken as they grieve through Hell's long night. 72

"God sees all, and your insight, blessèd being,
  makes itself one with His," I said, "and thus
  no thought or wish may hide beyond your seeing.   75

Why does your voice, then, which forever sings
  Heaven's delight as one with those Blest Flames
  who wrap themselves about with their six wings,   78

not grant my wish? Had I the intuition
  with which to read your wish as you read mine,
  I should not be still waiting for *your* question!"   81

"The greatest basin to which earth's waters flow
  —aside from the sea that girdles all the land—"
  his voice began when I had spoken so,   84

"extends so far against the course of the sun,
  between opposing shores, that at its zenith
  the sun must cross what first was its horizon.   87

I first saw light on that sea's shore between
  the Ebro and that river whose short course
  parts Tuscan from Genoese—the Magra, I mean.   90

Sunrise and sunset are about the same
  for Bougiah and my city, whose blood flowed
  to warm its harbor's waters when Caesar came.   93

My name—to such as knew it on the earth
　　was Folquet; here eternally my ray
　　marks all this sphere, as its ray marked my birth.　　96

Dido did not burn hotter with love's rage,
　　when she offended both Sichaeus and Creusa,
　　than I, before my locks grew thin with age.　　99

Nor she of Rhodopè who felt the smart
　　of Demophoön's deception, nor Hercules
　　when he had sealed Iole in his heart.　　102

But none repents here; joy is all our being:
　　not at the sin—that never comes to mind—
　　but in the All-Ordering and All-Foreseeing.　　105

Here all our thoughts are fixed upon the Love
　　that beautifies creation, and here we learn
　　how world below is moved by world above.　　108

But that you may take with you from this sphere
　　full knowledge of all it makes you wish to know,
　　I must speak on a little further here.　　111

You wish to know who is within this blaze
　　you see in all its splendor here beside me,
　　like purest water lit by the sun's rays.　　114

Know, then, that in it Rahab finds her good;
　　and that, one with our choir, she seals upon it
　　the highest order of beatitude.　　117

Of all Christ's harvest, her soul was the one
　　first summoned by this Heaven, on which the shadow
　　the earth casts rests the point of its long cone.　　120

It was fitting in every way that she should thus
   adorn one of these heavens as a palm
   of the high victory two palms won for us,   123

for she it was who helped win the first glory
   of Joshua's victory in the Holy Land
   (which seems to have slipped from the Pope's
                                    memory).   126

Your Florence—which was planted by the One
   who first turned on his Maker, and whose envy
   has given men such cause for lamentation—   129

brings forth and spreads the accursed flower of gold
   that changes the shepherd into a ravening wolf
   by whom the sheep are scattered from the fold.   132

And so the Gospels and Great Doctors lie
   neglected, and the Decretals alone
   are studied, as their margins testify.   135

So Pope and Cardinal heed no other things.
   Their thoughts do not go out to Nazareth
   where the blessèd Gabriel opened wide his wings. 138

But the Vatican, and the other chosen parts
   of Holy Rome that have been, from the first,
   the cemetery of those faithful hearts   141

that followed Peter and were his soldiery,
   shall soon be free of this adultery."

NOTES

1–6. THE PROPHECY OF CHARLES MARTEL. On the death of Charles Martel (1295) the throne of Naples passed to his son Caroberto, but in 1309 Robert the Wise (younger brother of Charles and, therefore, Caroberto's uncle) usurped the throne. Thus the direct line of Charles Martel lost the crown of Naples. Robert and his followers, however, will yet have cause to weep in the disastrous consequences of their deceptions and of the suffering inflicted upon Robert's subjects by his Spanish lieutenants. Dante does not specify what will cause their tears, but the subsequent history of the Kingdom of Naples left generous provision for any amount of mourning.

There is no wholly satisfactory identification of the Clemence Dante here addresses. Charles' wife was named Clemence, but she died in 1295, and Dante's words seem clearly addressed to a living person. Charles' mother was also called Clemence, and she lived until 1323, but she was customarily known as Maria of Hungary, the daughter of Rudolph I of Hapsburg. And Charles had a daughter named Clemence, but if Dante intended the daughter, it seems odd to refer to the father as "her Charles."

8. *the eternal being:* Charles.

13. *another of those splendors:* Cunizza da Romano (circa 1198–circa 1279), younger daughter of Ezzolino II, Count of Onora, and the cruelest of the Ghibelline tyrants. He is in Hell with the Violent against their Neighbors (*Inferno* XII, 110).

Cunizza was known as an outgoing woman, her tendencies attested by the fact that she had various lovers as well as three husbands. Sordello was one among her lovers (*Purgatorio* VI, 58 ff.). Among other bad choices, she willed her estate to Alessandro and Napoleone, Counts of Mangone, two of the worst sinners in Hell (*Inferno* XXXII, 41–60). There seems to be no way of knowing why Dante put her in Paradise. He must have credited her with a true contrition in her later years, and certainly he might have been moved to show that even a great sinner could find heaven's grace through repentance, but at best she would have been scheduled for more than twenty-one years in Purgatory. Her case may have been helped by the fact that in 1265 she manumitted a number of slaves who had been in bondage to her father and brothers.

15. *outward glow:* Dante regularly conceives the spirits of heaven as having an inner and an outer glow, of which only the outer is visible to him.

16. *as before:* As when Dante, with his eyes, asked of Beatrice's eyes their permission to talk to Charles Martel (VIII, 40–42).

19–21. Dante knows by now that the heavenly spirits know his thoughts without need for him to speak them, and that knowledge fills him with the expectation of joy. He asks Cunizza to give him that joy without delay, by demonstrating that she can address his unspoken thoughts.

22. *the unknown spirit:* Cunizza has not yet identified herself to Dante.

26–27. *Rialto:* The principal island of Venice, here taken for all of Venice. *the Brenta and Piave:* These rivers have their sources in the mountains north and northwest of Florence. The area so defined is Marca Trivigiana whose principal city is Treviso.

29. *a firebrand:* Ezzolino (or Azzolino), Cunizza's brother.

33. The flame of Venus is, of course, love.

34–36. *the fate that so arranged my lot:* Cunizza's amorous nature was the force of fate that shaped her lot. The crowd below (mortal men) may think it painful for her to recall her natural amorousness and the loose life to which it led her. Yet that same fire of passion, properly directed to the love of God, was also the source of her blessedness.

37 ff. *This bright and precious jewel:* Folquet of Marseilles, a troubadour poet who became a Cistercian monk, and who was Bishop of Toulouse from 1205 to 1231. He was a leader (as he informs Dante in lines 123–142) in the atrocious crusade against the Albigensians. The fame he left on earth was written darkly enough in Albigensian blood, but Cunizza (and, through her, Dante) seems here to honor him as one who inveighed against the false passions of the people of Marca Trivigiana, exhorting them to seek the pure and lasting fame of an honored memory.

40. *this centenary:* The year 1300 was a Jubilee year (see *Inferno* XVIII, 28–33, note). Dante is probably saying that five more centenaries will pass before Folquet's fame dies.

43–48. CUNIZZA'S PROPHECY. The Tagliamento and Adige are rivers. The land they bound is, approximately, the present Venetia. The Bacchiglione flows through this land a bit south of its center, passes by Vicenza and then Padua, and empties into the swamps behind Venice ("drains into the mud"). Dante's text can be variously interpreted but points clearly enough to the defeat of the Paduans outside Vicenza in 1314 by Dante's great patron, Can Grande della Scala. The duty the Paduans shunned was, in general, the observance of justice but, specifically, their allegiance to the empire as represented by Can Grande, the reigning Ghibelline.

49–51. Rizzardo da Cammino, Lord of Treviso ("where the Sile and Cagnano join"), was treacherously murdered in 1312 while playing chess. He was the son of "the good Gherardo" (*Purgatorio* XVI, 124 and 138), the son-in-law of Judge Nin (*Purgatorio* VIII, 53 ff.), and the husband of "my Giovanna" (*Purgatorio* VIII, 71).

52–60. The Malta here referred to was a papal prison near Lake Bolsena. The worst of its criminals had yet to commit a crime as foul as the one that would be committed by Alessandro Novella, Bishop of Feltro, who accepted a group of Ghibelline refugees from Ferrara as his guests, and then (in July of 1314) turned them over to Pino della Tosa, one of the Spanish agents of Robert of Naples, to be beheaded. Thus the Bishop fell to his place in Ptolomea among those who were treacherous against their guests. (Sinners in that category, bear in mind, did not await their death to begin their damnation, but fell instantly into the ice of Cocytus, their earthly bodies being assumed by fiends.)

The blood of the Ferrarans would fill a great urn, but this generous priest (an irony) will give it gladly in duty to his party (Guelph), and be it said (another and a savage irony) such gifts of blood will suit the way the people of Marca Trivigiana live.

61. *Thrones:* There is no established creed concerning the hierarchy of the angels but Dante sets forth their orders. Cunizza's words indicate that Dante conceives the informing spirits of Venus (and

probably of each of the spheres) to be Thrones. See also VIII, 35–37, note.

62–63. *so enlightened:* It is in the full illumination of God's judgment and wisdom that Cunizza has thought well to utter her prophecy. Clearly, however, she is the spokesman for all the spirits of this sphere.

64–66. To understand these lines, one should refer to VIII, 16–27 and 34–36, in which Dante describes how these souls dance their eternal delight in God.

67. *That other bliss:* Folquet. Dante does not yet know who he is, except as Cunizza referred to him in line 37 as "this bright and precious jewel."

70–71. *Up there:* In Heaven. *as here:* On earth.

73–81. Since the Heavenly Soul is one with God, it shares God's omniscience and no thought or wish may hide from it. Folquet, therefore, knows instantly what Dante is yearning to ask. Why then does he not speak at once? Had Dante the gift of Paradisal ominscience, he declares, he would not have waited so long to gratify whatever wish Folquet may have. Dante's wish, of course, is to know the spirit's identity. *those Blest Flames . . . six wings:* The Seraphim. "Each one had six wings; with twain he covered his face, and with twain he covered his feet, and with twain he did fly" (*Isaiah* vi, 2).

82–87. *the greatest basin . . . aside from the sea that girdles all:* The Mediterranean. Folquet conceives it as if he were standing in Spain; hence it extends against the course of the sun, from west to east. In common with most of his contemporaries Dante believed that the Mediterranean extended through 90° of latitude (it actually covers 42°): thus the sun at Zenith over Jerusalem would have Gibraltar as its horizon, and moving west, would be at zenith over what was at first its horizon.

88–92. *the Ebro:* The Spanish river. *the Magra:* Runs south into the Mediterranean for a bit over 40 miles (its short course) between Tuscany and Liguria (whose capital city is Genoa). Marseilles lies about halfway between the two rivers and is in almost the same latitude as Bougiah (or Bougie) in Algeria (5° E.). Thus the two cities would see the sun rise and set at almost the same time.

92–93. *blood flowed . . . when Caesar came:* In 49 B.C., when Caesar left Brutus to defeat the forces of Pompey at Marseilles while he himself "swooped down on Spain." (*Purgatorio* XVIII, 102).

94. *to such as knew it:* Cunizza introduced (the unidentified) Folquet (38–39) as one who "left great fame behind him." Folquet is careful to speak of himself in far more modest terms.

95–96. *my ray marks all this sphere:* Folquet is now one with God. His radiance, therefore, is impressed upon Venus (influencing it) as powerfully as the influence of Venus impressed itself upon him at his birth.

97–99. *Dido:* See *Inferno* V, 61–62, and note. Having conceived so violent a passion for Aeneas that she killed herself when he left, she wronged both Sichaeus, her dead husband, and Creusa, Aeneas's dead wife.

100–102. *she of Rhodopè . . . Demophoön:* Phyllis, daughter of King Sithon of Thrace (wherein rises Mount Rhodopè) was to marry Demophoön. When he did not arrive on the wedding day, she hanged herself and was changed into an almond tree. Demophoön (Ovid, *Heroides,* 2) narrates how the bridegroom arrived after a painful delay only to find that Phyllis had gone out on a limb.

101–102. *Hercules . . . Iole:* See *Inferno* XII, 67, note. Folquet's three references are all to mythic figures who died painfully for love.

104. *not at the sin—that never comes to mind:* When the purified soul reaches the Terrestrial Paradise it is bathed in the waters of Lethe and the very memory of sin is taken from it (*Purgatorio* XXXI, 91–102). Yet both Cunizza (30–36) and Folquet make the point that they do not regret their amorous natures, which once led them into carnality, because the same impulse later led them to the True Love. (See also *Purgatorio* XXXIII, 91–102, and note. There Dante, newly washed in Lethe, forgets that he was ever estranged from Beatrice, and she proves the sinfulness of his estrangement by the very fact that Lethe washed its memory from him.)

One might argue that the pure soul forgets sin in what might be called the active sense, recalling its existence only in a passive and conceptual way that has no power upon it. After every subtlety, however, there remains an unresolvable contradiction in Dante's handling of this point, and the contradiction arises directly from the narrator's necessity. In whatever way these souls are conceived, Dante has to give them something to talk about, and the narrator has never existed who can sustain a conversation about mankind without bringing sin into it.

109–112. Folquet is mind-reading here, as directed to in lines 73–81. He has satisfied Dante's unspoken question about his identity and his place in Heaven. He now continues by answering Dante's next unspoken question. Note that he does not promise to explain the total mysteries of the Third Heaven but only to satisfy all the questions that arise in Dante's mind (which is yet incapable of conceiving the ultimate mystery).

115. *Rahab:* When Joshua sent spies before him into Jericho, Rahab, a harlot of that city, hid them from the king's men and helped them to escape. Thus she helped the people of Israel to regain the promised land, and immediately following the crucifixion her soul (which must have been in Limbo) was summoned by the Third Heaven, the first of its elected.

119–120. *shadow . . . rests the point of its long cone:* Some scholars of Dante's time believed that the cone of the earth's shadow came to a point in the third sphere.

121–126. *as a palm:* As a trophy, *two palms:* Of Christ when he was nailed to the cross. It is fitting that Rahab should be the heavenly trophy of Christ's victory for she had helped Israel win its promised land. It is a pity, Dante has Folquet say, that the Pope cares so little for the Holy Land (he had done nothing to reestablish Christianity there after Acre, the last Christian stronghold, fell to the Saracens in 1291).

127. *the One:* Satan was, of course, the first to turn on God, and it was Mars who founded Florence (*Inferno* XIII, 143–150) but Dante's invective has a firm foundation in those church fathers who held that Mars and all the pagan gods were fiends.

130–132. *the accursed flower of gold:* The Florentine florin, a gold coin stamped with a lily. Dante's figure of a tree that bears magically evil flowers begins with "planted" in line 127. The power of gold transforms the shepherd (the Church, the Papacy in general, and

Boniface VIII in particular) so that he preys on the sheep he should lead and guard.

132–135. *Great Doctors:* The Church Fathers, givers of doctrine. *the Decretals:* The volumes of canon law. Gregory IX ordered the compilation of the first five volumes in 1234 and Boniface VIII had a sixth added. The margins of the Decretals testify (by being worn and covered with annotations) how seriously they were studied, for they covered the temporal rights and privileges of the Church's vast power and wealth, and a knowledge of canon law could make a shyster's fortune.

138. *where . . . Gabriel opened wide his wings:* At the Annunciation.

CANTO X

Ascent to the Sun—Doctors of the Church

The Fourth Sphere: The Sun—The First Garland
of Souls: Aquinas

Dante revels in the joy of God's creation and especially in the art
shown by the placement of *The Equinoctial Point*. So rejoicing, he
enters the *Sphere of the Sun,* unaware of his approach until he has
arrived.

A Garland of Twelve Souls immediately surrounds him and
Beatrice, the glory of each soul shining so brilliantly that it is vis-
ible even against the background of the Sun itself. These are
Twelve Doctors of the Church, philosophers and theologians whose
writings have guided the church in creed and canon law. Their
spokesman, appropriately, is *Thomas Aquinas.* He identifies the
souls in order around the ring.

When Aquinas has finished, the souls dance around Dante and
Beatrice, raising their voices in harmonies unknown except to
Heaven itself.

Contemplating His Son with that Third Essence
   of Love breathed forth forever by Them both,
   the omnipotent and ineffable First Presence   3

created all that moves in mind and space
   with such perfection that to look upon it
   is to be seized by love of the Maker's grace.   6

Therefore, reader, raise your eyes across
   the starry sphere. Turn with me to that point
   at which one motion and another cross,   9

and there begin to savor your delight
   in the Creator's art, which he so loves
   that it is fixed forever in His sight.   12

Note how the wheel on which the planets ride
  branches from there obliquely: only thus
  may the earth that calls to them be satisfied.   15

For if these two great motions never crossed,
  the influence of the heavens would be weakened
  and most of its power upon the earth be lost.   18

For if its deviation were to be
  increased or lessened, much would then be wanting,
  both north and south, from the earth's harmony.   21

Stay on at table, reader, and meditate
  upon this foretaste if you wish to dine
  on joy itself before it is too late.   24

I set out food, but you yourself must feed!
  For the great matters I record demand
  all my attention and I must proceed.   27

Nature's majestic minister, the Sun,
  who writes the will of Heaven on the earth
  and with his light measures the hours that run,   30

now in conjunction (as I have implied)
  with Aries, rode those spirals whose course brings him
  ever earlier from the eastern side.   33

And I was with the Sun; but no more aware
  of my ascent than a man is of a thought
  that comes to mind, until he finds it there.   36

It is Beatrice, she it is who leads our climb
  from good to better, so instantaneously
  that her action does not spread itself through time.   39

How radiant in its essence that must be
  which in the Sun (where I now was) shows forth
  not by its color but its radiancy.   42

Though genius, art, and usage stored my mind,
  I still could not make visible what I saw;
  but yet may you believe and seek to find!   45

And if our powers fall short of such a height,
  why should that be surprising, since the sun
  is as much as any eye has known of light?   48

Such, there, was the fourth family of splendors
  of the High Father who fills their souls with bliss,
  showing them how He breathes forth and engenders. 51

"Give thanks!" my lady said. "With all devotion
  give thanks to the Sun of Angels, by whose grace
  you have been lifted to this physical one!"   54

The heart of mortal never could so move
  to its devotion, nor so willingly
  offer itself to God in thankful love,   57

as mine did when these words had passed her lips.
  So wholly did I give my love to Him
  that she sank to oblivion in eclipse.   60

Nothing displeased, she laughed so that the blaze
  of her glad eyes pierced my mind's singleness
  and once again divided it several ways.   63

Splendors of living and transcendent light
  circle us now and make a glowing crown,
  sweeter in voice than radiant in sight.   66

Latona's daughter sometimes seems to us
  so banded when the vaporous air weaves round her
  the thread that makes her girdle luminous.   69

In Heaven's courts, from which height I have come,
  are many gems so precious and so lovely
  that they cannot be taken from the kingdom.   72

Of such those splendors sang. Who does not grow
  wings that will fly him there, must learn these things
  from the tidings of the tongueless here below.   75

When, so singing, those Sun-surpassing souls
  had three times turned their blazing circuit round us,
  like stars that circle close to the fixed poles,   78

they stood like dancers still caught in the pleasure
  of the last round, who pause in place and listen
  till they have caught the beat of the new measure.   81

And from within its blaze I heard one start:
  "Since the ray of grace from which true love is kindled—
  and then by loving, in the loving heart,   84

grows and multiples—among all men
  so shines on you to lead you up these stairs
  that none descend except to climb again;   87

whoever refused your soul, it being thirsty,
  wine from his flask, would be no freer to act
  than water blocked from flowing to the sea.   90

You wish to know what flowering plants are woven
  into this garland that looks lovingly
  on the lovely lady who strengthens you for Heaven.   93

I was a lamb among the holy flock
  Dominic leads to where all plenty is,
  unless the lamb itself stray to bare rock.   96

This spirit on my right, once of Cologne,
  was my teacher and brother. Albert was his name,
  and Thomas, of Aquinas, was my own.   99

If you wish, similarly, to know the rest
  let your eyes follow where my words shall lead
  circling through all this garland of the blest.   102

The next flame springs from the glad smile of Gratian
  who so assisted one court and the other
  that in him Heaven found good cause for elation.   105

The next to adorn our chorus of the glad
  was the good Peter who, like the poor widow,
  offered to Holy Church all that he had.   108

The fifth light, and the loveliest here, shines forth
  from so magnificent a love that men
  hunger for any news of it on earth;   111

within it is that mind to which were shone
  such depths of wisdom that, if truth be true,
  no mortal ever rose to equal this one.   114

See next the taper whose flame, when formerly
  it burned in mortal flesh, saw most profoundly
  the nature of angels and their ministry.   117

Within the lesser lamp next on my right
  shines the defender of the Christian Age
  whose treatise led Augustine toward the light.   120

Now if your mind has followed on my praise
  from light to light, you are already eager
  to know what spirit shines in the eighth blaze.   123

In it, for having seen the sum of good,
  there sings a soul that showed the world's deceit
  to any who would heed. The bones and blood   126

from which it was cruelly driven have their tomb
  down there in Cieldauro: to this peace
  it came from exile and from martyrdom.   129

See next the flames breathed forth by Isidore,
  by Bede, and by that Richard whose 'Contemplations'
  saw all that a mere man can see, and more.   132

The next, from whom your eyes return to me,
  is the glory of a soul in whose grave thoughts
  death seemed to be arriving all too slowly: 135

it is the flame, eternally elated,
  of Siger, who along the Street of Straws
  syllogized truths for which he would be hated."   138

Then as a clock tower calls us from above
  when the Bride of God rises to sing her matins
  to the Sweet Spouse, that she may earn his love,   141

with one part pulling and another thrusting,
  tin-tin, so glad a chime the faithful soul
  swells with the joy of love almost to bursting—   144

just so, I saw that wheel of glories start
  and chime from voice to voice in harmonies
  so sweetly joined, so true from part to part   147

that none can know the like till he go free
where joy begets itself eternally.

NOTES

1–3. The idea of Trinity will hardly be contained in a footnote, but note the essence of Dante's doctrine. The Father is the Creator. The Son is Wisdom—the Word of God. Together, they eternally breathe forth the Third Essence of Love, the Holy Ghost. Note, therefore, that it is forever being born.

7–27. THE PERFECTION OF THE CREATION. Dante summons the reader to ponder the perfection of God's creation as exemplified by the point of the vernal equinox. It is at this point that the Sun's ecliptic crosses the celestial equator into the northern hemisphere. The two great circles intersect at an angle of 23° 27′.

These two circles are the "one motion and another." (The Sun is now at the vernal equinox.) The apparent equatorial (or diurnal) motion is from east to west. The apparent order in which the signs of the Zodiac appear along the ecliptic is from west to east. It follows, therefore, that the influences of the planets, following the zodiacal path, vary from north to south of the equator (see below, note to 32–33), striking the earth variously but in a fixed progression that is part of God's inscrutable plan. Were the courses of the equator and the ecliptic to run parallel, or were the angles between them to change, the influences of the spheres would be weakened, and earth that stands ever in need of those influences ("earth that calls on them") would lose the full good of their powers.

This is the mystical foretaste Dante offers the reader, bidding him to stay at table and feed himself (i.e., study God's ways) while Dante pursues his demanding theme.

31. *as I have implied:* In lines 8–9 ff., where he said the sun was at the vernal equinox, at which point it must be in Aries.

32–33. *those spirals:* The path of the Sun seems to be a spiral (as may be noted when it is drawn on a globe) from the Tropic of Capricorn (the southern limit of the sun's motion) to the Tropic of Cancer (the northern limit). These Tropics are the latitudes 23° 27′ south and north respectively (the same angle at which the ecliptic crosses the equator). As the apparent spiral of the sun's course brings it toward the Tropic of Cancer, we see it rise earlier every day.

43–45. *Though genius, art, and usage stored my mind:* None of these resources of human understanding (reason) can make visible what faith alone can find.

48. *as much as any eye has known of light:* Dante (following Aristotle) sets the sun as the maximum of light the human eye can see and, therefore, the human mind can imagine. The sun-surpassing radiance of Heaven is, therefore, beyond human imagination.

49. *the fourth family:* The Fourth Sphere of the Blest.

51. *how He breathes forth and engenders:* Once more of the mystery of the Trinity. Through all Eternity God is conceived as creating the Son, in union with whom He eternally breathes forth the Holy Ghost.

52–54. *the Sun of Angels:* God. *this physical one:* The sun. As the sun lights man, so God lights the angels.

55–63. Note the allegorical possibilities. At the bidding of Beatrice (Revealed Truth) the man turns his mind so utterly to God that he forgets her until her joy in his absorption draws him back from single-minded devotion to an awareness of other (and necessarily lesser) things.

64. *transcendent:* Transcending the light of the sun.

67. *Latona's daughter:* The Moon. See *Purgatorio* XX, 130–132, note. In vaporous air the moon seems girdled with light. Dante's figure conceives the vapors as weaving the thread (of light) that makes her glowing girdle.

72. *that they cannot be taken from the kingdom:* In one sense, no description can take the idea of them from heaven to mortal imagination. In a second, they are treasures Heaven reserves to itself because man is unworthy and incapable of them.

74–75. *must learn . . . from the tidings of the tongueless:* i.e., not at all. Every human tongue is mute to speak the treasures of Heaven. One must go there himself (i.e., undertake the purification that leads to celestial sensibilities).

82–87. The speaker is Aquinas (see 97–99, note) and he has just announced nothing less than Dante's salvation.

89–90. *no freer to act than water:* Would not be acting according to his nature. The nature of the Celestial Soul is *caritas* and only an impediment outside itself can prevent it from giving love freely.

91–92. *what flowering plants:* What souls. *are woven into this garland:* Are in this company of souls that wreathe Beatrice round.

95. *Dominic:* St. Dominic, founder of the Dominican Order. He will be discussed at length in XII, 34ff.

97–99. *Thomas Aquinas:* Aquinas (1227–1274), known as the "Doctor Angelicus," was author of the *Summa theologica* (a principal source of Dante's learning), founder of Thomistic philosophy, and perhaps the most learned of Catholic theologians. He was not canonized until 1323, two years after Dante's death. Dante, therefore, was writing of Thomas, not of St. Thomas. As befits the modes of Heaven, Thomas does not mention his own name till he has identified the spirit on his right, a brother Dominican and his teacher. *Albert:* Albertus Magnus (circa 1200–1280), the "Doctor Universalis" who, with Aquinas, reestablished Aristotelian learning in Western thought. He was teaching in Cologne in 1248 when Aquinas went there to be his student. Albertus was canonized and proclaimed a Doctor of the Church in 1931.

100. *to know the rest:* Of the encircling souls.

103. *Gratian:* Or Gratianus. Twelfth-century scholar. It is for his *Decretum gratiani* that Aquinas credits him with correlating and harmonizing civil and ecclesiastical law (the "one court and another").

107. *the good Peter:* Petrus Lombardus. Born early in the twelfth century, Bishop of Paris 1159, died 1160. Called "Magister Sententiarum" because of his *Sententiarum libri IV,* a compilation of scriptures and texts of the church fathers. In a sense, he did for doctrine what Gratianus did for canon law, and Dante typically puts the two side by side. *like the poor widow:* In his preface to *Sententarium* Peter modestly compares himself to the poor widow in *Luke* xxi, 1–4, who gave her two mites (all she had) to the treasury of the church.

109–114. *The fifth light:* Solomon. *so magnificent a love:* As expressed in the "Song of Songs" which was thought to be the wedding hymn of the Church and God. *men hunger for any news:* Of Solomon's final fate. *I Kings* xi, 1–9, records the sins of Solomon's age and theologians of Dante's time debated whether he had been saved or damned. *if truth be true:* If Scripture (which is truth) be true. Hence: it certainly is true. *no mortal ever rose to equal this one:* Dante says, literally, "no second [equal] has risen." Adam, of course, knew God directly, and Christ was man-and-God. Both, therefore, surpassed Solomon. But Christ may be said to have descended and Adam to have issued from God, whereby they did not "rise." Whether or not Dante had these thoughts in mind, his words echo *I Kings* iii, 12: "that there was none like thee before thee, neither after thee shall any arrive like unto thee." The exact phrasing of this line is important for it will be referred to several times in the next three Cantos.

115. *whose flame:* The soul of Dionysus the Areopagite, converted by St. Paul (*Acts* xvii, 34) and wrongly believed in Dante's time to be the author of "The Celestial Hierarchy."

119. *the defender of the Christian Age:* Dante may intend here Paulus Orosius, fifth-century Spanish priest whose *Historiarum adversus paganos* defended the effect of Christianity upon the Roman Empire. Or he may intend Marius Victorinus, fourth-century Roman, who became a Christian theologian, and whose example was believed to have contributed to the conversion of St. Augustine.

123. *what spirit shines in the eighth blaze:* Boethius. Anicius Manlius Severinus Boethius was born in Rome circa 470, studied in Greece, became consul of Theodoric the Ostrogoth in 510, later to be imprisoned by Theodoric in Pavia on charges of treason and magic, and executed in 524. His *De consolatione philosophiae*, written in prison, is a work of pagan dignity that defends the joys of the good life without reference to any eternal reward. Despite its essential paganism, its influence upon the Middle Ages (and upon Dante) was enormous, among other reasons, as a source of late classical learning. In time the death of Boethius came to be thought of as a martyrdom. His remains were formally moved to a tomb in Pavia's

Cieldauro (Church of St. Peter) in the eighth century, and though never canonized, he grew to be locally revered as St. Severinus.

130. *Isidore:* Of Seville (circa 560–636). Became Archbishop of Seville circa 600. Canonized St. Isidore, 1598. Designated a Doctor of the Church, 1722. His major work, *Etymologiae,* was highly prized as an encyclopedia of medieval learning.

131. *Bede:* The Venerable Bede (circa 673–735). English Bible scholar and historian. The title of Venerable (the three orders of holiness are venerable, blessed, and saint, in mounting order) was conferred in the ninth century. Pope Leo declared him a Doctor of the Church in 1899.

131. *Richard:* Richard of St. Victor. Twelfth-century English mystic and theologian. Birthdate unknown; died circa 1173. He was called the Great Contemplater after one of his treatises, "De Contemplatione."

133. *from whom your eyes return to me:* Thus completing the round of the twelve doctors.

135. *death seemed to be arriving all too slowly:* In his eagerness to be done with the vanity of this world and to begin the eternal life.

137. *Siger:* Siger of Brabant. Born circa 1226. An outstanding Averroist philosopher, he taught philosophy at the University of Paris (which was then on *la rue de Feurre* or Street of Straws) and was cited for heresy in 1277 before the Grand Inquisitor of France (hence, "the truths for which he would be hated"). He fled to Orvieto to appeal his case to the Papal Court but was stabbed to death (circa 1283) by his secretary, probably in a mad fit.

140–141. *the Bride of God:* The Church. *the Sweet Spouse:* Christ.

CANTO XI

The Fourth Sphere: The Sun—Doctors of the Church
· The First Garland of Souls: Aquinas · Praise of St. Francis ·
Degeneracy of Dominicans

The spirits complete their song and their joyous dance and once
more gather around Dante and Beatrice.

Aquinas reads Dante's mind and speaks to make clear several
points about which Dante was in doubt. He explains that Provi-
dence sent two equal princes to guide the Church, St. Dominic,
the wise law-giver, being one, and St. Francis, the ardent soul,
being the other. Aquinas was himself a Dominican. To demon-
strate the harmony of Heaven's gift and the unity of the Do-
minicans and Franciscans, Aquinas proceeds to pronounce a
Praise of the Life of St. Francis. His account finished, he returns to
the theme of the unity of the Dominicans and Franciscans, and
proceeds to illustrate it further by himself lamenting the *Degen-*
eracy of the Dominican Order.

O senseless strivings of the mortal round!
  how worthless is that exercise of reason
  that makes you beat your wings into the ground!   3

One man was giving himself to law, and one
  to aphorisms; one sought sinecures,
  and one to rule by force or sly persuasion;   6

one planned his business, one his robberies;
  one, tangled in the pleasure of the flesh,
  wore himself out, and one lounged at his ease;   9

while I, of all such vanities relieved
  and high in Heaven with my Beatrice,
  arose to glory, gloriously received.   12

—When each had danced his circuit and come back
  to the same point of the circle, all stood still,
  like votive candles glowing in a rack.   15

And I saw the splendor of the blazing ray
  that had already spoken to me, smile,
  and smiling, quicken; and I heard it say: 18

"Just as I take my shining from on high,
  so, as I look into the Primal Source,
  I see which way your thoughts have turned, and why. 21

You are uncertain, and would have me find
  open and level words in which to speak
  what I expressed too steeply for your mind   24

when I said 'leads to where all plenty is,'
  and 'no mortal ever rose to equal this one.'
  And it is well to be exact in this.   27

The Providence that governs all mankind
  with wisdom so profound that any creature
  who seeks to plumb it might as well be blind,   30

in order that the Bride seek her glad good
  in the Sweet Groom who, crying from on high,
  took her in marriage with His blessèd blood,   33

sent her two Princes, one on either side
  that she might be secure within herself,
  and thereby be more faithfully His Bride.   36

One, in his love, shone like the seraphim.
  The other, in his wisdom, walked the earth
  bathed in the splendor of the cherubim.   39

I shall speak of only one, though to extol
  one or the other is to speak of both
  in that their works led to a single goal.   42

Between the Tupino and the little race
  sprung from the hill blessèd Ubaldo chose,
  a fertile slope spreads up the mountain's face.   45

Perugia breathes its heat and cold from there
  through Porta Sole, and Nocera and Gualdo
  behind it mourn the heavy yoke they bear.   48

From it, at that point where the mountainside
  grows least abrupt, a sun rose to the world
  as this one does at times from Ganges' tide.   51

Therefore, let no man speaking of that place
  call it *Ascesi*—'I have risen'—but rather,
  Oriente—so to speak with proper grace.   54

Nor was he yet far distant from his birth
  when the first comfort of his glorious powers
  began to make its warmth felt on the earth: 57

a boy yet, for that lady who, like death
  knocks on no door that opens to her gladly,
  he had to battle his own father's wrath.   60

With all his soul he married her before
  the diocesan court *et coram patre;*
  and day by day he grew to love her more.   63

Bereft of her First Groom, she had had to stand
  more than eleven centuries, scorned, obscure;
  and, till he came, no man had asked her hand: 66

none, at the news that she had stood beside
  the bed of Amyclas and heard, unruffled,
  the voice by which the world was terrified;   69

and none, at word of her fierce constancy,
  so great, that even when Mary stayed below,
  she climbed the Cross to share Christ's agony.   72

But lest I seem obscure, speaking this way,
  take Francis and Poverty to be those lovers.
  That, in plain words, is what I meant to say.   75

Their harmony and tender exultation
  gave rise in love, and awe, and tender glances
  to holy thoughts in blissful meditation.   78

The venerable Bernard, seeing them so,
  kicked off his shoes, and toward so great a peace
  ran, and running, seemed to go too slow.   81

O wealth unknown! O plenitude untried!
  Egidius went unshod. Unshod, Sylvester
  followed the groom. For so it pleased the bride!   84

Thenceforth this father and this happy lord
  moved with his wife and with his family,
  already bound round by the humble cord.   87

He did not grieve because he had been born
  the son of Bernardone; he did not care
  that he went in rags, a figure of passing scorn.   90

He went with regal dignity to reveal
  his stern intentions to Pope Innocent,
  from whom his order first received the seal.   93

Then as more souls began to follow him
  in poverty—whose wonder-working life
  were better sung among the seraphim—   96

Honorius, moved by the Eternal Breath,
  placed on the holy will of this chief shepherd
  a second crown and everflowering wreath.   99

Then, with a martyr's passion, he went forth
  and in the presence of the haughty Sultan
  he preached Christ and his brotherhood on earth;   102

but when he found none there would take Christ's pardon,
  rather than waste his labors, he turned back
  to pick the fruit of the Italian garden.   105

On the crag between Tiber and Arno then, in tears
  of love and joy, he took Christ's final seal,
  the holy wounds of which he wore two years.   108

When God, whose loving will had sent him forward
  to work such good, was pleased to call him back
  to where the humble soul has its reward,   111

he, to his brothers, as to rightful heirs
  commended his dearest Lady and he bade them
  to love her faithfully for all their years.   114

Then from her bosom, that dear soul of grace
  willed its return to its own blessèd kingdom;
  and wished its flesh no other resting place.   117

Think now what manner of man was fit to be
  his fellow helmsman, holding Peter's ship
  straight to its course across the dangerous sea.   120

Such was our patriarch. Hence, all who rise
　　and follow his command will fill the hold,
　　as you can see, with fruits of paradise.　　　　　123

But his flock has grown so greedy for the taste
　　of new food that it cannot help but be
　　far scattered as it wanders through the waste.　　126

The more his vagabond and distant sheep
　　wander from him, the less milk they bring back
　　when they return to the fold. A few do keep　　　129

close to the shepherd, knowing what wolf howls
　　in the dark around them, but they are so few
　　it would take little cloth to make their cowls.　　132

Now, if my words have not seemed choked and blind,
　　if you have listened to me and taken heed,
　　and if you will recall them to your mind,　　　　135

your wish will have been satisfied in part,
　　for you will see how the good plant is broken,
　　and what rebuke my words meant to impart　　　138

when I referred, a while back in our talk,
　　to 'where all plenty is' and to 'bare rock.' "

NOTES

15. *rack:* Dante says "candellier," which may be taken to mean
candlestick, but equally to mean the candle-racks that hold votive
candles in churches. The image of the souls as twelve votive candles
in a circular rack is certainly apter than that of twelve candles in sep-
arate candlesticks.

25–26. *lead to . . . all plenty:* X, 95. *no mortal ever:* X, 114.

28–42. INTRODUCTION TO THE LIFE OF ST. FRANCIS.
Compare the words of Bonaventura in introducing the life of St.
Dominic, XII, 31–45.

31. *the Bride:* The Church.

32. *crying from on high: Matthew* xxvii, 46, 50; *Mark* xv, 34, 37;
Luke xxiii, 46; and *John* xix, 26–30; all record Christ's dying cries
upon the cross.

34. *two Princes, one on either side:* St. Dominic and St. Francis. Do-
minic, on one side (line 39 equates his wisdom with the cherubic),
by his wisdom and doctrinal clarity made the church secure within
itself by helping to defend it against error and heresy. Francis, on the
other (line 37 ascribes to him seraphic ardor of love), set the exam-
ple that made her more faithfully the bride of Christ.

43–51. ASSISI AND THE BIRTH OF ST. FRANCIS. The pas-
sage, in Dante's characteristic topophiliac style, is full of local allu-
sions, not all of them relevant to St. Francis, but all describing the
situation of Assisi, his birthplace. Perugia stands to the east of the
upper Tiber. The Tiber at this point runs approximately north to
south. Mt. Subasio, a long and many spurred crest, runs roughly par-
allel to the Tiber on the west. Assisi is on the side of Subasio, and it
was from Assisi that the sun of St. Francis rose to the world, as "this
one" (the actual sun in which Dante and Aquinas are standing) rises
from the Ganges. The upper Ganges crosses the Tropic of Cancer, the
line of the summer solstice. When the sun rises from the Ganges,
therefore, it is at its brightest.

the Tupino: Skirts Mt. Subasio on the south and flows roughly
west into the Tiber. *the little race:* The Chiascio [KYAH-show] flows
south along the length of Subasio and empties into the Tupino
below Assisi. *blessèd Ubaldo:* St. Ubaldo (1084–1160), Bishop of Gub-
bio from 1129. He chose a hill near Gubbio as a hermitage in which
to end his days, but died before he could retire there. *Porta Sole:* Pe-
rugia's west gate. It faces Mt. Subasio. In summer its slopes reflect the
sun's ray through Porta Sole; in winter, covered with snow, they send
the cold wind. *Nocera* [NAW-tcheh-ra], *Gualdo* [GWAHL-doe]:
Towns on the other side of (behind) Subasio. Their heavy yoke may

be their subjugation by Perugia, or Dante may have meant by it the taxes imposed by Robert of Naples and his Spanish brigands.

51–54. It is such passages that certify the failures of all translation. *Ascesi,* which can mean "I have risen," was a common name for Assisi in Dante's day. *Oriente,* of course, is the point at which the sun rises. Let no man, therefore, call Assisi "I have risen" (i.e., a man has risen), but let him call it, rather, the dawning east of the world (a sun has risen).

55 ff. *yet far distant:* While he was still young. The phrasing continues the figure of the new-risen sun.

Francis, born Bernardone, was the son of a relatively prosperous baker and, early in life, assisted his father. In a skirmish between Assisi and Perugia he was taken prisoner and later released. On his return to Assisi (he was then twenty-four) he abandoned all worldly affairs and gave himself entirely to religious works.

a boy yet: Here, as in line 55, Aquinas is overdoing it a bit: twenty-four is a bit old for being a boy yet. *that lady:* Poverty. *his own father's wrath:* In 1207 (Francis was then twenty-five) he sold one of his father's horses along with a load of bread and gave the money to a church. In a rage, his father forced the church to return the money, called Francis before the Bishop of Assisi, and there demanded that he renounce his right to inherit. Francis not only agreed gladly but removed his clothes and gave them back to his father saying, "Until this hour I called you my father on earth; from this hour I can say in full truth 'our Father which art in Heaven.'"

he married: In his "Hymn to Poverty" Francis himself celebrated his union to Poverty as a marriage. He had married her before the diocesan court of Assisi, *et coram patre* (before the court, i.e., in the legal presence of, his father). The marriage was solemnized by his renunciation of all possessions.

64–66. *her First Groom:* Christ. *he:* St. Francis.

68. *Amyclas:* Lucan reported (see also *Il Convivio* IV, 13) how the fisherman Amyclas lay at his ease on a bed of seaweed before Caesar himself, being so poor that he had nothing to fear from any man. Not even this report of the serenity Mistress Poverty could

bring to a man, and not even the fact that she outdid even Mary in constancy, climbing the very cross with Christ, had moved any man to seek her in marriage.

79. *Bernard:* Bernard di Quintavalle, a wealthy neighbor, became the first disciple of Francis, kicking off his shoes to go barefoot in imitation of the master.

82–84. *unknown:* To men. Holy Poverty is the wealth none recognize, the plentitude none try. *Egidius . . . Sylvester:* The third and fourth disciples of Francis. Peter, the second disciple, seems not to have been known to Dante. *the groom:* Francis. *the bride:* Poverty.

87. *the humble cord:* Now a symbol of the Franciscans but then in general use by the poor as a makeshift belt.

88. *grieve:* At his humble origins.

93. *his order first received the seal:* In 1210. But Innocent III thought the proposed rule of the order so harsh that he granted only provisional approval.

96. *among the seraphim:* In the Empyrean, rather than in this Fourth Heaven.

97–99. *Honorius . . . second crown:* In 1223, Pope Honorius III gave his fully solemnized approval of the Franciscan Order.

100–105. In 1219, St. Francis and eleven of his followers made a missionary pilgrimage to Greece and Egypt. Dante, whose facts are not entirely accurate, may have meant that pilgrimage; or he may have meant Francis's projected journey to convert the Moors (1214–1215) when Francis fell ill in southern Spain and had to give up his plans.

106–108. In 1224, on a crag of Mt. Alvernia (on the summit of which the Franciscans have reared a commemorative chapel), St. Francis received the stigmata in a rapturous vision of Christ. He wore the wound two years before his death in 1226, at the age of (probably) forty-four.

109–117. The central reference here is to Dame Poverty. *her bosom:* The bare ground of Poverty. *no other resting place:* Than in the bare ground.

119. *his fellow helmsman:* St. Dominic. *Peter's ship:* The Church.

121–132. THE DEGERNERACY OF THE DOMINICANS IN DANTE'S TIME. Aquinas was a Dominican. As a master touch to symbolize the harmony of Heaven and the unity of Franciscans and Dominicans, Dante puts into the mouth of a Dominican the praise of the life of St. Francis. That praise ended, he chooses the Dominican to lament the degeneracy of the order. In XII, Dante will have the Franciscan, St. Bonaventure, praise the life of St. Dominic and lament the degeneracy of the Franciscans.

122. *his command:* The rule of the Dominicans. *will fill his hold:* With the treasures of Paradise. Dante is carrying forward the helmsman metaphor of lines 118–120, though the ship is now commanded by a patriarch. Typically, the figure changes at once to a shepherd-and-flock metaphor.

136. *in part:* In X, 95–96, in identifying himself as a Dominican, Aquinas said the Dominican rule "leads to where all plenty is" unless the lamb itself stray to "bare rock." In lines 25–26, above, he refers to these words and also to his earlier statements (X, 114) about Solomon's wisdom (that "no mortal ever rose to equal this one"). What he has now finished saying about the degeneracy of the Dominicans will satisfy part of Dante's wish (about "plenty" and "bare rock"). The other part of his wish (about "no mortal ever rose to equal this one") will be satisfied later.

137. *the good plant:* Of the Dominican rule strictly observed.

CANTO XII

The Fourth Sphere: The Sun—Doctors of the Church
The Second Garland of Souls: Bonaventure · Praise of
St. Dominic · Degeneracy of Franciscans

As soon as Aquinas has finished speaking the wheel of souls be-
gins to turn, and before it has completed its first revolution it is
surrounded by a *Second Garland of Twelve Souls*.

The spokesman of this second company is *St. Bonaventure*. In
the harmonious balances of Heaven the Dominican Aquinas had
spoken the praise of the life of St. Francis. In the same outgoing
motion of love the Franciscan Bonaventure now speaks the *Praise
of the Life of St. Dominic*. And as Aquinas had concluded by
lamenting the degeneracy of the Dominican Order, so Bonaven-
ture concludes his account with a *Lament for the Degeneracy of the
Franciscan Order*. He then identifies the other souls in his Garland.

So spoke the blessèd flame and said no more;
 and at its final word the holy millstone
 began revolving round us as before. 3

And had not finished its first revolution
 before a second wheel had formed around it,
 matching it tone for tone, motion for motion. 6

As a reflection is to the source of light,
 such is the best our sirens and muses sing
 to the chanting of those sheaths of pure delight. 9

As through thin clouds or mists twin rainbows bend
 parallel arcs and equal coloring
 when Juno calls her handmaid to attend— 12

the outer band born of the inner one,
 like the voice of that wandering nymph of love consumed,
 as vapors are consumed, by the summer sun— 15

whereby all men may know what God made plain
   in the pledge he gave to Noah that the waters
   of the great deluge would not come again—   18

just so, those sempiternal roses wove
   their turning garland round us, and the outer
   answered the inner with the voice of love.   21

And when the exalted festival and dance
   of love and rapture, sweet song to sweet song,
   and radiance to flashing radiance,   24

had in a single instant fallen still
   with one accord—as our two eyes make one,
   being moved to open and close by a single will—   27

from one of those new splendors a voice came;
   and as the North Star draws a needle's point,
   so was my soul drawn to that glorious flame.   30

Thus he began: "The love that makes me shine
   moves me to speak now of that other leader
   through whom so much good has been said of mine.   33

When one is mentioned the other ought to be;
   for they were militant in the same cause
   and so should shine in one light and one glory.   36

The troops of Christ, rearmed at such great cost,
   were struggling on behind the Holy Standard,
   fearful, and few, and laggard, and half lost,   39

when the Emperor who reigns eternally—
   of His own grace and not for their own merit—
   took thought of his imperiled soldiery;   42

and, as you have heard say, He sent His bride
  two champions by whose teachings and example
  the scattered companies were reunified.   45

In the land to which the West wind, soft and glad,
  returned each Spring to open the new leaves
  with which, soon, all of Europe will be clad,   48

at no great distance from the beat and bite
  of those same waves behind which, in its course,
  the sun, at times, hides from all mortal sight,   51

a fortunate village lies in the protection
  of the great shield on which two lions are,
  one subjugating and one in subjection.   54

Within its walls was born the ardent one,
  true lover and true knight of the Christian faith;
  bread to his followers, to his foes a stone.   57

His mind from the instant it began to be,
  swelled with such powers that in his mother's womb
  he made her capable of prophecy.   60

And when he and his Lady Faith before
  the holy front had married and endowed
  each other with new gifts of holy power,   63

the lady who had spoken for him there
  saw, in a dream, the wonder-working fruit
  that he and his inheritors would bear.   66

To speak him as he was, a power from Heaven
  was moved to give him the possessive form
  of His name unto Whom he was wholly given.   69

Dominicus he was called. Let him be known
  as the good husbandman chosen by Christ
  to help Him in the garden He had sown.   72

A fitting squire and messenger of Christ
  he was, for his first love was poverty,
  and such was the first counsel given by Christ.   75

Often his nurse found him in meditation
  at night on the bare floor, awake and silent,
  as if he were saying, 'This is my vocation.'   78

O Felix his father in true 'felicity!'
  O mother truly Joan, 'whom God has graced!'
  —if the names can be translated literally!   81

Not as men toil today for wealth and fame,
  in the manner of the Ostian and Taddeo,
  but for love of the true manna, he soon became   84

a mighty doctor, and began to go
  his rounds of that great vineyard where the vine,
  if left untended, pales and cannot grow.   87

Before that Seat where once the poor were fed
  and tended (now, through no fault of its own,
  but by its degenerate occupant, corrupted)   90

he did not ask the right to keep as pay
  three out of every six, nor a benifice,
  nor *decimas quae sunt pauperum Dei;*   93

but license in the sick world there below
  to battle for that seed from which are sprung
  the four and twenty plants that ring you now.   96

Then, will and doctrine joined, and in the light
  of apostolic office, he burst forth,
    like a torrent from a mountain vein, to smite   99

the stumps and undergrowths of heresy.
  And where the thickets were least passable,
    there his assault bore down most heavily.   102

And from him many rivulets sprang to birth
  by which the Catholic orchard is so watered
    that its little trees spring greener from the earth.   105

If such was the one wheel of the great car
  in which the Church rode to defend herself
    and win in open field her civil war,   108

you cannot fail to see with a clear mind
  the excellence of that other, about whom,
    before I joined you, Thomas was so kind.   111

But the track its great circumference cut of old
  is so abandoned that the casks are empty,
    and where there once was crust, now there is mold. 114

His family, that formerly used to go
  in his very footsteps, is so turned around
    that it prints toe on heel, and heel on toe.   117

Soon shall we see the harvest of these years
  of lazy cultivation, and hear the darnel,
    the storehouse shut against it, shed its tears.   120

Search our book leaf by leaf and you will see,
  I have no doubt, written upon some page:
    'I am today all that I used to be.'   123

But not at Casal' nor Acquasparta—there
   they come to keep our rule, and in the keeping
   one loosens it, one tightens it like a snare.   126

I am the life of Bonaventure, on earth
   of Bagnoregio, who in great offices
   always put back the things of lesser worth.   129

Illuminato and Augustine are here,
   two of the first-come of the barefoot poor.
   For the cord they wore God holds them ever dear.   132

The prior Hugo is here, and the deathless glow
   of Peter Mangiadore, and Peter of Spain
   whose light still shines in twelve small books below.   135

And the prophet Nathan, and the eternal part
   of Chrysostom, and Anselm, and that Donatus
   who gladly turned his hand to the first art.   138

Rabanus is also here; and here beside me
   shines the Calabrian abbot Joachim
   whose soul was given the power of prophecy.   141

The ardent courtesy of my holy brother
   and his apt praise of one great paladin
   moved me to say this much about the other   144

in emulous and loving eulogy;
   and so moved all these of my company."

NOTES

2. *the holy millstone:* The wheel of souls, called a millstone here
perhaps to suggest the ponderous turning of God's will (cf. the ex-

pression "the mills of the Gods") but also to describe their motion, for a millstone moves slowly when it starts to turn, and this wheel of souls had not completed its first revolution before it was surrounded by another wheel.

5. *a second wheel:* Of twelve more splendors. In the heavenly hierarchy these are probably a grade inferior to the souls of the first wheel (line 13: "the outer band born of the inner one"). The inner band, moreover, revolves nearer the center of the sun (Divine Illumination). Lines 10–18 certainly suggest that the two wheels are complementary to one another. The total of twenty-four may suggest a reference to the books of the Old Testament. (See *Purgatorio* XXIX, 64, note.)

10–18. The compounding of metaphors in this passage is characteristically Dantean. The twin rainbows were said to occur when Juno called her handmaiden (Iris) to attend her. Iris (the Rainbow) was the messenger of the Gods as well as being especially associated with Juno. Thus, when she attends her mistress she presents herself in a double splendor. Line 13 is based on Dante's belief that the outer band of a twin rainbow is a reflection of the inner band. This reflection is like the voice of Echo, an outer reflection of the inner (first) sound. Echo was the wandering nymph who wasted away for love of Narcissus (consumed by the fire of love as vapors are consumed by the Sun) until the gods changed her to a stone. The figure then shifts from classical mythology to the Bible, referring to *Genesis* ix, 8–17, in which God made a pact with Noah and his sons, promising that the Deluge would not be repeated, and hung the rainbow in the sky as token of His pledge.

28. *one of those new splendors:* St. Bonaventure. A Franciscan, he eulogizes St. Dominic and laments the decay of the Franciscan order, just as Aquinas, a Dominican, has eulogized St. Francis and lamented the decay of the Dominican order. Later, Bonaventure will identify the other souls of his circle (lines 130 ff.).

St. Bonaventure (1221–1274) was born Giovanni di Fidanza at Bagnoregio (now Bagnorea) near Lake Bolsena. He was a scholar saint and a leading theologian. He became Minister General of the Franciscan Order in 1257 and was created Cardinal Bishop of Albano in 1273. Much of his scholarship was carried out in France, where he died during the sessions of the second Council of Lyons. He was canonized in 1482 by Sixtus IV and pronounced sixth (Doctor Seraphicus) among the Doctors of the Church by Sixtus V in 1587.

31–45. INTRODUCTION TO THE LIFE OF ST. DOMINIC. Compare the words of Aquinas in introducing the Life of St. Francis (X, 28–42).

32. *that other leader:* St. Dominic.

33. *through whom:* The phrasing is obscure. Dante probably means that the earlier praise of St. Francis (Bonaventure's leader) is due to Dominic because his rule taught Aquinas such loving praises.

37–39. *rearmed:* By the blood of martyrs when persecution had all but scattered it. *the Holy Standard:* The Cross.

43. *as you have heard said:* In XI, 32 ff. *His bride:* The Church.

46–51. The land here referred to is Spain. In the sea beyond it, according to Dante's geography, the sun hides from all mortal sight when it is midnight in Jerusalem. For Dante, all of the earth's land area consisted of an arc of 180° from India to Spain with Jerusalem at the center, the other 180° of the earth's circumference being water. Thus, when the sun was at its furthest point from Jerusalem it shone only upon the watery wastes, hidden from the eyes of mortals.

52–54. *a fortunate village:* Calahorra, birthplace of St. Dominic, lies on the Ebro about 60 miles due south of the Bay of Biscay where it washes the westernmost point of the Spanish-French border. *the great shield:* Of the house of Castile. It is quartered and contains on one side a castle above a lion and on the other a lion above a castle, thus one lion is subjugating the castle and the other is being subjugated by it.

55 ff. LIFE OF ST. DOMINIC (1170–1221). Not all of the details Dante offers in his account of St. Dominic have a historic base. Dominic may have been born of an ancient family named Guzman, but little is known of his origins. He was an austere but undeviating man of mercy and with whole faith in pure doctrine. Beginning as an Augustinian, Dominic sought to overcome the heresies of the

Albigensians, partly in defense of the pure faith and partly to save them from the terrors of the crusade that eventually destroyed them in a hideous blood bath. He founded the Dominican Order with the special purpose of saving the Albigensians from destruction in this world and damnation in the next. In 1215 he won provisional papal approval of his order from Innocent III, and, in 1216, full confirmation by Honorius III. He died in Bologna in 1221 and was canonized in 1234. Unlike Francis, who dreaded learning as a corruptive force and praised the holy ignorance of the rude and simple mind, Dominic labored for purity of doctrine and founded his order for missionary scholars who were to go forth and preach the pure faith. Thus the Founding principles of the two great orders were in many senses opposed and yet complementary.

The notes that follow comment on Dante's version of the life of St. Dominic, not on the historical record:

58–60. The mind and soul form at the instant of conception and take on the gifts assigned by the influences of the spheres. While still in the womb, Dominic was said to be so gifted that his mother foresaw the Dominican Order in a dream of giving birth to a black and white dog. Black and white are the Dominican colors, and *"Domini canes"* translates "hounds of the Lord."

61–66. Dominic married the faith at the Baptismal font, each bringing the other a dowry of strength and of holy purpose. Following his baptism, his godmother is supposed to have dreamed that he had a star on his forehead, a sign that he would bring God's light to man.

67–75. "Dominic" is the possessive form of Latin *"Domine"* (the Lord). Note the triple use of "Christ" to rhyme with itself. Dante has not so rhymed before in the *Comedy*. He will again in XIV, XIX, and XXXII. He will not rhyme "Christ" with any other word because none is fit to be joined with that holy name. In a *tenzone* against Forese (who appears in *Purgatorio* XXXII) the younger Dante had once made use of what he probably came to think of as a sacrilegious rhyme on "Christ." This later device may be his way of making amends.

75–81. As noted above, little is known about Dominic's parents. The details of their names, like the tales of Dominic's prenatal powers, are the stuff of pious folk tales.

82–87. *the Ostian:* Enrico di Susa, who became Bishop of Ostia in 1271. *Taddeo:* Probably Taddeo d'Alderotto, a Florentine physician born circa 1215. The first was a successful scholar of canon law, the second of medicine. Both acquired money and fame as a result of their secular studies. Dominic, on the other hand, studied only for the true manna of spiritual knowledge in order that he might labor in the vineyard (the Church) in which the vines wither and grow pale if they are neglected.

88–96. Because of a decree against the founding of new Orders, Dominic had to plead for many years before he could win approval from the papal seat which is now (i.e., as of 1300) corrupted by Boniface VIII. Dominic did not ask permission to dispense church wealth (withholding two or three of every six coins for himself), nor for a benefice, nor for *decimas quae sunt pauperum Dei* (the tithes that belong to God's poor). He asked only for license to combat heresy, and thus to defend the seed of the true faith from which are sprung, as plants of the everlasting tree, the twenty-four doctors that surround Dante as Bonaventure speaks.

97–102. The reference here is to Dominic's years of labor against the Albigensian heresy. He joined a mission for that purpose as early as 1203. In 1206 he opened in France a mission house dedicated to saving Albigensian women from their heresy. In 1208 Innocent III declared a crusade against the Albigensian plain-folk (they were anti-church and among other major points of doctrine, denied the Resurrection). In seven years of savage warfare and massacres the Albigensians were wiped out. Thus, when Dominic was allowed in 1215 to found his Order of Preaching Friars, he had already been laboring for at least twelve years to wipe out heresy, not by the sword, but by winning the heretics back to the faith through his preachments.

106–111. *If such was the one . . . the excellence of that other:* Since the car (the chariot) must have two equal wheels if it is to work properly, the excellence of the one wheel (Dominic) testifies to the excellence of the other (Francis), about whom Aquinas spoke in XI.

122 ff. LAMENT FOR THE DECLINE OF THE FRANSISCAN ORDER. Bonaventure now laments the decline of his Franciscans as Aquinas earlier lamented the decline of the Dominicans. The core of this metaphor has changed from the chariot of the war to the two-wheeled cart in which peasants haul grapes from the vineyard. The circumference of this great wheel (the Franciscan order) no longer turns in its former track, going back and forth from the vineyard to the winery. Hence the grapes (souls? good works?) are not brought in, and in the barrels (salvation? rectitude? the church?) where once there used to gather the crust of sediment left by good wine, there is now only the mold that forms in empty barrels.

117. *toe on heel, and heel on toe:* Instead of walking, as the first disciples did, in the footsteps of St. Francis, the decayed Franciscans walk backward in them, leaving their toe prints on the heel of the true tracks, and their heel prints on the toes; hence, walking in the other direction.

118–120. *the harvest . . . of lazy cultivation:* Bonaventure's moral point and its symmetrical response to Aquinas's lament for the decline of the Dominican Order are clear enough, but historically, the original rule of St. Francis was so harsh that it was, in effect, banned by the church. Its severity had, in fact, caused a schism within the order even before the death of St. Francis. One group sought to modify the rule of absolute poverty. The other (the Zealots or Spiritual Franciscans from whom stemmed the Penitentes) insisted on the rule to the point of open conflict with church authority. In 1318, in fact, four of the Spirituals were burned for heresy when they refused to modify the original rule of St. Francis.

There is an odd irony in the history of the Franciscans. The piety, fervor, and absolute poverty of the early monks made its impression upon a pious people, who began to make rich gifts to the order. Inevitably, an administrator had to appear, and so the monks of poverty had to acquire stewards and accountants. St. Bonaventure sought to resolve this conflict by teaching that all the property given to the friars was the property of the church but was held for their use *(usus pauperis)* in their life and work.

This schism was the lazy cultivation that made a bad harvest inevitable. Given the nature of Bonaventure's teaching, the bad harvest (the darnel) would be those Franciscans who risked excommunication by insisting, against direct papal orders, on the unmitigated rule (though he would, of course, include those Franciscans who observed the modified rule too slackly. Darnel or rye grass or black caraway springs up among the cultivated grains. Its hard seeds, ground up with the edible grains and so eaten as bread, can cause nervous disorders. It (the damned souls?) must be weeded out carefully (by good cultivation) and kept out of the good grain, the storehouse (the order? the church? heaven?) shut against it.

121–123. *our books:* Used figuratively for the Franciscan Order. *some page:* Some brother, some member of the Order.

124–126. *Casal:* The Franciscan monastery at Casale in Monferato. Ubertino di Casale (1259–1338) was general of the chapter and, favoring the Spirituals, so tightened the rule that he was forced to leave the Order. *Acquasparta:* In Todi. From this monastery Matteo d'Acquasparta rose to be general of the Order in 1287 and cardinal in 1288. Under him the Franciscan rule was substantially relaxed.

THE SOULS OF THE SECOND GARLAND:

130. *Illuminato and Augustino:* Two of the early brothers. Illuminato accompanied St. Francis on his mission to the East. Augustino joined the order in 1210.

133. *The prior Hugo:* Hugo of St. Victor (1096?–1141). Born in Saxony, he went to the monastery of St. Victor in Paris in 1115, where he taught philosophy and theology. In 1133 he was made prior and given charge of all studies.

134. *Peter Mangiadore:* Of Troyes (1110–1179?), Dean of the Cathedral of Troyes, 1147–1164. His *Historia Scholastica* was long the standard work on Bible history. *Peter of Spain:* Became John XXI in 1276, died in 1277. He was born in Lisbon circa 1226. Among the twelve books here referred to was his well-known summary of logical principles, *Summulae logicales.*

136. *the prophet Nathan:* See *II Samuel* xii. Nathan spoke out against the sins of King David.

137. *Chrysostom:* The name in Greek means "Golden Mouth," a tribute to his oratorical power. He was John of Antioch (344?–407), Metropolitan of Constantinople. Like Nathan, he denounced the sins of the ruler. He was exiled for his pains by the Empress Eudoxia. *Anselm:* Born in Aosta, Lombardy, circa 1033. As Archbishop of Canterbury (from 1093) he fought the king on the question of the recognition of the Pope. Forced into exile in 1103, he returned to Canterbury in 1107, and died there in 1109. *Donatus:* Lived in Rome about the middle of the fourth century. He wrote commentaries on Terence and Virgil (the latter of which may have been what recommended him to Dante for his place here) and a book on grammar that was widely used in Dante's time. Grammar is "the first art" (first of the seven liberal arts that make up the trivium and quadrivium of the classical curriculum).

139. *Rabanus:* Rabanus Maurus (776?–856). Became Archbishop of Mainz in 847. Bible scholar, poet, and author of *De clericorum institutione,* a manual for clerics.

140. *Joachim:* Of Fiore (1132?–1202). A Cistercian mystic whose doctrines were especially popular among the Spiritual Franciscans who opposed Bonaventure. There is no historic evidence of his prophetic gift, and some of his preachments were specifically condemned by the Lateran Council in 1215 and by Alexander IV in 1256.

142–144. *my holy brother:* St. Thomas. *one great paladin:* St. Francis. *the other:* St. Dominic. The paladins were the twelve great champions who surrounded Charlemagne.

CANTO XIII

The Fourth Sphere: The Sun—The Intellect of the Faith:
Theologians and Doctors of the Church: Aquinas

The Twenty-Four blessèd spirits, moved by the concluding words
of Bonaventure, manifest themselves as a mystical constellation
while ringing forth a hymn of praise that fills all Heaven.

When the hymn has been sung Aquinas speaks again. He has
read Dante's mind and addresses its perplexity, explaining *Why
None Ever Rose to Equal Solomon's Wisdom.* He concludes with a
Warning Against Hasty Judgment.

If you would understand what I now write
  of what I saw next in that Heaven, imagine
  (and hold the image rock-fast in your sight)   3

the fifteen brightest stars the heavens wear
  in their living crown, stars of so clear a ray
  it pierces even the mist-thickened air;   6

imagine that Wain that on our heaven's breast
  lies night and day, because the tiller's turning
  causes no part of it to sink to rest;   9

imagine the bright mouth of the horn one sees
  flower from the axle star, around which spins
  the first wheel—and imagine all of these   12

forming two constellations, each a wreath
  (like that the daughter of King Minos made
  when through her limbs she felt the chill of death)   15

and imagine, last, that one wreath has its rays
  inside the other, and that both are turning
  around one center but in opposite ways.   18

So might you dimly guess (if mankind could)
  what actual stars, joined in their double dance,
  circled around the point on which I stood;   21

though such experiences outrun our knowing
  as the motion of the first and fastest heaven
  outruns the low Chiana's sluggish flowing.   24

There they sang no Bacchic chant nor Paean,
  but Three Persons in One Divine Nature
  and It and human nature in One Person.   27

The song and circling dance ran through their measure,
  and now those holy lights waited on us,
  turning rejoiced from pleasure to new pleasure.   30

The silence of these numina was broken
  by the same lamp from which the glorious life
  of God's beloved pauper had been spoken.   33

It said: "Since one sheaf has been thrashed, my brother,
  and the good grain of it has been put by,
  sweet love invites me now to thrash the other.   36

Into that breast, you think, from which was carved
  the rib that went to form the lovely cheek
  for whose bad palate all mankind was starved,   39

and into that the lance pierced when it made
  such restitution for the past and future
  that every guilt of mankind was outweighed,   42

as much of wisdom's light, to the last ray,
  as human nature can contain, He breathed
  by whose power they were clad in mortal clay.   45

And, therefore, you were puzzled when I came
  to the fifth light and said no mortal ever
  had matched the wisdom sheathed within its flame.   48

Now open your eyes to what I shall say here
  and see your thought and my words form one truth,
  like the center and circumference of a sphere.   51

All things that die and all that cannot die
  are the reflected splendor of the Form
  our Father's love brings forth beyond the sky.   54

For the Living Light that streams forth from the Source
  in such a way that it is never parted
  from Him, nor from the Love whose mystic force   57

joins them in Trinity, lets its grace ray down,
  as if reflected, through nine subsistant natures
  that sempiternally remain as one.   60

From thing to thing to the last least potencies
  the ray comes down, until it is so scattered
  it brings forth only brief contingencies;   63

and these contingencies, I would have you see,
  are those *generated things* the moving heavens
  bring forth from seeds or not, as the case may be.   66

The wax of these things, and the powers that press
  and shape it, vary; thus the Ideal seal
  shines through them sometimes more and sometime
                                         less.   69

So trees of the same species may bring forth
  fruit that is better or worse; so men are born
  different in native talent and native worth.   72

Were the wax most ready and free of every dross,
   and were the heavens in their supreme conjunction,
   the light of the seal would shine through without loss: 75

but nature scants that light in all it makes,
   working in much the manner of a painter
   who knows the true art, but whose brush hand shakes. 78

But if the Fervent Love move the Pure Ray
   of the First Power to wield the seal directly,
   the thing so stamped is perfect in every way. 81

So once a quickening of the dust of earth
   issued the form of the animal perfection;
   so once the Virgin Womb quickened toward birth. 84

Therefore I say that I am one with you
   in the opinion that mankind was never,
   nor will be, what it once was in those two. 87

Having said this much, I must yet go on
   or you would ask: 'How then can it be said,
   no mortal ever rose to equal this one?' 90

But to make clear what yet seems not to be,
   think who he was, and what it was that moved him
   to answer when God said, 'What shall I give thee?' 93

I speak these words that you may understand
   he was a king, and asked the Lord for wisdom
   in governing his people and his land, 96

and not to know the number and degree
   of our motor-angels, nor if a premised 'may'
   can ever conclude, in logic, 'this must be,' 99

nor if there is prime motion, nor if in the space
  of a semicircle a non-right triangle
  may be drawn with the diameter as its base.   102

Hence you may see that when I spoke before
  of unmatched wisdom, it was on royal prudence
  that the drawn arrow of my intention bore.   105

Note well that I said 'rose' when I spoke of it.
  Thus you will see I spoke only of kings,
  of whom there are many, though so few are fit.   108

Such were my words, and taken in this light
  they are consistent with all that you believe
  of our first father and of our Best Delight.   111

And lead weights to your feet may my words be,
  that you move slowly, like a weary man,
  to the 'yes' and 'no' of what you do not see.   114

For he is a fool, and low among his kind,
  who answers yea or nay without reflection,
  nor does it matter on which road he runs blind.   117

Opinions too soon formed often deflect
  man's thinking from the truth into gross error,
  in which his pride then binds his intellect.   120

It is worse than vain for men to leave the shore
  and fish for truth unless they know the art;
  for they return worse off than they were before.   123

Of this, Parmenides and Melissus bear
  their witness to all men, along with Bryson,
  and others who set out without knowing where;   126

so Arius, Sabellius, and their schools
  who were to Scripture like a mirroring sword,
  distorting the straight faces to mislead fools.   129

Men should not be too smug in their own reason;
  only a foolish man will walk his field
  and count his ears too early in the season;   132

for I have seen a briar through winter's snows
  rattle its tough and menacing bare stems,
  and then, in season, open its pale rose;   135

and I have seen a ship cross all the main,
  true to its course and swift, and then go down
  just as it entered its home port again.   138

Let Tom and Jane not think, because they see
  one man is picking pockets and another
  is offering all his goods to charity,   141

that they can judge their neighbors with God's eyes:
  for the pious man may fall, and the thief may rise."

NOTES

1–24. THE DANCE OF THE TWO GARLANDS. The passage,
though in Dante's most elliptical style, presents the basically simple
image of the two garlands of souls transformed into twin constella-
tions in the form of two concentric wheels revolving in opposite di-
rections around the point on which Dante is standing.

To envision the glory of the twenty-four stars (twelve and
twelve), the reader is invited to pick the fifteen brightest stars from
anywhere in heaven (4–6), to add to them the seven stars of the Big
Dipper (7–9), and to add the two bright stars from the mouth of the
Little Dipper (10–12).

All these are to be imagined as forming into the two circles, each like the Corona Borealis, which, according to legend, was made from the bridal wreath of Ariadne (daughter of King Minos) when, abandoned by Theseus, she is found by Dionysus and is taken to heaven to become his wife (13–15).

Put all these imaginings together and you may glimpse perhaps a shadow of the actual experience, for such things surpass mortal understanding by as much as the speed of the Primum Mobile surpasses the flow of the Chiana, a Tuscan river that, in Dante's time, wound sluggishly through swamplands that have since been drained (19–24).

8. *the tiller:* The Pole. It turns all the stars. Those of the Big Dipper, however, are so close to it that they never set, but lie night and day at the Celestial North Pole ("our heaven's breast").

25. *Paean:* Specifically a hymn to Apollo, though used generally for any pagan hymn.

30. *pleasure to new pleasure:* From the pleasure of praising God to the pleasure of serving Him in an act of *caritas.*

31. *numina:* A numen (pl. numina) is a divine spirit or a god conceived as a person.

32. *the same lamp:* St. Thomas Aquinas.

33. *God's beloved pauper:* St. Francis.

34–36. At the end of XI, Thomas had finished explaining his use of "where all plenty is." He paused in XII for Bonaventure to give the counterpoint to his Franciscan eulogy and Dominican lament. That first sheaf of understanding, then, has been thrashed (the grains of truth extracted from the straw). Now he is moved by love to thrash the second sheaf, separating from Dante's error (the straw) the truth about the wisdom of Solomon, and of Aquinas's earlier words (X, 114) "no mortal ever rose to equal this one."

38. *the lovely cheek:* Cheek, in conjunction with rib and breast, results in a somewhat anatomically strewn figure of speech, but is meant to stand here as a synecdoche for Eve, the part standing for the whole, while specifically referring to the part of her that contained the sinful palate.

40. *and into that:* That breast (of Christ).

47. *the fifth light:* Solomon. (See X, 109–114).

48 ff. THE WISDOM OF SOLOMON. Aquinas proceeds to explain why "no mortal man ever rose to equal this one" in wisdom, for Aquinas's statement had perplexed Dante, who had immediately concluded (as we shall see) that Aquinas was implying that Solomon was wiser than Christ and than Adam, though that could not be.

Aquinas parses the question in meticulous Scholastic detail in order to clear Dante's misconception, explaining, in essence, that though Adam and Christ-the-man were wiser than Solomon, containing more of the light of God, they were *direct* creations of God, whereas Solomon was a *secondary* creation, arising from Nature. Thus, Solomon sprang from the earth ("rose"), whereas Adam and Christ-the-man sprang directly from God and were apart from mortal creation.

53. *Form:* The Platonic Form. Idea.

55–58. *The Living Light:* The Son, as the Wisdom of mankind. *the Source:* The Father as Creator. *the love:* The Holy Ghost.

59–60. *nine subsistant natures:* The nine orders of angels that attend the heavenly spheres.

61–63. *thing:* Actuality. (It. *atto.*). The Scholastic term for "that which actually exists." *potency:* That which does not exist but that has the power of coming into being. *contingency:* What could exist (what could have actuality) but does not.

66. *from seeds or not:* See *Purgatorio* XXVIII, 69, and 109–120, and note, for Dante's theory of wind-sown generative "virtues."

67–69. *the wax:* The matter that is available for the formation of contingencies. The term is used here metaphorically. It is not part of Scholastic terminology. *the powers that press:* The influences of the heavens. "Press" continues the "seal-in-wax" metaphor. *the ideal Seal:* A metaphoric equivalent of the Ideal Form of Plato, here, the Divine Concept. It is perfect and unchangeable but, descending through the constant changes of the Spheres to the flux of matter, it is transmitted and received in a necessarily diminished way. Thus the Divine Idea shines through all things, and through some more than through others, but never perfectly.

79–81. The rendering of the original lines is much disputed, but their general sense is clear. Secondary creation, as Aquinas has explained, is never entirely perfect. Direct creation, on the other hand, is necessarily so. In lines 52–60 Aquinas explained direct creation as the ray of the Father and of the Son conjoined in Trinity. Here the force of the periphrasis is to cite all the Trinity in One, the Fervent Love being the Holy Ghost, the Pure Ray being the Son, and the First Power being the Father.

83. *the animal perfection:* The perfection of animal existence (as contrasted, perhaps, to angelic existence). In its ideal form this perfection was embodied in Adam and in Christ-the-man, as direct creations.

86. *in the opinion:* Which Aquinas has read in Dante's mind.

88. *those two:* Adam and Christ-the-man.

90. *this one:* Solomon.

91. *but to make clear what yet seems not to be:* Aquinas knows everything that passes in Dante's mind. Thus, he not only instructs but knows instantly how much of the instruction has registered; the perfect, if supernatural, teacher.

93. *'What shall I give thee?':* After Solomon went to Gideon and offered up a thousand burnt offerings, the Lord appeared in a dream and asked what gift he would choose. Solomon asked for the wisdom with which to rule his people. *I Kings* iii, 4–14.

97–102. THE WISDOM SOLOMON DID NOT SEEK. Aquinas cites a number of propositions that engaged medieval learning. *motor-angels:* The angels that moved the spheres. How many they were, and of what degree (e.g., Principalities or Thrones) provided the subject of many disputations. *may . . . this must be:* Any qualification of the premise must, logically, be reflected in the conclusion. The premise "x may be" can never lead to the conclusion "x must be," but logicians kept trying in ingenious ways to derive a "must be" from a "may be." *if there is prime motion:* Prime motion would be uncaused motion. The learned question here would be whether or not such motion can exist. *semicircle . . . non-right angle:* Euclid demonstrated that any triangle whose base is the diameter of a circle and

whose apex is on the circumference of that circle must be a right tri-
angle. Medieval mathematicians, however, tried to theorize a non-
right triangle to these specifications.

Hence, all these examples are of the wisdom required for playing
abstract and learned games, as opposed to the wisdom Solomon
sought in order to deal justly with God's people.

Earlier in his life, Dante himself had sometimes been drawn to
metaphysical hairsplitting. Here he is renouncing all such, as he had
earlier renounced his overreliance on natural philosophy, in order to
seek the greater truths of faith.

103–108. The reference here is, once again, to X, 109–114: "No
mortal ever rose to equal this one." Aquinas is explaining that the
"arrow of his intention" was sighted only upon the qualities of royal
prudence. It was in that order of wisdom (and not, for example, in
metaphysical speculation) that Solomon was unequaled.

And that specific intent, Aquinas adds, Dante may see for himself
if he will recall that Aquinas had said "rose" to equal. That usage
could apply only to kings, one gathers, since only kings may be said
to "rise" above the masses of mankind. In another sense, neither
Christ-the-man and Adam, being direct creations, could have
"risen."

Such fine-spun parsing of a construction that could have had sev-
eral meanings may leave the modern reader uneasy and lead him to
miss the point. Dante conceives these spirits as direct participants in
God's omniscience and infallibility. Their every word, therefore, is
exactly chosen and must be studied meticulously.

It is not their words that lack clarity but Dante's understanding
that lacks vision. Their very use of language, for that matter, is a con-
cession to Dante, akin to their willingness to manifest themselves to
him, not as they ultimately are, but in the closest approximation that
Dante can grasp. Since their knowledge is a direct ray from God,
their understanding is reflected from one to the other, through God,
with no need of words.

111. *our first father:* Adam. *our Best Delight:* Christ.

112 ff. AQUINAS REPROACHES DANTE. Dante had jumped
to a conclusion. Because he failed to understand what Aquinas had

said, he concluded that Aquinas had contradicted the truth in speaking of Solomon. Now that the contradiction has been resolved, Aquinas warns him not to be in a hurry to decide "yes" or "no" in matters that surpass his understanding.

117. *on which road:* Whether the road of affirmation or of denial.

123. *worse off:* Because they will have left their ignorance only to fall into error.

124–126. THE FOOLOISH PHILOSOPHERS: All three of the philosophers here mentioned were refuted by Aristotle in the *Organon* (*Sophistici Elenchi* I, 10) and that is probably all Dante knew of them. Parmenides taught that all things come from and return to the Sun. Melissus, a disciple of Parmenides, taught that there is no motion in the universe but only an appearance of motion. Bryson labored devotedly and at great length to square the circle.

127–129. THE HERETICAL PHILOSOPHERS. Arius, an Alexandrian priest (died in 336) taught that the Son, having been created by the Father, could not be one with Him. Sabellius advanced the Monarchian heresy that there is no real distinction between Father and Son and that the Trinity was merely a succession of modes in which a single person appears. Little is known about him except that he was probably born in Libya and that he died about 265.

139–143. *Tom and Jane:* Anyone in general. (Dante says: *"donna Berta or ser Martino."*) It is easy for people in general, observing that one man acts sinfully and another piously, to conclude that the sinful man will be damned and the pious one saved. But that could be a hasty judgment. No man should let himself believe that he can foresee another's fate with the eyes of Divine Omniscience. The pious man may fall from grace (as even Solomon turned to idolatry in his old age and risked damnation) or a thief may repent and win his seat in heaven.

CANTO XIV

The Fourth Sphere: The Sun—The Two Circles of Souls ·
Philosophers and Theologians · Solomon

Ascent to Mars—The Third Circle of Souls · Warriors of God

The Fifth Sphere: Mars—The Vision of Christ on the Cross

Thomas Aquinas has finished speaking. Now, anticipating the
wish Dante has not yet realized is his own, Beatrice begs the dou-
ble circle of Philosophers and Theologians to explain to Dante
the state in which the blessèd will find themselves after the *Res-
urrection of the Flesh.* The radiant spirit of *Solomon* answers.

As Solomon finishes his discourse and the souls about him cry
"Amen!" Dante becomes aware of a *Third Circle of Souls,* higher
and more radiant even than the first two. Its radiance dawns
slowly and indistinctly at first, and then suddenly bursts upon
him. Only then does he realize that he and Beatrice have been
ascending and that he has entered the *Fifth Sphere, Mars.* The souls
he had seen in the third great circle are those of the *Warriors of
God.* There Dante beholds, shining through the Sphere of Mars
(in about the way the rays of a star sapphire shine within the
stone), the *Vision of Christ on the Cross.*

"The water in a round vessel moves about
   from center to rim if it is struck from within,
   from rim to center if it is struck from without."   3

—Such was the thought that suddenly occurred
   to my rapt mind when the immortal ray
   of Thomas had pronounced its final word,   6

occasioned by the likeness to the flow
   of his speech and my lady's, she being moved
   to speak when he had done, beginning so: 9

"There is another need this man must find
   the holy root of, though he does not speak it,
   nor know, as yet, he has the thought in mind.   12

Explain to him if the radiance he sees flower
   about your beings will remain forever
   exactly as it shines forth in this hour;   15

and if it will remain so, then explain
   how your restored eyes can endure such brilliance
   when your beings have grown visible again."   18

As dancers in a country reel flush brighter
   as they spin faster, moved by joy of joy,
   their voices higher, and all their gestures lighter—   21

so at my lady's prompt and humble plea
   the sacred circles showed yet greater joy
   in their dance and in their heavenly harmony.   24

Those who mourn, here, that we must die to gain
   the life up there, have never visualized
   that soul-refreshing and eternal rain.   27

That One and Two and Three that is eternal,
   eternally reigning in Three and Two and One,
   uncircumscribed, and circumscribing all,   30

was praised in three great paeans by each spirit
   of those two rings, and in such melody
   as would do fitting honor to any merit.   33

And I heard, then, from the most glorious ray
   of the inner circle, a voice as sweetly low
   as the angel's must have sounded to Mary, say: 36

"Long as the feast of Paradise shall be,
  so long shall our love's bliss shine forth from us
  and clothe us in these radiant robes you see.   39

Each robe reflects love's ardor shining forth;
  the ardor, the vision; the vision shines down to us
  as each is granted grace beyond his worth.   42

When our flesh, made glorious at the Judgment Seat,
  dresses us once again, then shall our persons
  become more pleasing in being more complete.   45

Thereby shall we have increase of the light
  Supreme Love grants, unearned, to make us fit
  to hold His glory ever in our sight.   48

Thereby, it follows, the vision shall increase;
  increase the ardor that the vision kindles;
  increase the ray its inner fires release.   51

But as a coal, in giving off its fire,
  outshines it by its living incandescence,
  its form remaining visible and entire;   54

so shall this radiance that wraps us round
  be outshone in appearance by the flesh
  that lies this long day through beneath the ground;   57

nor will it be overborne by so much light;
  for the organs of the body shall be strengthened
  in all that shall give increase of delight."   60

And "Amen!" cried the souls of either chain
  with such prompt zeal as to make evident
  how much they yearned to wear their flesh again;   63

perhaps less for themselves than for the love
  of mothers, fathers, and those each soul held dear
  before it became an eternal flame above.   66

And lo! all round me, equal in all its parts,
  a splendor dawned above the splendor there
  like a horizon when the new day starts.   69

And as, at the first coming on of night,
  new presences appear across the sky,
  seeming to be, and not to be, in sight;   72

so did I start to see Existences
  I had not seen before, forming a ring
  around the other two circumferences.   75

Oh sparkling essence of the Holy Ghost!
  How instantly it blazed before my eyes,
  defeating them with glory, their function lost!   78

But Beatrice let herself appear to me
  so glad in beauty, that the vision must lie
  with those whose glory outdoes memory.   81

From her I drew again the power of sight,
  and looked up, and I saw myself translated,
  with her alone, to the next estate of light.   84

I was made aware that I had risen higher
  by the enkindled ardor of the red star
  that glowed, I thought, with more than usual fire.   87

With all my heart, and in the tongue which is
  one in all men, I offered God my soul
  as a burnt offering for this new bliss.   90

Nor had the flame of sacrifice in my breast
  burned out, when a good omen let me know
  my prayer had been received by the Most Blest;   93

for with such splendor, in such a ruby glow,
  within two rays, there shone so great a glory
  I cried, "O Helios that arrays them so!"   96

As, pole to pole, the arch of the Milky Way
  so glows, pricked out by greater and lesser stars,
  that sages stare, not knowing what to say—   99

so constellated, deep within that Sphere,
  the two rays formed into the holy sign
  a circle's quadrant lines describe. And here   102

memory outruns my powers. How shall I write
  that from that cross there glowed a vision of Christ?
  What metaphor is worthy of that sight?   105

But whoso takes his cross and follows Christ
  will pardon me what I leave here unsaid
  when *he* sees that great dawn that rays forth Christ. 108

From arm to arm, from root to crown of that tree,
  bright lamps were moving, crossing and rejoining.
  And when they met they glowed more brilliantly.   111

So, here on earth, across a slant of light
  that parts the air within the sheltering shade
  man's arts and crafts contrive, our mortal sight   114

observes bright particles of matter ranging
  up, down, aslant; darting or eddying;
  longer and shorter; but forever changing.   117

And as a viol and a harp in a harmony
  of many strings, make only a sweet tinkle
  to one who has not studied melody;   120

so from that choir of glories I heard swell
  so sweet a melody that I stood tranced,
  though what hymn they were singing, I could not
                                tell.   123

That it was raised in lofty praise was clear,
  for I heard "Arise" and "Conquer"—but as one
  may hear, not understanding, and still hear.   126

My soul was so enraptured by those strains
  of purest song, that nothing until then
  had bound my being to it in such sweet chains.   129

My saying so may seem too bold at best,
  since I had not yet turned to those dear eyes
  in which my every yearning found its rest.   132

But think how the living seals of every beauty
  grow stronger toward their heights, and though I had
                                      not
  turned to those others yet in love and duty,   135

reason may yet dismiss the charge I bring
  against myself in order to dismiss it;
  and see the holy truth of what I sing;   138

for my sacred pleasure in those sacred eyes
  can only become purer as we rise.

NOTES

1–9. Dante and Beatrice are standing in the center of a double circle of souls that forms, so to speak, a rim around them. The rim suggests to Dante the flow of ripples in a round basin filled with water. If the basin is struck from the outside, the ripples flow toward the center, growing smaller. In Dante's fancy, the sound of Thomas's voice had flowed in this way, from rim to center. Now Thomas falls still and Beatrice speaks from the center, her voice seeming to flow outward like ripples from the center to the rim.

10–18. *another need:* To know the truth of the resurrection of the flesh. Dante has not spoken this thought. He does not yet know, in fact, that it is forming in his mind, but Beatrice knows he is about to think to ask how it will be after the Day of Judgment if these souls retain their superhuman radiance after they have resumed their bodies (grown visible again). How will their restored human eyes be able to bear such radiance both within and without?

22. *prompt:* Beatrice entered her plea in Dante's behalf even before he knew it was what he wished. It hardly seems possible to be prompter.

27. *rain:* Of light.

35. *a voice:* Solomon.

36. *as the angel's must have sounded:* At the Annunciation.

40. *robe:* In which each spirit is clad.

40–42. As ever in Dante, many degrees of being exist within each category. The brilliance in which these souls are robed is in proportion to (reflects) the degree of ardor (of *caritas*) that burns in each. That intensity, in turn, reflects the intensity of each soul's beatific vision. And the vision is granted to each soul by God's grace, in proportion to the worth of the individual soul. But that grace is more than even such great souls as these can merit: it is God's gift to man beyond man's merit.

67–81. THE THIRD RING OF SOULS. There is no way of assigning an exact symbolism to this third ring of souls, though three of anything is a natural unity in Dante. The third circle appears above the other two and outshines even their glory. The third circle appears dimly and slowly at first, then bursts upon Dante's vision just as he and Beatrice soar into the next higher heaven (of Mars). The third circle is also identified as the "sparkling essence of the Holy Ghost" (line 76). It is reasonable, then, to think of the earlier two circles of Philosophers and Theologians as being identified with the Father and the Son, the law and the wisdom of the Trinity, surmounted and encompassed by its ardor. So interpreted, the shining of the third circle becomes a first view of the souls of the Sphere of Mars, the heaven of God's warriors; and the two spheres (of the Sun and of Mars) combine into a symbolism of the Trinity.

82–84. *from her:* Divine Revelation restores Dante's vision. *translated:* The ascent, despite the slow dawning of the vision of the Third Circle of Souls, is here presented as being instantaneous. *with her alone:* With Beatrice, leaving the spirits of the Fourth Heaven behind. *to the next estate:* The Fifth Heaven, the Sphere of Mars.

88–90. Dante waits for no prompting from Beatrice but offers his soul in thanks to God, offers it as wholly as if it were a burnt offering sent aloft in the consuming fire (ardor of soul) of sacrifice. *the tongue which is one in all men:* The tongue of true prayer. Men may phrase it in different languages, but its essence is always the same.

94 ff. THE VISION OF CHRIST ON THE CROSS. Embedded in the Sphere of Mars (much like the rays of a star sapphire but with a magnitude on the order of the Milky Way) a cross forms on the Heaven of Mars, and in a ruby glow (the redness of Mars and the blood of Christ's sacrifice are both indicated here), Christ himself shines forth.

96. *Helios:* Greek for "sun" and specific to Apollo. Dante is praising God for the glory in which he arrays His vision.

100. *that sphere:* Mars.

102. *a circle's quadrant lines:* A quadrant is one fourth of a circle. The lines that describe the four quadrants form a cross within a ring.

103–108. *Christ . . . Christ . . . Christ:* Dante never rhymes "Christ" with anything but itself, no word being worthy of being so paired.

109. *that tree:* The Cross.

111. *And when they met they glowed more brilliantly:* The lights Dante sees are souls. Their radiance is the flame of *caritas* within them. Whenever two or more meet there their love of one another flares the brighter.

112–117. THE FIGURE OF MOTES IN A RAY OF SUN. Having begun his figure on a galactic scale, Dante shifts to the scale of earthly particles dancing in a ray of sun that strikes across a darkened room. The shift is dramatic and the figure of motes in sunlight not only apt in itself but apt again to set the scale of the galactic vision, the souls, in their enormous dimension, being so far from Dante that they are seen as motes.

127–140. DANTE'S RAPTURE. Hitherto, Dante has found his bliss in Beatrice, and it has been to her eyes that he has turned as each new vision awed him. Here, however, he is so enraptured by the vision of the cross and by the power of the music that he has not turned to Beatrice. He has even declared that nothing in all that has gone before has filled him with such bliss.

Shall he then be accused of ignoring Beatrice? Of neglecting her, his ardor cooled? He brings the charge against himself only that he may dismiss it. His joy in her can only become purer and more intense as they ascend to the heights of the glorious mystery.

In one allegorical sense, of course, there is the perfect beauty, beyond even Divine Revelation, of the thing revealed. The Heavenly Soul, subsumed into the body of God, becomes its own revelation. In that sense, even Beatrice must be outgrown, as Virgil was, though the comparison is questionable, the one relation being finite and the other infinite. Beatrice cannot be outgrown: she has her place in God, as Dante is aspiring to his. When she does leave him at the height of Heaven, it is to reassume her throne in God. She does not disappear but takes her place, and as Dante grows closer to God he grows closer to Beatrice. Thus, to look away from Beatrice toward God is to turn the more closely to Beatrice.

131. *those dear eyes:* Of Beatrice.

133–135. *living seals:* The Heavens. Their influences stamp themselves, as a signet does in wax, upon the souls of men. *those others:* The eyes of Beatrice.

CANTO XV

The Fifth Sphere: Mars—The Warriors of God · Cacciaguida

The souls of the great cross stop their singing in order to encourage Dante to speak, and one among them descends to the foot of the cross like a shooting star, glowing with joy at the sight of Dante. It is, as Dante will discover, *Cacciaguida,* Dante's own great-great-grandfather.

Cacciaguida addresses Dante as "Blood of mine," and though he already knows Dante's thoughts, he begs his descendant to speak them for the joy of hearing his voice.

Dante does as he is bid, and Cacciaguida, in answer to Dante's request, identifies himself, gives an *Account of Ancient Florence,* and explains how he followed *Conrad* in the Crusades, *Became a Knight,* and died in battle passing from *Martyrdom to Bliss.*

Good will, in which there cannot fail to be
   the outgoing love of right (just as we find
   self-seeking love in all iniquity),   3

stopped the sweet trembling harp, and let fall still
   the blessèd viol, upon whose many strings
   the Hand of Heaven plays Its sacred will.   6

How shall those beings not heed a righteous prayer
   when, to encourage me to speak my wish,
   they stopped with one accord, and waited there?   9

Justly they mourn in their eternal wasting
   who, in their love for what does not endure,
   stripped off the hope of this love everlasting.   12

As through the pure sky of a peaceful night
   there streaks from time to time a sudden fire,
   and eyes that had been still move at the sight,   15

as if they saw a star changing its post
   (except that none is gone from where it started,
   and blazed its little while, and soon was lost)—   18

so, in a trail of fire across the air,
   from the right arm to the foot of the great cross,
   a star streaked from the constellation there.   21

Nor did that gemstone leave its diadem.
   Like fire behind an alabaster screen,
   it crossed those radiant ranks, still one with them.   24

Just so did the shade of ancient Ilium
   (if we may trust our greatest muse) go forth
   to greet Aeneas in Elysium.   27

"O sanguis meus, o superinfusa
   gratia Dei, sicut tibi, cui
   bis unquam coeli ianua reclusa?"   30

So spoke that radiance as I stared wide-eyed.
   Then I turned my eyes back to my blessèd lady,
   and between those two souls I stood stupefied,   33

for such a fire of love burned in her eyes
   that mine, I thought, had touched the final depth
   both of my Grace and of my Paradise.   36

Then, radiating bliss in sight and sound,
   the spirit added to his opening words
   others I could not grasp: they were too profound.   39

Nor did the spirit's words elude my mind
   by his own choice. Rather, his thoughts took place
   above the highest target of mankind.   42

And when the bow recovered from the effect
  of its own ardor, and its words arced down
  nearer the target of our intellect,   45

the first on which my straining powers could feed
  were: "Praised be Thou, O Triune Unity
  which showeth me such favor in my seed!"   48

Continuing: "The sight of you assuages
  a long dear hunger that grew within this lamp
  from which I speak, as I perused the pages   51

of the Great Book where neither black nor white
  can ever change. I give thanks to this spirit
  whose love gave you the wings for this high flight. 54

You believe that what you think rays forth to me
  from the Primal Intellect, as five and six,
  if understood, ray forth from unity.   57

And for that reason you do not inquire
  who I may be, nor why I am more joyous
  than the other spirits of this joyous choir.   60

And you are right: for here in Paradise
  greatest and least alike gaze in that Mirror
  where thoughts outsoar themselves before they rise. 63

But, that the Sacred Love in which I wake
  to the eternal vision, and which fills me
  with a sweet thirst, you may the sooner slake, 66

let your own voice, assured, frank, and elated
  sound forth your will, sound forth your soul's desire,
  to which my answer is already fated!"   69

I turned to Beatrice and while I still
  sought words, she heard, and smiled such glad assent
  the joy of it gave wings to my glad will.   72

Thus I began: "When the First Equipoise
  shone forth to you, love and the power to speak love
  became in each of you an equal voice;   75

because the Sun that warmed and lighted you
  contains its heat and light so equally
  that though we seek analogies, none will do.   78

But mortal utterance and mortal feelings—
  for reasons that are evident to you—
  have no such equal feathers to their wings.   81

I, then, being mortal, in the perturbation
  of my unequal powers, with heart alone
  give thanks for your paternal salutation.   84

I do indeed beseech you, holy flame,
  and living topaz of this diadem,
  that you assuage my hunger to know your name."   87

"O leaf of mine, which even to foresee
  has filled me with delight, I was your root."
  —So he began in answer to my plea.   90

And then: "The first to take your present surname
  (whose soul has crawled the first round of the mountain
  a century and more), he who became   93

father of your grandfather, was my son.
  You would do well, by offering up good works,
  to shorten his long striving at his stone.   96

Florence, within her ancient walls secure—
  from them she still hears *tierce* and *nones* ring down—
  lived in sweet peace, her sons sober and pure.   99

No golden chains nor crowns weighed down her spirit,
  nor women in tooled sandals and studded belts
  more to be admired than the wearer's merit.   102

A father, in those days, was not terrified
  by the birth of a daughter, for marriage and marriage
                            portion
  had not escaped all bounds on either side.   105

No mansions then stood uninhabited.
  No Sardanapalus had yet arrived
  to show what may be done in hall and bed.   108

Montemario had not yet been outshone
  by your Uccellatoio, which having passed it
  in the race up, shall pass it going down.   111

Bellincion Berti, with whom I was acquainted,
  went belted in leather and bone; and his good wife
  came from the mirror with her face unpainted.   114

I have seen the lords of Vecchio and of Nerli
  content to wear plain leather, and their wives
  working the spindle and distaff late and early.   117

Fortunate they! And blest their circumstance!
  Each sure of her own burial place; none yet
  deserted in her bed because of France.   120

One watched the cradle, babbling soft and low
  to soothe her child in the sweet idiom
  that is the first delight new parents know.   123

Another, spinning in her simple home,
  would tell old tales to children gathered round her,
  of Troy, and of Fiesole, and of Rome.   126

A Cornelia or Cincinnatus would amaze
  a modern Florentine as a Cianghella
  or a Lapo would have startled men in those days.   129

To so serene, so fair a townsman's life,
  to a citizenry so wedded in good faith,
  to such sweet dwelling, free of vice and strife,   132

Mary gave me—called in the pain of birth—
  and in your ancient Baptistry I became
  a Christian—and Cacciaguida, there on earth.   135

Moronto and Eliseo my brothers were.
  My wife came from the valley of the Po.
  The surname you now bear derives from her.   138

I served with Conrad in the Holy Land,
  and my valor so advanced me in his favor
  that I was knighted in his noble band.   141

With him I raised my sword against the might
  of the evil creed whose followers take from you—
  because your shepherds sin—what is yours by right. 144

There, by that shameless and iniquitous horde,
  I was divested of the flesh and weight
  of the deceitful world, too much adored   147

by many souls whose best hope it destroys;
  and came from martyrdom to my present joys.

NOTES

4–6. Dante does not say "harp" and "viol" but "lyre" and "strings." I take him to be referring to XIV, 117, and repeat the phrasing of that line to reinforce the reference. In any case, it is the spirits themselves who are the instruments, and it is God's Will (the Hand of Heaven) that plays upon them. Now, however, as an act of heavenly *caritas,* they have foregone the bliss of their singing and wait silently to be the more readily at Dante's service.

7–12. Since *caritas* is the essence of Heaven, it is the joy of the blessèd to hear and to grant righteous prayers. It is fitting, therefore, that the damned mourn forever, having deliberately cast from themselves, for the sake of temporal satisfactions, the everlasting love that would have received them with such eager joy.

22–24. The soul whose glory Dante sees flashing like a falling star is compared first to a gem on a ribbon or diadem, and then to a fire moving behind an alabaster screen. The soul does not leave the blessèd company, but moves through it, so rapidly and so brightly that it seems to be a falling star. Dante is standing at the foot of the great cross. Thus, the spirit approaches him from within it, remaining inside the cross, but at the point closest to Dante.

25–27. *Ancient Ilium:* Anchises, i.e., "the ancient king of Ilium." *Aeneid* VI, 684 ff., narrates the meeting of Anchises and Aeneas in the Elysian Fields. *Muse:* For "poet." Virgil.

28–30. "O blood of mine! O ever abundant grace of God poured over you! To whom was the gate of Heaven ever thrown open twice, as it is to you?" *twice:* Now, while Dante is still in the flesh, and again after his death. St. Paul was borne up in a dream to the Third Heaven, but Dante has come in the flesh. The speaker is Cacciaguida (cah-cha-GWEE-da), Dante's great-great-grandfather. The details of Cacciaguida's life are best presented piecemeal, in the notes of the conversation that follows. Note, however, that Cacciaguida lived in the middle and later twelfth century when the spoken language was still basically Latin. The reference to Virgil and to the *Aeneid* makes it doubly felicitous that he begin his remarks in Latin.

31–36. Dante is astonished by the fact that this new soul addresses him as "Blood of mine!" He turns to Beatrice (Revelation) and sees her eyes light with such bliss that he believes he has experienced the final joy of Heaven. Beatrice, of course, is radiant with her foreknowledge of Dante's pleasure when he learns the identity of the new soul.

37–39. *in sight and sound:* By the sight of his radiance and by the quality of his voice. *added to his opening words:* some commentators have taken this phrasing to signify that Cacciaguida continued in Latin. He may have done so but that can hardly be Dante's point, for Latin would have posed no problem of understanding. There is, rather, a much richer point to be made. Cacciaguida left the earth about a century before this meeting. His long absorption into the Divine Intellect has given him infinite insights and has made natural to him modes of thought beyond mortal understanding. He must learn, therefore, to adjust his speech to Dante's understanding, and he begins by overshooting it.

What he has been absorbed into is, of course, omniscience, and omniscience, one might argue logically enough, would have no need to learn by trial and error. Yet, as a touch of characterization, his first inability to speak on Dante's level is masterful.

42. *target:* Not only does his thought exist at a higher level than any arrow of human thought could reach, but higher even than man could think of placing the target.

48. *seed:* Line of descent.

52. *the Great Book:* Of fate. *black nor white:* To alter the black would be to change what is written. To alter the white would be to add to or subtract from what is written. If neither can be changed, no least change is possible.

53. *this spirit:* Beatrice.

55. Dante is asserting, as a principle of mathematics, that all numbers (Five or Six, for example) derive from One. So all knowledge derives from the Primal Thought, which is unity.

62. *the greatest and least alike:* All souls in Paradise brim full of the most bliss they can achieve or conceive, and all are united in the body of God. Yet, as everywhere in Dante, degrees of difference are

meticulously observed. Perhaps this state of things will seem contradictory to human reason, but we are here dealing with revelation. And certainly one can accept the premise that God's grace, while giving to each its fill, gives one soul a greater capacity than another.

63. *where thoughts outsoar themselves before they rise:* I have had to yield to a rhyme-forced metaphor. Dante's text, rendered literally, would read: "In which, before you think it, your thought outspreads itself."

64–69. Cacciaguida knows Dante's wish and what the answer will be, but has a sweet thirst to hear Dante's voice: an understandable grandfatherly sentiment.

73–87. DANTE'S REPLY TO CACCIAGUIDA. Cacciaguida has asked that Dante speak in his "own voice, assured, frank, and elated." In one sense, then, he has asked the poet Dante to rejoice Heaven with the power of poetry. Dante replies with a passage so superbly balanced that the temptation to cite it as an example of Dante's highest style is counterbalanced only by the fact that he achieves such heights so regularly.

The First Equipoise: God, in whom all attributes co-exist equally, as light and heat co-exist in the sun. When the spirits of the Blessèd are subsumed into the body of God, they, too, share this fullness of equal powers. Thus, their feelings of love and their ability to express those feelings are equal to one another in their fullness. Mortal man's powers of feeling, on the other hand, outrun his powers of utterance. In the perturbation of his unequal powers, therefore, Dante can give thanks only with his heart. Thus, hearing Cacciaguida address him as *"sanguis meus"* (his "paternal salutation") he is more deeply moved than he has power to express.

88–89. *"O leaf of mine . . . I was your root":* Dante seems not to have known his lineage prior to Cacciaguida, who here describes himself as the root of the family tree of which Dante is the present leaf. The metaphoric tree can foresee little continuity from a leaf, and certainly "branch of mine" might have promised more for the future. In "leaf," Dante may have meant to express his transience and smallness as compared to Cacciaguida's eternal glory. *foresee:* Dante uses *"aspettando"* (awaiting). But since Heavenly souls can foresee what they wait for—and rhyme demanding—I have thought this rendering reasonable.

91–96. *present surname:* The surname Alighieri (then Aldighiero) is thus identified as having originated with Cacciaguida's son. The name occurs in a Florentine document of 1189. This Aldighiero (father of Bellincione, who fathered Dante's father) was still alive in 1201 though his date of death is not known. "A century and more," therefore, is a bit too long. *first round of the mountain:* Of Purgatory. The ledge of the Proud. Pride may have been a hereditary failing of the Alighieri, or Dante may be further recognizing his own weakness. (Cf. *Purgatorio* XIII, 133–138.)

97. *her ancient walls:* The original Roman walls. In 1173 a new ring of walls was completed, and others were added in 1284.

98. *from them . . . tierce and nones:* The church called La Badia was built on the old Roman walls. This church rang all the canonical hours (including *tierce* and *nones*).

103–105. In Dante's time, Florentine girls were married in childhood, before they were ten in some cases, and with such enormous dowries that it was said a man with one daughter was impoverished and a man with two ruined. *on either side:* The marriage custom escaped all bounds of moderation, on one side because the girls were too young, and on the other because the dowery demands were too great.

106. *no mansions then stood uninhabited:* Mansions might be empty because wealthy Florentines kept great suites and halls for ostentatious display, rather than to live in; or because dissolute living had destroyed ancestral fortunes and hereditary palaces had to be closed for lack of maintenance; or because the owners (like Dante) had been forced into exile. Dante probably intends all of these reasons, for all are part of the degeneracy he has Cacciaguida lament.

107–108. *Sardanapalus:* King of Assyria from 667 to 626 B.C. He is cited as the type of the luxurious and libertine debauché of the harem. *in hall and bed:* i.e., "indoors" (by way of debauchery and of riotously expensive display).

109–111. *Montemario:* (Mon-teh-MAHR-i-o): A hill with a commanding view of Rome. *Uccellatoio* (Oo-tchell-ah-TOY-oh): A hill with a similar view of Florence. The splendor of the view from the Uccellatoio had not yet outdone the view from Montemario, but just as Florence is rising faster than Rome, so will she plunge to ruin faster.

112–113. *Bellincion Berti:* A nobleman of some importance, honorary citizen of Florence, and father of "the good Gualdrada" (see *Inferno* XVI, 38, note). *belted in leather and bone:* i.e., simply—a leather belt with a bone clasp rather than ornamented stuff with a jeweled clasp.

115. *Vecchio* (Veh-kyo); *Nerli* (NEHR-lee): Both were Guelph lords of Cacciaguida's time and leading citizens of Florence.

119. *sure of her own burial place:* As Dante was not, having been exiled. As, by implication, few later Florentines could be, since any of them might find himself banished.

120. *because of France:* In both of two possible senses. Florentine bankers and merchants often traveled to France, hence they were often out of town. But in France, too, they learned vices for which they abandoned their wives even when they were back in Florence.

122. *the sweet idiom:* Baby talk.

127–129. Dante is contrasting a man and woman of decayed Florence to a man and woman of republican Rome. *Cornelia:* Daughter of Scipio Africanus and mother of the Roman paragons, the Gracchii. Dante saw her in Limbo (*Inferno* IV, 128). *Cincinnatus:* See VI, 46–48, note. *Cianghella:* (Chan-GHELL-ah) A Florentine woman married to a lord of Imola. She died about 1330, having acquired a reputation for a sharp tongue, a haughty extravagance, and an easy bed. *Lapo:* Lapo Saltorello. A Florentine poet and lawyer noted for his extravagant living. He and Dante were banished in the same decree of March 10, 1302.

133–134. *Mary . . . called in the pain of birth:* Sense: Cacciaguida's mother, in the throes of her birth pains, cried out a plea to the Virgin Mary, who thereupon granted him life and sweet dwelling in ancient Florence. *Baptistry:* Of San Giovanni. See *Inferno* XIX, 17–18, and note.

136–138. There is no historic record of any of the persons here mentioned.

139. *Conrad:* Dante says "the Emperor Conrad." (Conrad III, reigned 1137–1152.) He went crusading in 1147 and was defeated at Damascus. He never visited Florence, however, whereas Conrad II (reigned 1024–1039) knew Florence well. Conrad II crusaded against the Saracens in Calabria. Dante has probably run the two Conrads into one.

143–144. *the evil creed:* Islam. *because your shepherds sin:* See *Inferno* XXVII, 82 ff. Because of bad popes (such as Boniface VIII) the Holy Land, which Dante held to be rightfully Christian, was left to Islam. In Dante's view, a proper pope would have called for a crusade and hacked it free of un-Godly hands.

149. *from martyrdom to my present joys:* To call a death in battle a "martyrdom" may be stretching the meaning of the word. In any case, Cacciaguida, having died fighting for the faith—for God— seems to have mounted directly to his place in Heaven. (Cf. the Islamic belief that true believers who die in battle mount instantly to heavenly bliss.)

CANTO XVI

The Fifth Sphere: Mars—The Warriors of God: Cacciaguida

Dante thrills with pleasure on learning that his ancestor had been
elevated to knighthood, and feeling the power of pride of ances-
try even in Heaven, in which there is no temptation to evil, he
has a new insight into the family pride in which mortals glory.
Moved by pride, Dante addresses Cacciaguida with the formal
"voi," an affectation at which Beatrice, half amused, admonishes
him with a smile.

Dante then asks Cacciaguida for details of his birth and an-
cestry and of *The History of Early Florence.* Cacciaguida, as if to
warn Dante away from pride of ancestry, dismisses the question
of his birth and of his forebears as a matter best passed over in si-
lence, and proceeds to a detailed account of the lords and people
of Florence in the days when her bloodlines and traditions had
not been diluted by the arrival of new families. It is to this "mon-
grelization" of the Florentines that Cacciaguida attributes all the
subsequent degeneracy of Florence.

O trivial pride of ours in noble blood!
  that in possessing you men are possessed,
  down here, where souls grow sick and lose their good, 3

will never again amaze me, for there, too,
  where appetite is never drawn to evil—
  in Heaven, I say—my own soul gloried in you! 6

You are a mantle that soon shrinks and tears.
  Unless new cloth is added day by day,
  time will go round you, snipping with its shears! 9

I spoke again, addressing him with that *"voi"*
  whose usage first began among the Romans—
  and which their own descendants least employ— 12

at which my Lady, who stood apart, though near,
  and smiling, seemed to me like her who coughed
  at the first recorded fault of Guinevere.   15

"You are my father," I started in reply.
  "You give me confidence to speak out boldly.
  You so uplift me, I am more than I.   18

So many streams of happiness flow down
  into my mind that it grows self-delighting
  at being able to bear it and not drown.   21

Tell me, then, dear source of my own blood,
  who were your own forefathers? when were you born?
  and what transpired in Florence in your boyhood?   24

Tell me of St. John's sheepfold in those days.
  How many souls were then within the flock,
  and which of them was worthy of high place?"   27

As glowing coals fanned by a breath of air
  burst into flames, so did I see that light
  increase its radiance when it heard my prayer.   30

And as its light gave off a livelier ray,
  so, in a sweeter and a softer voice—
  though not in the idiom we use today—   33

it said: "From the day when *Ave* sounded forth
  to that in which my mother, now a saint,
  being heavy laden with me, gave me birth,   36

this flame had come back to its Leo again
  to kindle itself anew beneath his paws
  five hundred times plus fifty plus twenty plus ten.   39

My ancestors and I were born in the place
  where the last quarter of the course begins
  for those who take part in your annual race.   42

Of my fathers, be content with what you have heard.
  Of who they were and whence they came to Florence
  silence is far more fitting than any word.   45

Of men who could bear arms there were counted then,
  between Mars and the Baptist, the fifth part
  of what may be mustered there from living men.   48

But the citizenry, now mongrelized by the blood
  of Campi, of Certaldo, and of Figghine,
  was pure then, down to the humblest planer of wood. 51

Oh how much better to have been neighbors of these
  of whom I speak, and to have Trespiano
  and Galuzzo still fixed as your boundaries,   54

than to have swallowed them and to bear the stink
  of the yokel of Aguglione, and of Signa's boor
  who still has eyes to swindle and hoodwink.   57

Had the world's most despicable crew not shown
  a hard stepmother's face and greed to Caesar
  but been a loving mother, one who is known   60

as a Florentine, and who trades in goods and debt,
  would be back in Simifonti, where his grandsire
  once gypsied in the streets for what he could get.   63

Montemurlo would still be owned by its own counts,
  the Cerchi would be in the parish of Acone,
  and in Valdigreve, still, the Bondelmounts.   66

It has always been a fact that confusion of blood
  has been a source of evil to city-states,
    just as our bodies are harmed by too much food;   69

and that a bull gone blind will fall before
  a blind lamb does. And that one sword may cut
    better than five has been proved in many a war.   72

If you will think of Luni and Urbisaglia,
  how they have passed away, and how, behind them,
    are dying now Chiusi and Sinigaglia,   75

it should not be too hard to comprehend,
  or strange to hear, that families dwindle out,
    when even cities come at last to an end.   78

All mankind's institutions, of every sort,
  have their own death, though in what long endures
    it is hidden from you, your own lives being short.   81

And as the circling of the lunar sphere
  covers and bares the shore with never a pause,
    so Fortune alters Florence year by year.   84

It should not, therefore, seem too wondrous strange
  to hear me speak of the good Florentines
    whose fame is veiled behind time's endless change.   87

I knew the Ughi, the Catellini, the line
  of the Greci, Filippi, Ormanni, and Alberichi—
    illustrious citizens, even in decline.   90

I knew those of Sannella, and those of the Bow,
  and the Soldanieri, Ardinghi, and Bostichi;
    as grand as they were ancient, there below.   93

Not far from the portal that now bears the weight
  of such a cargo of new iniquity
  as soon, now, will destroy the ship of state,   96

once lived the Ravignani, from whom came
  Count Guido Guerra, and whoever else
  has since borne Bellincione's noble name.   99

The della Pressa were already furnished
  with knowledge of how to rule, and Galigaio
  had his gold hilt and pommel already burnished.   102

Great already were the lands of the vair,
  Sacchetti, Guiochi, Fifanti, Barucci, and Galli
  and of those who blush now for the stave affair.   105

The trunk that bore the many-branched Calfucci
  had grown already great; already called
  to the curule were Sizii and Arrigucci.   108

How great I have seen them who are now undone
  by their own pride! And even the balls of gold—
  in all great deeds of Florence, how they shone!   111

So shone the fathers of that gang we see
  in the bishop's palace when your See falls vacant,
  fattening themselves as a consistory.   114

That overweening and presumptuous tribe—
  a dragon to all who run from it, a lamb
  to any who stand and show a tooth or bribe—   117

were coming up, though still so parvenu
  Donato was hardly pleased when his father-in-law
  made him a relative of such a crew.   120

The Caponsacchi had come down by then
  from Fiesole to market; the Infangati
  and Giudi were established as good townsmen.   123

And here's an astonishing fact, though little known:
  in ancient times a gate of the inner wall
  was named for those of the Pera, now all gone.   126

All those whose various quarterings display
  the staves of the great baron whose name and worth
  are kept alive every St. Thomas' Day   129

owe him the rank and privilege they enjoy,
  though one who binds those arms with a gold fringe
  makes common cause today with the hoi polloi.   132

Gualterotti and Importuni were then well known.
  And Borgo would still be a peaceful place
  had it not acquired new neighbors from Montebuon'. 135

The line from which was born your grief and strife
  because of the righteous anger that ruined you,
  and put an end to all your happier life,   138

was honored in itself and its allies.
  O Buondelmonti, what ill you did in fleeing
  its nuptials to find comfort in other ties!   141

Many would still be happy whom we now pity,
  had God seen fit to let the Ema drown you
  on the first day you started for the city.   144

But it was fitting that to the broken stone
  that guards the bridge, Florence should offer a victim
  to mark the last day's peace she has ever known.   147

With such as these, and others, my first life's years
  saw Florence live and prosper in such peace
  that she had, then, no reason to shed tears.   150

With such as these I saw there in my past
  so valiant and so just a populace
  that none had ever seized the ensign's mast   153

and hung the lily on it upside down.
  Nor was the red dye of division known."

NOTES

1. *in noble blood:* Pride of birth into a family with patents of no-
bility.

6. *my own soul gloried in you:* On hearing that Cacciaguida had
been knighted by (whichever) Conrad. The point is curiously made.
Despite the statements of many of Dante's commentators, who were
probably working backward from Dante's own claim rather than
from any historical record, there is no recorded evidence either that
Cacciaguida had been knighted, or even that he had served in the
crusades. Dante may be following a family legend, or he may be in-
venting his own claim to nobility, the latter an oddly uncelestial act
of pride. Dante, in any case, hastens to disclaim any real merit in the
possession of noble ancestry unless the descendants labor to main-
tain the family's true nobility of soul.

10–12. *voi:* The second person plural. It seems to have come
into use as the deferential form of address to a single person in
about the third century A.D., but Dante is following the popular be-
lief of his time that it was first used in addressing Caesar when he
assumed all the high offices of the Republic and so became, in ef-
fect, many personages in one. English does not distinguish between
"tu" (you-singular) and *"voi"* (you-plural) except perhaps in the di-
alect of the southern states where "you" (singular) and "you-all"
(plural) is standard. *least employ:* The modern Romans, always a
mannerless lot, made the least use of this polite or deferential form.

The "you" that begins each of the three sentences in lines 16–18 is this *"voi."*

13–15. Beatrice notes Dante's foible in using the *"voi"* form and admonishes him with a half-amused smile that reminds him of the wife of Mallehaut (see *Inferno* V, 124–134, and notes) who coughed when she first saw Guinevere with Launcelot.

25. *St. John's sheepfold:* Florence. John the Baptist was its patron saint.

34. *Ave:* Hail. The first word spoken to Mary by the Angel of the Annunciation.

37–39. *this flame:* Mars. *its Leo:* Astrologers asserted various special connections between Mars and Leo. Both were classified as "hot and dry." And Leo is the constellation of the Lion, the warlike and heraldic beast perhaps closest to the god of war.

39. THE DATE OF CACCIAGUIDA'S BIRTH. The Annunciation took place on March 25. Scartazzini cites a text of Dante's time that sets the Martian year at 686.94 days. That figure multiplied by 580 and divided by the 365.2466 days of the earth year (as Scartazzini asserts, my mathematics floundering in his wake) yields as a birthdate January 25, 1091. Even Scartazzini does not complicate his computations by entering a correction for various calendar reforms. In any case, Cacciaguida is thought to have died when he was about 56.

40–42. The annual race was run in Florence on June 24, the Feast of St. John. "Quarter" here signifies "quarter of a town," as in "Latin Quarter." Scholars disagree as to the course of the race and the exact quarter Dante had in mind. Porta San Piero is generally favored by the commentators.

43. *Of my fathers:* This much in answer to Dante's first question, and also as a rebuke to Dante for his pride of ancestry, but note, too, that this answer covers Dante's own ignorance of his remoter ancestry.

47. *between Mars and the Baptist:* To be between Mars and the Baptist signifies, in effect, to be in Florence, the statue of Mars on the Ponte Vecchio and the Baptistry of St. John marking two of the limits of Florence in Cacciaguida's time. In 1300 Florence had a popu-

lation of about 70,000, of which (according to a doubtful estimate by Scartazzini) about 30,000 were able to bear arms.

50. *of Campi, of Certaldo* (tchehr-TAHL-doh) *and of Figghine* (fee-GHEE-neh): All are nearby places a self-righteous Florentine would think of as the backwoods. Florence was on the main highway of invasion from the north. Inevitably, therefore, many tribal strains were joined in its people. Dante is seldom temperate in his views of outsiders.

52–57. *those of whom I speak:* In line 50. *Trespiano:* A crossroads village now at the edge of Florence, but in Cacciaguida's time an hour's walk away on the road to Bologna. *Galuzzo:* A village at about the same distance on the road to Siena. *the yokel of Aguglione* (ah-goo-LYOW-neh): Baldo d'Aguglione. His family name traces to a "backwoods" castle in Val di Pesa, but he became a power in Florence. He was probably involved in the swindles Dante cites in *Purgatorio* XII, 100–105. On September 3, 1311 he issued a decree recalling a number of Florentine exiles but left Dante's name off the list, whereby, of course, he put himself on Dante's list to be registered as a stink in Heaven. *Signa's boor:* Fazio dei Morubaldini of Signa (SEE-nyah), a hamlet near Florence. Fazio was a lawyer of Dante's time with a considerable reputation as a grafter, swindler, and barrator.

58–59. *crew:* The clergy. *Caesar:* Here as a symbol of temporal government. Sense: Had the church been a loving mother in temporal affairs.

60. *one who is known:* Dante may have had a specific person in mind but many Florentines, old-line and parvenu, traded as merchants and pawnbrokers. Dante seems to charge all such evil commerce to the influx of new families that resulted from the political scheming of the church.

62. *Simifonti:* A castle and town in Valdessa captured by Florence in 1202.

64. *Montemurlo:* A castle between Pistoia and Prata. It formerly belonged to the counts Guidi (see *Inferno* XXX, 76–77). In 1254, unable to defend the castle against the Pistoians, the counts sold it to Florence.

65. *the Cerchi* (TCHEHR-kee); *Acone* (ah-CON-eh): is in Val di Sieve. In Dante's time, the Cerchi had become leaders of the White Party in Dante's own soidisant ancestral quarter of Porta San Piero.

66. *Valdigreve:* South of Florence where the Buondelmonti had a castle called Montebuoni. In 1135 the castle was taken from them by the Florentines and they were forced to move into Florence, where they became powerful in Borgo Sant' Apostolo.

67. *confusion of blood:* The admixture of new blood lines to those of an old established population.

73–75. Cacciaguida is citing examples of dead or enfeebled cities; the first two are already dead, the second two are dying. *Luni:* An ancient city on the Magra at the northern boundary of Tuscany, already a ruin in Dante's time. *Urbisaglia* (oor-bee-SAH-lyah): In the March of Ancona; not quite dead in Dante's time. *Chiusi* (KYOO-zee); Ancient Clusium. In Val di Chiana. *Sinigaglia* (see-nee-GAH-lyah): On the coast north of Ancona. Both were ravaged by malaria in Dante's time, but both have survived their prophesied extinction.

84. *so Fortune alters Florence:* Now raising her on the flood, now letting her down on the ebb. Fortune, of course, is Dame Fortune.

88–90. *Ughi* (OO-ghee), *etc.:* Cacciaguida lists six solid old families of the first half of the eleventh century and says they were illustrious even in their decline. In 1300 these families had finished declining and were extinct, at least as influential voices in Florentine affairs.

91. *those of the Bow:* The family dell' Arca. They and the other four families here cited were numerous and powerful in Cacciaguida's time. In Dante's time the dell' Arca clan was extinct; the Soldanieri, a Ghibelline clan, still existed but had been banished; and the descendants of the other three clans had lost power and social standing.

94. *the portal:* Of San Piero, where the Cerchi ruled in Dante's time (see line 65) showing the destruction of Florence.

97–99. *Ravignani . . . Count Guido Guerra . . . Bellincione:* Bellincione (bell-een-TCHOE-neh) Berti dei Ravignani (rah-vee-NYAH-nee) was praised in XV, 112–114. Count Guido Guerra VI was praised in *Inferno* XVI, 37–39, though he is damned among the sodomites. He was a great grandson of Bellincione, who was the father of Good Gualdrada. Through another daughter, his name descended to many members of the Adimari family (see Filippo Argenti, *Inferno* VIII, 32, note, and note to line 119 below).

100. *della Pressa:* An emergent family (in Cacciaguida's time) who had been elected to govern some of the nearby territories of Florence. Their descendants were charged with betraying the Florentines at Montaperti (for which see *Inferno* X, 86, and note to 32–51).

101. *Galigaio* (gal-ee-GUY-oh): A noble family of Porta San Piero, here said to have been already of the knighthood ("gold hilt and pommel") in Cacciaguida's time, but reduced to the rank and file by 1300.

103. *vair:* A fur, usually of a small squirrel. Represented in heraldry by rows of little bells. It appeared on the arms of the Pigli (PEE-lyee), a family of Porta San Pancrazio.

104. A continuation of the early eleventh-century Florentine social register.

105. *those who blush now for the stave affair:* The Chiaramontesi of Porta San Piero. See *Purgatorio* XII, 100–105, note.

106. *Calfucci* (kahl-FOO-tchee): Were collateral with the Donati. Dante's wife, Gemma, was a Donati.

108. *the curule:* A chair in which only the highest officers of Rome might sit. Here used to indicate highest rank. *Sizii* (see-TZEE-yee) *and Arrigucci* (ah-ree-GOO-tchee): Neither family was extinct by Dante's time, but the first was nearly so, and the second much reduced.

110. *balls of gold:* From the arms of the Lamberti. Mosca, one of this line, is in the Bolgia of the Sowers of Discord (*Inferno* XXVIII, 106, and note).

112. *so shone the fathers of that gang we see:* As the Lamberti once shone in every great deed of Florence so shone (in evil deeds) the Visdomini and the Tosinghi, hereditary patrons and defenders of the episcopal see and palace. Whenever the see fell vacant, they were in

charge of episcopal affairs until a new bishop was elected. Dante here accuses them of forming themselves into a private consistory in order to fatten themselves on the resources of the see.

115. *That . . . tribe:* The Adimari. Dante had special reasons for disliking them. When Dante was banished, Boccaccio Adimari took over his forfeited estates and resisted every effort to rescind the decree of banishment.

119. *Donato . . . his father-in-law:* Bellincione married the good Gualdrada to Umbertino Donati of the family of the Counts Guidi. He then married another daughter to the upstart Adimari, thus relating the two families. The Donati refused to acknowledge kinship.

121–123. *Caponsacchi . . . Giudi . . . Infangati:* Three Ghibelline families, once well established, but much diminished by Dante's time. Is it only coincidence that these three names mean, at root, Head-in-a-sack, Judases (or Jews), and Covered-with-mud? Could Dante be suggesting that these Johnny-come-latelies were as outlandish as their names in comparison with the old-line Florentines?

125. *the inner wall:* The first (Roman) wall of the city. Cacciaguida is saying that Dante would know the long-vanished della Pera family was an ancient one, but not that it traced back to the very founding of Florence.

127–132. Hugh of Brandenburg, known in Italy as Ugo il Grande, marchese di Toscano, was the Imperial Vicar of Tuscany. Thus he was the voice of Imperial authority and order (see note to *Purgatorio* VI, 100) and Tuscany's chief Ghibelline. His arms bore seven staves, which are variously reproduced in the arms of "all those" families he raised to knighthood and fortune (among them the Giandotti, Pulci, della Bella, and Neri). He died on St. Thomas' Day, 1006, and it is still part of the festival of St. Thomas to offer solemn prayer to Ugo in the Abbey he built in Florence. *though one who binds those arms:* Giano (DJAH-no) della Bella. He was exiled in 1295 and was no longer making common cause with the hoi polloi. But Dante, though he had to become a Guelph once there were no more Ghibellines in Florence, still has his only political hope in the party of the Emperor and will not miss a chance to condemn the great Ghibelline families that identified themselves with the cause of vulgar independence.

133. *Gualterotti and Importuni:* Guelph families of Borgo Santo Apostolo, great in Cacciaguida's time, but common workingmen in Dante's.

136. *new neighbors from Montebuon':* The Buondelmonti. Cacciaguida goes on to describe the grief and disorder they brought to Florence. Their houses were next to those of the Gualterotti and Importuni.

136–138. *The line:* Of the Amidei. A great family related to the Lamberti and allied to many noble families of Florence. Despite the fact that it was of much higher rank, it betrothed one of its daughters to Buondelmonte dei Buondelmonti, who broke off the nuptials in order to marry a daughter of the Donati. The Amidei, in "righteous anger" at this affront by a man of lower rank, held a council of war. It was at this council that Mosca dei Lamberti (*Inferno* XXVIII, 106, and note) declared, "A thing done has an end." As a result Buondelmonti was murdered at the foot of the statue of Mars in 1215. As a result of that murder Florence, previously united, became divided into Guelph and Ghibelline factions, and was plunged into civil war, thereby ending its "happier life."

143. *the Ema:* A river bounding the lands from which the Buondelmonti were dispossessed before they came to Florence.

145–147. *the broken stone:* The mutilated statue of Mars. It is fitting, says Cacciaguida in bitter irony, that Florence should mark its return to the rule of Mars by offering up the blood of a victim at the foot of the mutilated statue of its first pagan patron.

153–154. Cacciaguida means that the Florentines had never been defeated in war. It was a custom to mock the vanquished by flying their captured flags upside down on the mast. The lily was, of course, the emblem of France.

155. The ancient standard of Florence bore a white lily on a red field. In 1251 the Guelphs changed their standard to a red lily on a white field, the Ghibellines preserving the original. Thus there were two Florentine standards and division had dyed the lily red. The "red dye," of course, is also the blood spilled in war.

CANTO XVII

The Fifth Sphere: Mars—The Warriors of God: Cacciaguida

Beatrice and Cacciaguida already know what question is burning in Dante's mind, but Beatrice nevertheless urges him to speak it, that by practicing Heavenly discourse he be better able to speak to men when he returns to Earth. So urged, Dante asks Cacciaguida to make clear the recurring *Dark Prophecies of Dante's Future.*

Cacciaguida details *Dante's Coming Banishment from Florence,* identifies the patrons Dante will find, and assures Dante of his future fame. He warns Dante not to become bitter in adversity assuring him that the Divine Comedy, once it becomes known, will outlive the proudest of the Florentines and bring shame to their evil memories for ages to come.

Like him who went to Clymene to learn
   if what he had heard was true, and who makes fathers
   unwilling to yield to their sons at every turn—   3

such was I, and such was I taken to be
   by Beatrice and by the holy lamp
   that, earlier, had changed its place for me.   6

Therefore my lady: "Speak. And let the fire
   of your consuming wish come forth," she said,
   "well marked by the inner stamp of your desire;   9

not that we learn more by what you say,
   but that you better learn to speak your thirst,
   that men may sooner quench it on your way."   12

"Dear root of my existence, you who soar
   so high that, as men grasp how a triangle
   may contain one obtuse angle and no more,   15

you grasp contingent things before they find
  essential being, for you can see that focus
  where all time is time-present in God's mind.   18

While I was yet with Virgil, there below,
  climbing the mountain where the soul is healed,
  and sinking through the dead world of its woe,   21

dark words of some dark future circumstance
  were said to me; whereby my soul is set
  four-square against the hammering of chance: 24

and, therefore, my desire will be content
  with knowing what misfortune is approaching;
  for the arrow we see coming is half spent."   27

—Such were the words of my reply, addressed
  to the light that had spoken earlier; and with them
  as Beatrice wished, my own wish was confessed.   30

Not in dark oracles like those that glued
  the foolish like limed birds, before the Lamb
  that takes our sins away suffered the rood;   33

but in clear words and the punctilious style
  of ordered thought, that father-love replied,
  concealed in and revealed by his own smile: 36

"*Contingency,* whose action is confined
  to the few pages of the world of matter,
  is fully drawn in the Eternal Mind;   39

but it no more derives *necessity* . . .
  from being so drawn, than a ship dropping down river
  derives its motion from a watcher's eye.   42

As a sweet organ-harmony strikes the ear,
  so, from the Primal Mind, my eyes receive
  a vision of your future drawing near.   45

As Hippolytus left Athens, forced to roam
  by his two-faced and merciless stepmother,
  just so shall you leave Florence, friends, and home.   48

So is it willed, so does it already unfold,
  so will it soon be done by him who plots it
  there where Christ is daily bought and sold.   51

The public cry, as usual, will blame you
  of the offended party, but the vengeance
  truth will demand will yet show what is true.   54

All that you held most dear you will put by
  and leave behind you; and this is the arrow
  the longbow of your exile first lets fly.   57

You will come to learn, how bitter as salt and stone
  is the bread of others, how hard the way that goes
  up and down stairs that never are your own.   60

And what will press down on your shoulders most
  will be the foul and foolish company
  you will fall into on that barren coast.   63

Ingrate and godless, mad in heart and head
  will they become against you, but soon thereafter
  it will be they, not you, whose cheeks turn red.   66

Their bestiality will be made known
  by what they do; while your fame shines the brighter
  for having become a party of your own.   69

Your first inn and first refuge you shall owe
  to the great Lombard whose escutcheon bears
  the sacred bird above, the ladder below.   72

In such regard and honor shall he hold you,
  that in the act of granting and requesting,
  what others do late, shall be first between you two.   75

With him you will see another, born of this star
  and so stamped by the iron of its virtues
  that he shall be renowned for deeds of war.   78

The world has not yet noticed him: these spheres
  in their eternal course above his youth
  have turned about him now only nine years.   81

Before the Gascon sets his low intrigue
  to snare high Henry, men will start to speak
  of his disregard of money and fatigue.   84

The knowledge of his magnanimities
  will spread so far that men will hear of it
  out of the mouths of his very enemies.   87

Look you to him and his great works. The fate
  of many shall be altered by his deeds,
  the rich and poor exchanging their estate.   90

And write this in your mind but remain silent
  concerning it . . ."—and he said things about him
  to astonish even those who shall be present.   93

Then added: "Son, these are the annotations
  to what was told you. These are the snares that hide
  behind a few turns of the constellations.   96

But do not hate your neighbors: your future stretches
  far beyond the reach of what they do
  and far beyond the punishment of wretches."   99

—When, by his silence, that blessèd soul made clear
  that he had finished passing his dark shuttle
  across the threads I had combed for him there,   102

I then, as one who has not understood
  longs for the guidance of a soul that sees,
  and straightway wills, and wholly loves the good: 105

"Father, I do indeed see time's attacks
  hard spurred against me to strike such a blow
  as shall fall most on him who is most lax.   108

And it is well I arm myself with foresight.
  Thus, if the dearest place is taken from me,
  I shall not lose all place by what I write.   111

Down through that world of endless bitter sighs,
  and on the mountain from whose flowering crown
  I was uplifted by my lady's eyes,   114

and then through Heaven from ray to living ray,
  I have learned much that would, were it retold,
  offend the taste of many alive today.   117

Yet if, half friend to truth, I mute my rhymes,
  I am afraid I shall not live for those
  who will think of these days as 'the ancient times.' "   120

The light in which my heaven-found treasure shone
  smiled brighter in its rapture, coruscating
  like a gold mirror in a ray of sun;   123

then answered me: "A conscience overcast
  by its own shame, or another's, may indeed
  be moved to think your words a bitter blast.   126

Nevertheless, abjure all lies, but match
  your verses to the vision in fullest truth;
  and if their hides are scabby, let them scratch!   129

For if your voice is bitter when first tested
  upon the palate, it shall yet become
  a living nutriment when it is digested.   132

This cry you raise shall strike as does the wind
  hardest at highest peaks—and this shall argue
  no little for your honor, as you will find.   135

Therefore you have been shown—here in these spheres,
  there on the mount, and in the valley of woe—
  those souls whose names most ring in mortal ears;   138

for the feelings of a listener do not mark
  examples of things unknown, nor place their trust
  in instances whose roots hide in the dark;   141

nor will men be persuaded to give ear
  to arguments whose force is not made clear."

NOTES

1–3. *him who went to Clymene:* Phaeton, son of Clymene and
Apollo. Epaphus had told him Apollo was not his father and the boy
had run to his mother to be reassured. Phaeton makes all fathers
chary of yielding too readily to their sons by his example in per-
suading Apollo to let him drive the chariot of the Sun. Apollo con-
sented but Phaeton was not strong enough to control the horses.

They bolted and the Sun was about to burn Earth and sky when Zeus stopped the chariot with a thunderbolt, killing Phaeton. Thus the reluctance Phaeton teaches fathers is for the good of the sons.

6. *changed its place:* In descending to the foot of the cross.

7–12. The mixed metaphor with which Beatrice opens is once again based on the impress of a signet in wax. Here the fire is the wax and inner desire the signet. She and Cacciaguida (and all the heavenly souls) already know Dante's mind and their knowledge of it cannot be increased by his speaking, but by encouraging him to discourse on a heavenly level, Beatrice is preparing him the better to speak his soul's need when he returns to earth, in order that men may be moved to the good he urges.

13–18. Sense of this passage: "You grasp the future as easily as men grasp a problem in geometry, for your sight is fixed upon God's mind, in which all time is one and present." *root:* Dante uses *"piota,"* which may mean "root, soil around a root, sod, turf, or sole of the foot."

16. *contingent things:* Contingency, in Scholastic terminology, is "that which could or could not exist." Contingency is dependent upon the action of *necessity* (that which must necessarily exist). Contingent being is possible, finite, and secondary. Necessary being is certain, infinite, and primary.

29. *to the light:* To Cacciaguida.

31–32. *that glued the foolish like limed birds:* Bird-lime, a highly viscous substance, is spread on boughs and used to trap birds much as flies are trapped on fly paper. Dante compares the sayings of pagan oracles to that lime, in which the pagan world let itself be trapped before the Lamb of Christ suffered to set men free of such traps.

36. *his own smile:* "Smile" is used here for "gladness of spirit"—a regular usage in the *Paradiso*. That gladness is revealed to Dante by the brightening of the flame that hides Cacciaguida from Dante's view. Thus he is both concealed in and revealed by the brighter shining of his bliss.

37–42. Divine foreknowledge of *contingency* does not confer *necessity* because man is given free will. The nature of free will within the workings of omniscient prevision is a point of faith and must be referred to the mysteries rather than to reason.

46. *Hippolytus:* Son of Theseus and the Amazon Antiope. He rejected the advances of his stepmother, Phaedra, and she, accusing him of what she herself wanted, turned Theseus against him. Theseus not only drove him from home but called on Poseidon for vengeance and Poseidon sent a bull from the sea to kill Hippolytus as he was driving his chariot along the shore. Ovid tells the story in *Metamorphoses* XV, 487 ff. Through Cacciaguida, Dante is, of course, protesting that the charges brought against him were as false and self-seeking as Phaedra's against Hippolytus.

Dante, as a high official of Florence and a leader of the Whites, was charged, vaguely and inconclusively, with grafting. The "Anonimo Fiorentino," a nearly contemporary fourteenth-century commentary, says that part of the charge brought against Dante was his "opposition to the Holy Mother Church," which in this case is, clearly enough, another way of saying "opposition to the politics of Pope Boniface VIII."

50–51. *him who plots it:* Boniface VIII, if not in person and with Dante specifically in mind, then through his corrupt agents and evil policies. *where Christ is daily bought and sold:* Rome, i.e., the Vatican.

52–53. *you of the offended party:* Both Dante and his party, the Whites.

53–54. *the vengeance truth will demand:* Truth will take its vengeance by punishing those who are guilty. In so doing, it will bear witness to what is true. Throughout this passage (from line 46) Boniface VIII is compared to Phaedra. (See *Inferno* XII, 12–18, and note.) For the force of the comparison it is well to bear in mind that Phaedra was born of a foul beast (the Minotaur) and a queen so lecherous that she crept into a wooden cow in order to be taken by the bull. Phaedra later committed suicide, overcome by her guilt, her death clearing the name of Hippolytus. Hippolytus, curiously enough, survived a shift of legend and appears in Catholic hagiography as St. Hippolytus or St. Hippolyte.

62. *the foul and foolish company:* Dante seems to be alluding to his own party, the Whites. As a fallen leader, he seems to feel his party has betrayed him. In any case there seems to be nothing to hope for from political parties. In line 69 Cacciaguida praises him for having become his own party of one.

63. *that barren coast:* Of exile.

65–66. *soon thereafter . . . cheeks turn red:* The same sort of machinations that led to Dante's banishment led Florence into foolish wars and bloody internal disorders that left the Florentines with more than enough reasons for blushing. The Whites in particular suffered many humiliations and bloody defeats.

69. *A party of your own:* In 1266, the Ghibellines were driven forever from Florence (see *Inferno* X, 32–51, note). The Guelphs, thereupon, divided into Whites and Blacks, and Dante became a member of the Whites' ruling council. At the end of 1301 the Blacks elected a new *podestà,* and on January 27, 1302, while Dante was on a mission to Rome, the Blacks published a decree fining him 5,000 florins and banishing him for two years. On March 10, not having appeared to pay his fine, Dante was banished permanently, and sentenced to death if he returned. In 1303, the Whites, joined now with the remnants of the Ghibellines, were gathering forces for an assault on Florence, and Dante was their ambassador at the court of Bartolomeo della Scala, Lord of Verona. At that time Boniface VIII died, and was succeeded by Benedict XI, who sent a cardinal to Florence to negotiate a settlement. With that hope in view, Dante remained affiliated with the Whites. The Blacks, however, resisted all negotiation, and the Whites prepared an attack that was repulsed with heavy losses at La Lastra, above Florence, July 20, 1304. Dante seems to have felt that the internal bickerings of the Whites had caused the carnage, and it was probably after La Lastra that he withdrew, damning Blacks and Whites together, to become a one-man party of his own.

71 ff. THE SCALIGERI (DELLA SCALA). The ancient nobel family of the Scaligeri (its German branch was named Scaliger) ruled over Verona and later acquired the office of Imperial Vicar of Tuscany. Alberto died in 1301 and was succeeded, in order, by his three sons: Bartolomeo, died 1304; Alboino, died 1311; Francesco (Can Grande), who shared power with Alboino beginning in 1308, became sole lord of Verona in 1311, and died in 1329. (Dante died in 1321.) Francesco was Dante's great patron and the lord on whom Dante based some of his hope of peace and order in Italy. (See *Inferno* I, 95, and note.) *the great Lombard:* Francesco. *the sacred bird:* The

eagle. The arms of the Scaligeri displayed a ladder *(scala)* below an eagle.

73–75. *Others ask first and give later.* But between Bartolomeo and Dante (as, note, among the souls of Heaven) the giving shall be first and any request (of service from the other) shall come late, the service having already been freely offered.

76. *another:* Can Grande. He won no particular renown as a warrior. "Of war" (line 78) does not occur in Dante. It is my own rhyme-forced addition. Yet to be stamped by the influence of Mars, praised by one of the warriors of God, and to be hailed, as Dante may have intended, as the Greyhound that shall hunt down and destroy evil, can only be appropriate to a warrior, even when the war record is missing. Perhaps Dante was still hoping ahead from the time of (as distinct from time "in") the writing, for Can Grande was then in power.

81. *nine years:* Earth years. Cacciaguida does not say nine "times." Nine Martian years would equal about seventeen earth years and Can Grande was nine years old on March 9, 1300. (Note that March is "Mars month.")

82–83. *the Gascon . . . high Henry:* The Gascon is Clement V (see *Inferno* XIX, 77–79, and note. Also *Purgatorio* XXXII, 149–150). He succeeded Boniface VIII to the Papal throne in 1305, and to the baptismal font of Hell in 1314. Henry VII of Luxembourg, Emperor 1308–1313 (see *Purgatorio* VII, 96, and note), was the main prop of Dante's hopes for a general peace and for the end of his exile. Clement invited him to Rome with fair promises but threatened to excommunicate him in 1312. "Before," therefore (line 82), means "before 1312." By that time Can Grande was twenty-one, had been joint lord of Verona for four years, and sole lord for one. *men will start to speak:* Dante says, literally, "sparks of his virtue will appear."

92–93. *him:* Can Grande. *those who shall be present:* To bear witness to the astonishing things Cacciaguida prophesies to Dante while enjoining him not to repeat them.

96. *a few turns:* Probably intended as daily rather than annual revolutions. At the Easter season of 1300 Dante was less than two years from his banishment.

108. *on him who is most lax:* Who has least foreseen and fore-armed himself.

110. *the dearest place:* Florence.

112. *that world:* Hell.

113. *flowering crown:* The Earthly Paradise.

CANTO XVIII

The Fifth Sphere: Mars—The Courageous: Cacciaguida ·
Great Warriors of God

Ascent to Jupiter

The Sixth Sphere: Jupiter—The Just and Temperate Rulers ·
The Vision of the Flashing Lights and of the Eagle

Beatrice comforts Dante, who is pondering the bitter and the
sweet of Cacciaguida's prophecy, then instructs him to turn back
to Cacciaguida, who proceeds to name among the souls who
form the Cross of Mars *The Great Warriors of God*. They flash like
shooting stars along the arms of the cross. Finished, Cacciaguida
reascends to his original place in the right arm and the whole
choir resumes its hymn.

Dante turns back to Beatrice, sees her grow yet more beauti-
ful, and knows they have made the *Ascent to the Sixth Sphere*. He
sees the pale glow of Jupiter replace the red glow of Mars and in
that silvery sheen he sees *The Vision of Earthly Justice,* a spectacu-
lar arrangement of lights that spell out a message, letter by letter,
and then form as an *Eagle* (The Empire) ornamented by glowing
lilies (France).

Moved by this vision of Justice, Dante prays that these souls of
Heavenly Justice will visit their wrath upon the corrupt Pope,
who, like a money-changer in the temple, denies the sacraments
of God's people by excommunication and interdiction, in order
to sell back to them what is rightfully theirs. So, for the love of
money does the successor of Peter and Paul betray holy office.

Now that holy mirror rejoiced alone,
    rapt in its own reflections; and I tasted
    the bitterness and sweetness of my own.   3

My guide to God said: "Turn your thoughts along
    a happier course. Remember I dwell near
    the One who lifts the weight of every wrong."   6

I turned to the loving sound of my soul's aid,
  and the love my eyes beheld in her sacred eyes
  I leave unsaid—not only am I afraid   9

my powers of speech fail, but my memory
  cannot return so far above itself
  unless Another's grace be moved to guide me.   12

This much of what I felt I can report—
  that as I looked at her my will was freed
  of every other wish of any sort,   15

for the Eternal Bliss that rayed down whole
  into my Beatrice, shone back from her face
  and its reflection there gladdened my soul.   18

And with a smile so radiant that my eyes
  were overcome, she said then: "Turn and listen:
  not in my eyes alone is Paradise."   21

As, here on earth, the face sometimes reveals
  the wish within, if it is wished so strongly
  that all the soul is gripped by what it feels—   24

so, in the flaming of the holy ray
  to which I turned, I read the inner will,
  and knew that it had something more to say.   27

It spoke thus: "In this fifth limb of the tree
  whose life is from its crown, and bears forever,
  and never sheds a leaf, I would have you see   30

elected spirits who, in the world's use,
  before they came to Heaven, were so renowned
  their great worth would make greater every Muse.   33

Look at the arms of the cross. As the swift flame
  within a flame does, so, within that choir,
  shall flash the splendor of each soul I name."   36

I saw along the cross a streak of light
  as he pronounced the name of Joshua:
  nor did the saying reach me before the sight.   39

And at the name of the great Maccabee
  I saw another, spinning; and the string
  that whirled that top was its own ecstasy.   42

And just as hunters follow their falcons' flights,
  so, at the names of Charlemagne and Roland,
  my rapt attention followed two more lights.   45

Then William of Orange, and then Rinoard
  drew my eyes after them along that cross.
  And then the good duke Godfrey, and Robert
                    Guiscard.   48

Then, moving once more through those lights, the light
  that had come down to greet me, let me hear
  its art among the choir of Heaven's height.   51

I turned to my right to learn from Beatrice,
  whether by word or sign, what I should do,
  and I beheld her eyes shine with such bliss,   54

with such serenity, that she surpassed
  the vision of every other accustomed beauty
  in which she had shone, including even the last.   57

And as a man, perceiving day by day
  an increase of delight in doing good,
  begins to sense his soul is gaining way—   60

so, seeing that Miracle surpass the mark
  of former beauty, I sensed that I was turning,
  together with Heaven, through a greater arc.   63

And such a change as fair-skinned ladies show
  in a short space of time, when from their faces
  they lift the weight of shame that made them glow— 66

such change grew on my eyes when I perceived
  the pure white radiance of the temperate star—
  the sixth sphere—into which I was received.   69

Within that jovial face of Paradise
  I saw the sparkling of the love that dwelt there
  forming our means of speech before my eyes.   72

As birds arisen from a marshy plain
  almost as if rejoicing in their forage
  form, now a cluster, now a long-drawn skein—   75

so, there, within their sheaths of living light,
  blest beings soared and sang and joined their rays,
  and *D,* then *I,* then *L* formed on my sight.   78

First they sang and moved to their own song;
  then having formed themselves into a letter,
  they stopped their song and flight, though not for long. 81

O holy Pegasean who consecrates
  the power of genius, giving it long life,
  as it, through you, gives life to cities and states—   84

so fill me with your light, that as it shines
  I may show forth their image as I conceive it:
  let your own power appear in these few lines!   87

In five times seven vowels and consonants
  they showed themselves, and I grasped every part
  as if those lights had given it utterance.   90

The first words of that message as it passed
  before me were *DILIGITE IUSTITIAM.*
  QUI IUDICATIS TERRAM were the last.   93

Then, in the fifth word, at the final *M*
  they stayed aligned, and silvery Jupiter
  seemed to be washed in a gold glow around them.   96

More lights descended then and took their place
  on top of the *M,* and sang, as I believe,
  a hymn to the Good that draws them to Its grace.   99

Then—just as burning logs, when poked, let fly
  a fountain of innumerable sparks
  (from which fools used to think to prophesy)—   102

more than a thousand of those lights arose,
  some to a greater height, some to a lesser,
  each to the place the Sun that lit it chose.   105

And as each took its place in that still choir
  I saw the head and shoulders of an eagle
  appear in the fixed pattern of that fire.   108

The One who paints there needs no guide's behest.
  He is Himself the guide. From Him derives
  the skill and essential form that builds a nest.   111

The other sparks, at first content to twine
  in the form of golden lilies round the *M*
  now moved a bit, completing the design.   114

O lovely star, how rich a diadem
  shown forth to let me understand our justice
  flows to us from the heaven you begem.   117

Therefore I pray the mind that initiated
  your power and motion, to observe the source
  of the smoke by which your ray is vitiated;   120

that it be moved to anger once again
  against the buyers and sellers in the temple
  whose walls were built of blood and martyr's pain.   123

O soldiery of Heaven to whose array
  my mind returns, pray for all those on earth
  who follow bad example and go astray.   126

In earlier eras wars were carried on
  by swords; now, by denying this man or that
  the bread the Heavenly Father denies to none.   129

But you who scribble only to scratch out,
  remember that Peter and Paul, who died for the
                                              vineyard
  you trample, still defend the good you flout.   132

Well may you say: "My heart's wish is so set
  on the image of the saint who lived alone
  and who was forced to give his head in forfeit,   135

as if it were a favor at a ball—
  what do I care for the Fisherman or old Paul!"

NOTES

1–3. *that holy mirror:* Cacciaguida. The image is of the blest soul
as a mirror and reflector of God's ray. (Cf. XIV, 40–42.) *the bitterness:*

Of the prophesied exile and of the triumph of his enemies. *the sweetness:* Of prophesied poetic fame.

4–6. Beatrice tells Dante to put away the bitter part of his thoughts (of revenge). She reminds him that she is close to God whose justice rights all wrongs, and that she will always be there as his protector. Her allegorical function as Divine Revelation is, of course, especially relevant here.

12. *Another's:* God's.

13–18. The vision of God's eternal bliss, rayed directly into Beatrice's eyes, and so reflected to Dante, fills his soul entirely and drives from it all thoughts of seeking revenge for the wrongs done him.

17. *face:* As he often does, Dante uses *aspetto* ("face") to mean "eyes."

25. *the holy ray:* Cacciaguida.

34. *Look at the arms of the cross:* Cacciaguida is speaking from within the base of the cross. He wants Dante to look up to the arms.

38 ff. THE GREAT WARRIORS OF GOD. Joshua, succeeding Moses, led Israel into the promised land. Judas Maccabaeus freed Israel from the Syrian tyranny. Charlemagne, in driving the Moors out of Europe, restored the Empire and freed the Spanish church. Roland (Orlando in Italian) was the nephew of Charlemagne and his greatest knight. (See *Inferno* XXXI, 17, note.) William of Orange, hero of various medieval French romances, was the ideal of the Christian knight and was said to have died a monk. Rinoardo Rainouart served under William as his chief lieutenant. He was reputed to have been a convert from paganism and to have died in holy orders but he, like William, is largely a legendary figure. Godfrey or Gottfried of Bouillon was the leader of the first crusade and became the first Christian king of Jerusalem. He died in 1100. Robert Guiscard, son of Tancred d'Hauteville, a Norman war leader, joined with his brothers in 1046 to war against the Saracens in southern Italy, becoming duke of Puglia and of Calabria. He died in 1085.

39. *nor did the saying reach me before the sight:* i.e., the naming and the flashing of these souls take place in the same instant.

49–63. THE ASCENT TO JUPITER. As usual the transition to the next sphere is rapid. Cacciaguida returns to his place in the right arm of the cross and joins with the choir when it resumes its singing. (Cf. XV, 7–12, and note.) Beatrice becomes still more beautiful and still more radiant and Dante senses that he has entered the next Heaven.

57. *including even the last:* The phrasing is unusual but unusually exact. Beatrice grows more beautiful and more radiant with each new ascent. Now, entering the sixth Heaven, her new beauty exceeds not only her accustomed beauty, but even its own last manifestation (see lines 7–12) which Dante lacked power to describe.

61. *that Miracle:* Beatrice.

63. *through a greater arc:* It is unlikely that such a change of motion would register on merely human senses, but each ascending sphere must, necessarily, revolve through a greater arc than the last, being farther from the center.

64–69. Dante has just passed from the redness of Mars to the whiteness of Jupiter, and in about the time it takes a fair-skinned lady to grow pale again when she recovers from a blush of shame, his eyes adjust to the new radiance. Whatever Dante understood of the ability of ladies to recover from a sense of shame, his intent is clear, and the mood of the image is appropriate if the reader will visualize one of those quick flushes of innocence and maiden modesty much admired in the courtly tradition, though rare in ours.

68. *the temperate star:* Ptolemy described Jupiter as a temperate mean between hot Mars and cold Saturn. Appropriately, it serves as the Heaven of the wise and just—souls who were the models of proportioned and temperate being.

70. *jovial:* The other name of Jupiter is, of course, Jove. Dante is punning, intending both "Jove" and "jovial."

72. *our means of speech:* The alphabet.

70 ff. DANTE'S VISION OF THE WISE AND JUST. Dante's conception here was unprecedented in his times, but the modern reader can grasp it easily by conceiving the vision as a huge moving electric sign of the sort called "spectaculars." The lights of the sign are the radiances of the spirits themselves. Those lights first spell out a message, one letter at a time. The last word of the message is then transformed into an eagle, which is then ornamented by further re-

combinations of the lights. In the Canto that follows the eagle will move its beak and speak, and then, taking flight, circle around Dante.

78–99. THE ALPHABET MESSAGE. The message formed by the lights, beginning with the letters *D*, and *I*, and *L* running to thirty-five letters, is: *DILIGITE IUSTITIAM QUI IUDICATIS TERRAM*—"Love righteousness, ye that are judges of the earth."

82. *Pegasean:* The Muses drink from the spring called Hippocrene that sprang from the earth where Pegasus struck it with his hoof. The nine Muses together may properly be called Pegaseans. Dante uses the singular form, perhaps to invoke the Muses generally.

88–90. *five times seven:* The thirty-five letters of the spelled-out message. *they:* The souls within their sheaths of light. *as if those lights had given it utterance:* I do not know why hearing a letter spoken should make it more "graspable" than seeing it flash across the sky, but Dante, a primitive art critic at best, was always filled with awe by the sort of visual representation that seemed to make the viewer hear what he was seeing. (Cf. *Purgatorio* X, 52–60.)

95–96. *silvery Jupiter:* Jupiter was reputed to have a silvery sheen that set it apart from other white stars. The souls, however, are encased in sheaths of golden light.

102. *prophesy:* By asking a question (for example, "How many years shall I live?"), then poking the fire, and counting the sparks to get an answer.

104–105. *greater . . . lesser . . . to the place the Sun that lit it chose:* See once more XIV, 40–42. It is the Sun (God) who decrees the pattern of the eagle, assigning to each soul its place in the pattern according to the amount of grace It rays forth to each.

109–11. The general meaning of this passage is clear enough: God is the creator whose creation is guided by no other, Himself being the guide. The last line, however, is in Dante's densest style. "Essential form" is a Scholastic term equivalent to "form" in the Platonic sense. "Nest," I think, must be taken as a lovely symbol of the way in which God's art fills His creation. Birds, though they know nothing about architecture, draw from God the skill (the virtue) that enables them to build intricate and beautiful nests. So, by extension, are all the arts of this world derived from the guidance of the Unguided.

112. *The other sparks:* "Innumerable sparks" shot up from the vision and "more than a thousand of them" rose to form the head and shoulders of the eagle. The other sparks first wove lilies around the *M;* then, moving a little, completed the body of the eagle by filling out the body of the original *M.* If the letter is visualized in the rounded form common in medieval manuscripts and much like our lower case "m," and if the head and shoulders of an eagle are drawn in above the "m," it takes little imagination to visualize how the "m" could form the eagle's body. In the figure below, the dotted lines suggest the manner of the change.

113. *lilies:* Could not fail to suggest the French monarchy, as the Eagle could not fail to suggest the Empire. Dante may very well mean that, were wisdom and justice to rule, France should adorn the Empire in union with it instead of following its own divisive course.

115–117. *O lovely star:* Jupiter. Earthly justice is an effect of its influence upon men. It is the ideal of earthly justice the souls have been expressing in their flashing message and in the symbolism of the eagle and of the lilies.

122. *the temple:* The Church. Dante, at sight of the Imperial Eagle of justice, is move to inveigh against papal avarice and corruption. "M," as various commentators have pointed out, is the first letter of

Monarchia. In *De Monarchia,* I, 11, Dante had argued: "Justice is possible only under a [good] monarchy." If this inference from the *M* is valid (and Dante was, in fact, much given to such devices) we are once more on the theme of a spiritual church within a strong temporal empire as the one hope of Europe.

123. *blood:* If the original text reads "sangue." Some texts read *"segni"* ("signs," of which the English rendering would be "signs/portents/miracles/prophecies").

126. *bad example:* Of papal corruption.

128–129. *now, by denying . . . the bread:* The bread of God's grace, particularly as received through the sacraments. By denying the sacraments through excommunications and interdictions, the papacy wages war against peace and justice, forcing men and states to buy back the sacraments that should rightfully be theirs.

130. *you:* Dante uses the singular form *"tu."* He must, therefore, be referring to a single evil pope. If he is speaking as of 1300 that pope would, of course, be Boniface VIII. *scribble only to scratch out:* Instead of preparing bulls that will clarify God's intent to all time, the evil popes merely scribble excommunications, interdictions, and denials of justice in order to cancel them again for a fee.

134. *the image of the saint:* John the Baptist. But in a bitter irony, Dante portrays the corrupt popes as having their hearts set not on the saint but on his image, for it was stamped on the Florentine gold florin. Thus their love of St. John is the love of money. *who lived alone:* In the desert. (See *Luke* i, 80.)

135–136. *his head in forfeit . . . favor at a ball:* The daughter of Herodias so pleased Herod with her dancing that he offered her "whatsoever she would ask." She asked for the head of John the Baptist on a charger, and against his own inclination Herod kept his word (*Matthew* xiv, 1–11; *Mark* vi, 21–28).

137. *the Fisherman:* St. Peter. Used here as a familiar and contemptuous term. *old Paul:* St. Paul. Again the form of address shows lack of respect.

CANTO XIX

The Sixth Sphere: Jupiter—The Just and Temperate
Rules · The Eagle

The Eagle made up of the many souls of the Just and Temperate
Rulers moves its beak and speaks as if it were a single entity, an-
nouncing that it is the chosen symbol of *Divine Justice*. Dante is
afire to understand the nature of the Divine Justice and begs the
Eagle to explain it, but he is told that the infinity of God's excel-
lence must forever exceed his creation, and that none may
fathom His will, whereby it is presumptuous of any creature to
question the Divine Justice. Man must be content with the guid-
ance of Scripture and with the sure knowledge that God is per-
fect, good, and just.

Dante had once pondered the justice of denying salvation to
virtuous pagans. The Eagle tells him it is not for him to sit in
judgment on God's intent. It affirms that except as he believes in
Christ no soul may ascend to Heaven, yet it adds that the virtu-
ous pagan shall sit nearer Christ than many another who takes
Christ's name in vain.

The Eagle concludes with a *Denunciation of the Bestialized
Kings of Christendom* in 1300.

Before me, its great wings outspread, now shone
  the image of the eagle those bright souls
  had given form to in glad unison.   3

Each seemed a little ruby in the sky,
  and the sun's ray struck each in such a way
  the light reflected straight into my eye.   6

What I must now call back from memory
  no voice has ever spoken, nor ink written.
  Nor has its like been known to fantasy.   9

For I saw and heard the beak move and declare
  in its own voice the pronouns "I" and "mine"
  when "we" and "ours" were what conceived it there.   12

"For being just and pious in my time,"
  it said, "I am exalted here in glory
  to which, by wish alone, no one may climb;   15

and leave behind me, there upon the earth,
  a memory honored even by evildoers,
  though they shun the good example it sets forth."   18

Just as the glow of many living coals
  issues a single heat, so from that image
  one sound declared the love of many souls.   21

At which I cried: "O everlasting blooms
  of the eternal bliss, who make one seeming
  upon my sense of all your many perfumes—   24

my soul has hungered long: breathe forth at last
  the words that will appease it. There on earth
  there is no food with which to break its fast.   27

I know that if God's justice has constructed
  its holy mirror in some other realm,
  your kingdom's view of it is not obstructed.   30

You know how eagerly I wait to hear;
  you know the what and wherefore of the doubt
  I have hungered to resolve for many a year."   33

Much as a falcon freed of hood and jess
  stretches its head and neck and beats its wings,
  preening itself to show its readiness—   36

so moved the emblem that was all compounded
  of praises of God's grace; and from it, then,
  a hymn they know who dwell in bliss resounded.   39

Then it began to speak: "The One who wheeled
  the compass round the limits of the world,
  and spread there what is hidden and what revealed,   42

could not so stamp his power and quality
  into his work but what the creating Word
  would still exceed creation infinitely.   45

And this explains why the first Prideful Power,
  highest of creatures, because he would not wait
  the power of the ripening sun, fell green and sour.   48

And thus we see that every lesser creature
  is much too small a vessel to hold the Good
  that has no end; Itself is Its one measure.   51

Therefore, you understand, our way of seeing,
  which must be only one ray of the Mind
  that permeates all matter and all being,   54

cannot, by its very nature, be so clear
  but what its Author's eye sees far beyond
  the furthest limits that to us appear.   57

In the eternal justice, consequently,
  the understanding granted to mankind
  is lost as the eye is within the sea: 60

it can make out the bottom near the shore
  but not on the main deep; and still it is there,
  though at a depth your eye cannot explore.   63

There is no light but from that ever fresh
  and cloudless Halcyon; all else is darkness,
  the shadow and the poison of the flesh.   66

By now, much that was hidden from your view
  by the living Justice of which you used to ask
  so many questions, has been shown to you.   69

For you used to say, 'A man is born in sight
  of Indus' water, and there is none there
  to speak of Christ, and none to read or write.   72

And all he wills and does, we must concede,
  as far as human reason sees, is good;
  and he does not sin either in word or deed.   75

He dies unbaptized and cannot receive
  the saving faith. What justice is it damns him?
  Is it his fault that he does not believe?'   78

—But who are you to take the judgment seat
  and pass on things a thousand miles away,
  who cannot see the ground before your feet?   81

The man who would split hairs with me could find
  no end of grounds for questioning, had he not
  the Scriptures over him to guide his mind.   84

O earthbound animals! minds gross as wood!
  Itself good in Itself, the Primal Will
  does not move from Itself, the Supreme Good!   87

Only what sorts with It is just. It sways
  toward no created good, but of Itself
  creates all Good by sending forth Its rays."   90

As a stork that has fed its young flies round and round
   above the nest, and as the chick it fed
   raises its head to stare at it, still nest-bound—   93

so did that blessèd image circle there,
   its great wings moved in flight by many wills,
   and so did I lift up my head and stare.   96

Circling, it sang; then said: "As what I sing
   surpasses your understanding, so God's justice
   surpasses the power of mortal reasoning."   99

Those blazing glories of the Holy Ghost
   stopped, still formed in the sign that spread the honor
   of Rome across the world, to its last coast,   102

grew still, then said: "To this high empery
   none ever rose but through belief in Christ,
   either before or after his agony.   105

But see how many now cry out 'Christ! Christ!'
   who shall be farther from him at the Judgment
   than many who, on earth, did not know Christ.   108

Such Christians shall the Ethopian scorn
   when the two bands are formed to right and left,
   one blest to all eternity, one forlorn.   111

What shall the Persians say to your kings there
   when the Great Book is opened and they see
   the sum of their depravities laid bare?   114

There shall be seen among the works of Albert,
   that deed the moving pen will soon record
   by which Bohemia shall become a desert.   117

There shall be seen the Seine's grief for the sin
  of that debaser of the currency
  whose death is waiting for him in a pig's skin.   120

There shall be seen the pride whose greed confounds
  the mad Scot and the foolish Englishman
  who cannot stay within their proper bounds.   123

There, the debaucheries and the vain show
  of the Spaniard and the Bohemian who knew
  nothing of valor, and chose not to know.   126

And there, the cripple of Jerusalem:
  a 1 put down to mark the good he did,
  and then, to mark his villainies, an *M*.   129

There, the baseness and the greedy rage
  of the watchdog who patrols the burning island
  on which Anchises closed his long old age;   132

and to make clear how paltry is his case,
  his entry will be signs and abbreviations
  that the record may say much in little space.   135

And there the filthy deeds shall be set down
  of his uncle and his brother, each of whom
  cuckolded a great family and a crown.   138

There shall be marked for all men to behold
  Norway's king and Portugal's; and Rascia's,
  who lost most when he saw Venetian gold.   141

Oh happy Hungary, had she suffered all
  without more griefs ahead! Happy Navarre
  were she to make her peaks a fortress wall!   144

And every Navarrese may well believe
  the omen of Nicosìa and Famagosto
  whose citizens have present cause to grieve   147

the way their beast, too small for the main pack,
  keeps to one side but hunts on the same track."

NOTES

10–12. The eagle, though composed of many souls, speaks as a single entity, so symbolizing the unity of these souls in God.

15. *by wish alone:* No soul may earn such glory by its own merit, but only by the gift of God's grace. (See XIV, 42.)

18. *it:* The memory of those who lived in justice and piety.

25. *breathe forth:* i.e., speak, but phrased in this way in order to continue the figure of flowers breathing forth their perfumes.

26–27. *on earth . . . no food:* Mortal understanding cannot satisfy Dante's hunger to know the nature of God's justice.

28–33. DANTE'S QUESTION ON THE NATURE OF DIVINE JUSTICE. The question is best understood by referring to IX, 61–63. "On high are mirrors (you say 'Thrones') and these reflect God's judgment to us." "On high" as spoken by Cunizza in the sphere of Venus could mean "in Jupiter" or somewhere higher. Whatever the rendering of this point, Dante is asking for nothing less than an explanation of the nature of God's Justice. In reply, he is given many particulars by the way, but the sum of it is that God's Justice is inscrutable and that the question is unanswerable. Not even these enormously elevated souls can know the full answer.

40–45. THE INFINITY OF GOD'S EXCELLENCE. Great as is God's creation, the Word (*Logos,* the creating source) cannot create what it does not Itself infinitely exceed.

46. *the first Prideful Power:* Satan. He was first among all created things, yet (as above) infinitely below his creator. His sin of pride was in wishing to equal God (instead of ripening and growing more perfect in His light) and therefore he fell green and sour.

52. *our:* Some texts read "your," but such a reading would imply that only mortals are inferior to God, whereas the eagle's point is that all parts of His creation (including the angels and the souls of the blest) are infinitely inferior to God. In line 59 the eagle does speak of what would be "your world" (mankind). There it has changed the grounds of the discussion and is explicating the difference between heavenly and mortal understanding—a second infinity of difference that does not invalidate the first.

65. *Halcyon:* God. His revelation is the one light. By comparison, the light of the intellect is a darkness and leads to error (the shadow) and to sin (the poison) of the flesh.

68–69. *of which you used to ask so many questions:* About the nature of divine justice. See lines 25–33.

80. *a thousand miles away:* Is not intended as a map measurement but as a general way of saying "a great distance." From God, as one may understand. From the man by Indus' water. And from both.

82. *with me:* With the eagle, as the heavenly symbol of God's justice. There would be endless grounds for doubts and fine arguments had not Scripture set forth all a man need know about Divine Justice.

91–96. A double long-tail simile: as the stork did, so did the image; as the chick did, so did Dante.

95. *by many wills:* By the conjoined wills of all the gemlike souls that make up the image of the eagle.

97–99. The harmonies and the language of the hymn are beyond Dante's powers of comprehension. He, like a fledgling stork, gapes up at what is beyond him. And so is it with his grasp of Divine Justice.

101. *stopped:* Their circling.

102–105. Note how adroitly this pause serves to mute the effective but no longer needed image of the mother stork circling its chick, and to sound in its place the majesty of the eagle.

105. *before:* By belief in the promised Messiah. *after:* By belief in the risen Christ. It is by allowing a place in Heaven to what may be called the "Messianic Christians" that Dante can seat such souls as Solomon's in Heaven.

104–108. As before, Dante rhymes the name of Christ only with itself.

108. *the many who did not know Christ:* So in part to answer Dante's doubts about the virtuous Hindu. All the Virtuous Pagans, to be sure, will be closer to Christ in Limbo than those professing Christians who damned themselves. But since Dante has allowed one pagan (Virgil) to ascend to the Earthly Paradise, it is perhaps his understanding that the Virtuous Pagans will be settled there after the Judgment. Higher, as the eagle has declared in line 104, they cannot go, though in *Purgatorio* I, 74–75, Cato of Utica is marked for special blessing in the resurrection.

109. *Ethiopian:* Used as a generic term for all pagans.

110. *when the two bands:* At the seat of Judgment when the sheep and the goats are set to Christ's right and left hands.

112. *Persians:* Another generic term for pagans.

115. *Albert:* Albert I, Emperor from 1298 to 1308. He is the "German Albert" of *Purgatorio* VI, 97 ff. He invaded Bohemia in 1304. As of 1300, therefore, the pen must wait four years before it moves to record his deed.

118–120. *the Seine:* For France, generally. *that debaser of the currency:* Philip the Fair (see *Purgatorio* VII, 109, and note; and XX, 85–93, and note). He debased the coinage to finance his wars and brought misery to France. Dante, it is well to remember, punished counterfeiters (*Inferno* XXX) not out of love of money, but because a sound coinage was an essential principle of social order. *death . . . in a pig's skin:* In 1314, in the course of a royal hunt, a wild boar ran under Philip's horse. Philip was thrown and died soon after of his injuries. Dante certainly relishes such a way of bringing down the mighty and evil.

121–123. *greed:* For more land. *Scot . . . Englishman:* The Scottish and English kings in their endless border wars.

124–126. *the Spaniard:* Probably Ferdinand IV. *the Bohemian:* Probably Wenceslaus IV (see *Purgatorio* VII, 102, note). With or without specific identification, Dante's general point is clear.

127–129. *cripple of Jerusalem:* Charles II of Anjou, known as Charles the Lame (see VIII, 82, note; *Purgatorio* VII, 124–129, and *Purgatorio* XX, 79, note). He was King of Jerusalem only by the act of giving himself that title. In the Book of Judgment his virtues will be marked by the number 1 and his villainies by the letter *M* (a thousand).

131–132. *the watchdog:* Frederick II of Sicily (see *Purgatorio* III, 115). *burning island:* Sicily. *on which Anchises:* He died at Drepanum, modern Trapani.

133. *paltry:* So paltry a man could not be allowed much space in the book of the Recording Angel, but his life was so evil that his sins will have to be written down in signs and abbreviations in order to squeeze them all in.

137–138. *his uncle and his brother:* King James of Majorca, brother of James I of Aragon; and James II of Aragon, son of James I. Each disgraced the crown he wore; both disgraced the house of Aragon. *cuckolded:* They disgraced their family and their kingdom from within, as a wife does when she cuckolds her husband.

140. *Norway's king:* In 1300, Hacon VII. *Portugal's:* Dionysus. *Rascia's:* Orosius II. Rascia was part of Serbia. Orosius seems to have altered the metal content of Venetian money on a substantial scale. *lost most:* His falsifying of the currency would slate him for a meeting with Master Adam in Hell (see *Inferno* XXX).

142. *Hungary:* Andrew III, a good king, ruled in 1300. Hungary had endured many ruinous wars. If only her sufferings were all behind her, as of course they are not.

143–144. *Navarre:* The ancient kingdom of what is now southern France and northern Spain. Joanna of Navarre married Philip the Fair of France in 1284 but remained sole ruler of Navarre. After her death in 1304, her son Louis inherited Navarre, and when his father died in 1314, he became Louis X, king of France and Navarre. So Navarre passed under French rule, the bitterness of which they were to learn in full. Hence, they would have been happier had they armed the mountains around them (the Pyrenees) as fortress walls for keeping out the French.

145–149. *Nicosìa and Famagosta:* The two principal cities of Cyprus. *Their beast:* Henry II of the French house of Lusignan was king of Cyprus in 1300, a man given to debaucheries for which the people paid dearly. Every Navarrese would have done well in 1300 to have taken him as an example of French rule and of what Navarre would suffer when it passed under the French crown. *the main pack:* Of the bestialized kings of Christendom. Henry is too small a beast to run in the main pack but he runs along to one side of it on the track of the same bestialities.

CANTO XX

*The Sixth Sphere: Jupiter—The Just and Temperate
Rulers · The Eagle*

The eagle pauses briefly and the spirits of the blest sing a hymn,
not as one symbolic entity, but each in its own voice. The hymn
ended, the Eagle resumes speaking in its single voice, and identi-
fies as the chief souls of this sphere those lusters that compose its
eye. In order they are: *David, Trajan, Hezekiah, Constantine, William
of Sicily,* and *Ripheus.*

Dante is astonished to find Trajan and Ripheus in Heaven,
both of whom he had thought to be pagans, but the Eagle ex-
plains how by the special grace of God Ripheus was converted
by a vision of Christ a millennium before His descent into the
flesh, and Trajan was returned from Limbo to his mortal body
long enough to undergo conversion to Christ and to allow his
soul to mount to Heaven.

So once again for Dante's doubts about the virtuous Hindu
and God's justice, for who can say how many more God has so
chosen to his grace? The Eagle concludes with a praise of God's
predestined justice, rejoicing even in the limitation of its own
knowledge, resting in the assurance that the unknown conse-
quences of God's will cannot fail to be good.

When the sun, from which the whole world takes its light,
  sinks from our hemisphere and the day fades
  from every reach of land, and it is night;   3

the sky, which earlier it alone had lit,
  suddenly changes mode and reappears
  in many lights that take their light from it.   6

I thought of just that change across night's sill
  when that emblem of the world and of its leaders
  had finished speaking through its sacred bill;   9

for all those living lights now shone on me
  more brightly than before, and began singing
  a praise too sweet to hold in memory.   12

O heavenly love in smiling glory wreathed,
  how ardently you sounded from those flutes
  through which none but the holiest impulse breathed. 15

When then those precious gems of purest ray
  with which the lamp of the sixth heaven shone
  let their last angel-harmony fade away,   18

I seemed to hear a great flume take its course
  from stone to stone, and murmur down its mountain
  as if to show the abundance of its source.   21

And as the sound emerging from a lute
  is tempered at its neck; and as the breath
  takes form around the openings of a flute—   24

just so, allowing no delay to follow,
  the murmur of the eagle seemed to climb
  inside its neck, as if the neck were hollow.   27

There it was given voice, and through the bill
  the voice emerged as words my heart awaited.
  And on my heart those words are written still.   30

"Look closely now into that part of me
  that in earth's eagles can endure the Sun."
  the emblem said, "—the part with which I see.   33

Of all the fires with which I draw my form
  those rays that make the eye shine in my head
  are the chief souls of all this blessèd swarm.   36

The soul that makes the pupil luminous
  was the sweet psalmist of the Holy Ghost
  who bore the ark of God from house to house: 39

now, insofar as he himself gave birth
  to his own psalms, he is repayed in bliss,
  and by that bliss he knows what they are worth.   42

Of the five that form my eyebrow's arc, the one
  whose glory shines the closest to my beak
  consoled the widow who had lost her son;   45

now he understands what price men pay
  who do not follow Christ, for though he learns
  the sweet life, he has known the bitter way.   48

The next in line on the circumference
  of the same upper arch of which I speak,
  delayed his own death by true penitence;   51

now he knows that when a worthy prayer
  delays today's event until tomorrow,
  the eternal judgment is not altered there.   54

The third, to give the Shepherd sovereignty,
  (with good intentions though they bore bad fruit)
  removed to Greece, bearing the laws and me;   57

now he knows the evil that began
  in his good action does not harm his soul
  although it has destroyed the world of man.   60

And him you see upon the arc beneath
  was William of that land that mourns the life
  of Charles and Frederick, as it mourns his death;   63

now he knows how heaven's heart inclines
  to love a just king, as he makes apparent
  by the radiance with which his being shines.   66

Who would believe in the erring world down there
  that Ripheus the Trojan would be sixth
  among the sacred lusters of this sphere?   69

Now he knows grace divine to depths of bliss
  the world's poor understanding cannot grasp.
  Even *his* eye cannot plumb that abyss."   72

Like a lark that soars in rapture to the sky,
  first singing, and then silent, satisfied
  by the last sweetness of its soul's own cry—   75

such seemed that seal of the Eternal Bliss
  that stamped it there, the First Will at whose will
  whatever is becomes just what it is.   78

And though my eagerness to know shone clear
  as colors shining through a clearest glass,
  I could not bear to wait in silence there;   81

but from my tongue burst out "How can this be?"
  forced by the weight of my own inner doubt.
  —At which those lights flashed in new revelry.   84

And soon then, not to keep me in suspense,
  the blessèd emblem answered me, its eye
  flashing a yet more glorious radiance.   87

"I see that you believe these things are true
  because I say them. Yet, you do not see how.
  Thus, though believed, their truth is hidden from you. 90

You are like one who knows the name of a thing
  whose quiddity, until it is explained
  by someone else, defies his understanding.   93

By every living hope and ardent love
  that bends the Eternal Will—by these alone
  the Kingdom of Heaven suffers itself to move.   96

Not as men bend beneath a conqueror's will.
  It bends because it wishes to be bent.
  Conquered, its own benificence conquers still.   99

You marvel at the first and the fifth gem
  here on my brow, finding this realm of angels
  and gift of Christ made beautiful by them.   102

They did not leave their bodies, as you believe,
  as pagans but as Christians, in firm faith
  in the pierced feet one grieved and one would grieve. 105

One rose again from Hell—from whose dead slope
  none may return to Love—into the flesh;
  and that was the reward of living hope;   108

of living hope, whose power of love made good
  the prayers he raised to God to bring him back
  to life again, that his will might be renewed.   111

And so the glorious soul for whom he prayed,
  back in the flesh from which it soon departed,
  believed in Him who has the power to aid.   114

Believing, he burst forth with such a fire
  of the true love, that at his second death
  he was worthy of a seat in this glad choir.   117

The other, by that grace whose blessings rise
  out of so deep a spring that no one ever
  has plumbed its sources with created eyes,   120

gave all his love to justice, there on earth,
  and God, by grace on grace, let him foresee
  a vision of our redemption shining forth.   123

So he believed in Christ, and all his days
  shunning the poisonous stink of pagan creeds,
  he warned the obstinate to change their ways.   126

More than a thousand years before the grace
  of baptism was known, those maids you saw
  at the right wheel, stood for him in its place.   129

Predestination! Oh how deep your source
  is rooted past the reach of every vision
  that cannot plumb the whole of the First Cause!   132

Mortals, be slow to judge! Not even we
  who look on God in Heaven know, as yet,
  how many He will choose for ecstasy.   135

And sweet it is to lack this knowledge still,
  for in this good is our own good refined,
  willing whatever God Himself may will."   138

In these words the blest emblem of that sphere
  gave me these gentle curatives of love
  with which my clouded vision was made clear.   141

And as the skillful harpist, string by string,
  makes every cord attend on a good singer,
  adding a greater pleasure to the singing;   144

so, I recall, that as it spoke to me
    these paradisal words, the holy lights
    of Trajan and Ripheus in sweet harmony,   147

as if they blinked their eyes with one accord,
    made their flames pulse in time with every word.

NOTES

1–12. THE DAY AND NIGHT IMAGE AND THE HEAVENLY
EAGLE. The metaphor is subtle but its essence simple. The symbolic
eagle (as a unity projected by many blessèd wills) stops speaking
through its bill as a single entity and a hymn rings forth not from the
eagle, but from the many lustrous beings who compose it. Each of
these beings is now giving voice to its joy not through the symbol
but from itself.

This change Dante compares to the twin faces of the heavens: by
day there is the one direct light of the Sun (a unity, as with the
Eagle); by night there is the shining of many heavenly bodies, all of
which (according to Dante's astronomy) glow not from within
themselves but by reflecting the light of the Sun (as these souls glow
by reflecting God's ray).

our hemisphere: The land mass of the world, all of it north of the
equator, and all contained in an arc of 180° from India to Spain.
Thus, when the sun is 90° west of Spain it lights only the waters on
the other side of the earth and all the land mass is dark.

31. *that part:* The eye. The Eagle is once again speaking as a uni-
fied entity. The ancients believed that the eagle could look straight
into the sun. Note that only one eye is mentioned. The symbolic
eagle must be conceived as appearing in heraldic profile, despite the
fact that it flew a circle around Dante's head in the previous canto.

38. *the sweet psalmist:* David. See *Inferno* IV, 58.

40–42. The first thought here, a simple one, is that the measure
of his present bliss (the reward being proportionate to the act) lets
David know the true worth of his psalms. That thought is compli-
cated by the parenthetical "insofar, *etc.*" Since the Holy Ghost moved

in David, Dante seems to be saying, some of his psalms sprang from
It, and his present bliss cannot be repayment to him for an act of
the Holy Ghost. As Dante pointed out in VI, 118–120, part of the
delight of each heavenly soul consists in knowing that his bliss is ex-
actly equal to his merits.

43. *the one:* Trajan. See *Purgatorio* X, 70–90.

48. *he has known the bitter way:* Trajan had been long in Limbo.
See note to 106 ff., below.

49–54. Hezekiah, offering a true repentance on his death bed,
was allowed to live for fifteen more years (*II Kings,* xx, 1–11; *II
Chron.* xxxii, 24–26; *Isaiah* xxxviii, 1–7). *now he knows:* To what
extent prayer may vary the preordained divine plan without altering
it. These lines are best understood by referring to *Purgatorio* VI,
28–51. Few readers will have remembered the point Dante left open
in those lines, but Dante seems never to forget. To read him is to
experience mind in extraordinary order.

55–60. The Emperor Constantine. With the purest of intentions
(so Dante's version of it) Constantine ceded the Western Empire to
the Church (the Shepherd) and moved his seat of Empire to Greece,
bearing with him Roman law and "me" (the Roman Eagle). See
Purgatorio XXXII, 124–129; *Inferno* XIX, 109–111, and notes.

Constantine learns in Heaven that the evil consequences of a
good action (or the good consequences of an evil action) do not
change the nature of the original action—a point made by Aquinas
in his *Summa.*

62. *William:* William II (the Good), king of the Two Sicilies from
1166 to 1189. He was the last of the house of Tancred. In Dante's
time, the kingdom of Naples passed to Charles the Lame (XIX, 127)
and the Kingdom of Sicily to Frederick II (XIX, 131). Sicily mourns
its present evil as it mourns the passing of its happiness with the
death of William.

65. *as he makes apparent:* The degree of brilliance flashed forth by
each soul is the measure of its relative bliss. William, by shining more
brightly than most there, shows that he is more blest than most.

68. *Ripheus:* Virgil mentioned him once (*Aeneid* II, 426 ff.) as
the one most just man among the Trojans and as the one who most

loved the right. No more is known of him, and Dante is thus free (see below) to invent a pre-Christian conversion for him. *sixth:* Dante says "fifth" among those who make up the eyebrow. Beginning with David as the eyeball, such a count would rank Ripheus sixth among the souls of this sphere; and, rhyme dictating, I have so rendered the passage.

89. *see how:* See how these things can be true.

92. *quiddity:* i.e., "thingness" or "whatness." In Scholastic terminology: "that which causes a thing to be what it is."

94–99. These paradoxes are, of course, the language of the mystery: God is unmovable but God is love and as love moves Him, He yields gladly to it, conquering by His act of love.

102. *and gift of Christ:* Not in Dante's text but necessary for the line and clearly implicit in what the Eagle is saying. Trajan and Ripheus, having been pagans, would not have had the gift of Christ's redemption. It is for this reason that Dante marvels at finding them in Heaven.

103–105. Ripheus and Trajan, as the Eagle will explain, did not "leave their bodies" as pagans but as Christians and firm believers, one (Trajan) in the pierced feet (the Crucifixion) that had already taken place; the other (Ripheus) in the Crucifixion yet to come.

106–117. THE RESURRECTION AND CONVERSION OF TRAJAN. Dante follows a legend that Gregory I (Pope from 590 to 604 and later St. Gregory) prayed so ardently for the salvation of Trajan that God's voice replied "I grant pardon to Trajan." Since God so granted, it was, of course, predestined that he should so grant. Trajan, therefore, could never have been truly damned, for no prayer can help the damned. But since none may go from Hell to Heaven (with the exception of those souls Christ took with him in the Harrowing of Hell), it was necessary to restore Trajan to the flesh long enough to permit his conversion to Christ.

108. *living hope:* Of Gregory.

120. *created eyes:* Nothing God has created can plumb the mystery of its creator. Compare lines 130–132 below.

121–129. THE CONVERSION OF RIPHEUS. Unhampered by any historical record, Dante creates a legend of Ripheus as a Christian before the fact. Granted a vision of Christ to come, he believed utterly and was saved. In place of baptism (over a thousand years before baptism came into being) the three maids who stood at the right wheel of the Chariot of the Church in the Pageant of the Terrestrial Paradise (i.e., the Three Theological Virtues) stood as his godmothers in some equivalent ritual (see *Purgatorio* XXIX, 121 ff.).

132. *that cannot plumb:* As, certainly, no human vision can. As even the chosen souls of Heaven cannot.

135. *how many He will choose:* Had Dante cared to, he could have made a rather accurate guess as to God's intention when he reached the Empyrean. In XXX, 128–132, he tells us that few seats are left open in Paradise (Judgment Day will take place when the last throne of Heaven is filled). And in XXXII, 25–27, he has St. Bernard point out the empty thrones, the number of which Dante might reasonably have guessed, though had he done so he would have found himself prophesying the end of the world within fairly tight limits, a prophecy Dante wisely chose not to utter. Poetry is, among other things, the art of knowing what to leave out.

CANTO XXI

The Seventh Sphere: Saturn—The Contemplative:
Peter Damiano

Beatrice and Dante enter the Sphere of Saturn. *Beatrice Does Not
Smile* in her new bliss to announce their arrival, for her radiance
would then be such that Dante's mortal senses would be con-
sumed, as Semele was consumed by the Godhead of Jupiter.
Rather, Beatrice announces that they are there and commands
Dante to look into the crystalline substance of that Heaven for
the vision he will see of the *Souls of the Contemplative.*

Dante turns and beholds a vision of a *Golden Ladder* on which
countless Splendors arise and descend wheeling like birds in
flight. That host of the blessèd descends only as far as a given
rung, but one radiance among them draws closer to Dante and
indicates by its radiance that it is eager to bring him joy. It is the
soul of *Peter Damiano,* a Doctor of the Church, renowned for a
severely ascetic life even in high church office. Peter Damiano
explains to Dante that *The Mystery of Predestination* is beyond the
reach of all but God, and that men should not presume to grasp
it. He concludes with a *Denunciation of Papal Corruption,* and at
his words, all the souls of Saturn fly down to form a ring around
him and thunder forth *Heaven's Righteous Indignation* at evildoers.
So loud is their cry that Dante cannot make out their words, his
senses reeling at that thunderclap of sound.

My eyes were fixed once more on my lady's face;
   and with my eyes, my soul, from which all thought,
   except of her, had fled without a trace.   6

She did not smile. "Were I to smile," she said,
   "You would be turned to ash, as Semele was
   when she saw Jupiter in his full Godhead;   3

because my beauty, which, as it goes higher
  from step to step of the eternal palace,
  burns, as you know, with ever brighter fire;   9

and if it is not tempered in its brightening,
  its radiance would consume your mortal powers
  as a bough is shattered by a bolt of lightning.   12

We have soared to the Seventh Splendor, which is now
  beneath the Lion's blazing breast, and rays
  its influence, joined with his, to the world below.   15

Now make your eyes the mirror of the vision
  this mirror will reveal to you, and fix
  your mind behind your eyes in strict attention."   18

Could any man conceive what blessèd pasture
  my eyes found in her face when I turned away,
  at her command, to find another nurture—   21

then would he know with what a rush of bliss
  I obeyed my heavenly escort, balancing
  one side and the other, that joy against this.   24

Within the crystal that bears round the world
  the name of its great king in that golden age
  when evil's flag had not yet been unfurled,   27

like polished gold ablaze in full sunlight,
  I saw a ladder rise so far above me
  it soared beyond the reaches of my sight.   30

And I saw so many splendors make their way
  down its bright rungs, I thought that every lamp
  in all of heaven was pouring forth its ray.   33

As grackles flock together at first light,
  obeying a natural impulse to move as one
  to warm their night-chilled feathers in glad flight;   36

after which, some go off and do not come back,
  others return to the points from which they came,
  and others stay with the flock in its wheeling track;   39

—just such an impulse seemed to work among
  those sparkling essences, for they flocked together
  the instant they had reached a certain rung.   42

One that came nearest where we stood below
  then made itself so bright I said to myself:
  "I well know with what love for me you glow!"   45

But she from whom I await the how and when
  of my speech and silence, was still; and despite my yearning
  I knew it was well to ask no questions then.   48

She saw in the vision of Him who sees all things
  what silence held my eager tongue in check,
  and said to me: "Give your soul's impulse wings!"   51

"O blessèd being hidden in the ray
  of your own bliss," I said in reverence,
  "I am not worthy, but for her sake, I pray,   54

who gives me leave to question, let me know
  why you, of all this sacred company,
  have placed yourself so near me, here below;   57

and tell me why, when every lower sphere
  sounds the sweet symphony of Paradise
  in adoration, there is no music here."   60

"Your sight is mortal. Is not your hearing, too?"
 he said. "Our song is still for the same reason
 Beatrice holds back her smile—for love of you.   63

Only that I might make your spirit gladder
 by what I say and by the light that robes me,
 have I come so far down the sacred ladder.   66

Nor was it greater love that spurred me: here
 as much—and more—love burns in every soul,
 as the flaming of these radiances makes clear.   69

But the high love that makes us prompt to serve
 the Judge who rules the world, decrees the fate
 of every soul among us, as you observe."   72

"O sacred lamp," I said, "I understand
 that in this court glad love follows the will
 of Eternal Providence, needing no command;   75

but the further point I cannot grasp is this:
 why, among all these blisses with whom you dwell,
 were you alone predestined to this office?"   78

Before I finished speaking, that lamp of grace
 like a millstone at full speed, making an axle
 of its own center, began to spin in place.   81

And then the Love within the lamp replied:
 "I feel the ray of God's light focused on me.
 It strikes down through the ray in which I hide.   84

Its power, joined to my own, so elevates
 my soul above itself, that I behold
 the Primal Source from which it emanates.   87

My bliss flames only as that ray shines down.
  As much of glory as I am given to see
  my flame gives back in glory of its own.   90

But in all Heaven, the essence most aglow,
  the Seraph that has God in closest view,
  could not explain what you have asked to know.   93

The truth of this is hidden so far down
  in the abyss of the Eternal Law,
  it is cut off from all created vision.   96

Report what I have said when you are back
  in the mortal world, that no man may presume
  to move his feet down so profound a track.   99

On earth the mind is smoke; here, it is fire.
  How can it do there what it cannot do
  even when taken into heaven's choir?"   102

I left that question, his own words having thus
  prescribed me from it; and, so limited,
  was content to ask him humbly who he was.   105

"Not far from your own birthplace, row on row
  between Italy's two shores, peaks rise so high
  that on them thunder sounds from far below.   108

A humpback ridge called Catria rises there.
  Beneath it stands a holy hermitage
  once given entirely to meditation and prayer."   111

So, for the third time now, that soul of grace
  began to speak, continuing: "I became
  so rooted in God's service in that place,   114

I lived on lenten olive-food alone
   and bore both heat and cold indifferently,
   rejoicing ever more in contemplation. 117

Once that cloister sent here, sphere on sphere,
   harvests of souls. Now all its works are vain
   as, soon now, righteous punishment shall make clear. 120

I was Peter Damiano there, and became
   Peter the Sinner by the Adriatic
   in the abbey sacred to Our Lady's name. 123

Little was left me of my mortal course
   when I was chosen and summoned to wear the hat
   that seems forever to pass from bad to worse. 126

Cephas, and the great ark of the Holy Ghost
   once came among mankind barefoot and gaunt,
   eating by chance, with charity as their host. 129

But now your pastors are so bloated and vain
   they go propped on either side, with a man before
   and another coming behind to bear the train. 132

They cover even their mounts with the cloaks they wear
   so that two beasts move under a single hide.
   O Heavenly Patience, how long will you forebear!" 135

As he spoke these words, I saw more ardors yearning
   downward in circling flight, from rung to rung;
   and grow more radiant with every turning. 138

Round him they came to rest, and all burst forth
   in unison of love: a cry so loud
   the like of it has not been heard on earth. 141

Nor could I understand it, for the peal
  of that ominous thunder made my senses reel.

NOTES

5. *as Semele was:* Semele loved Jupiter (Zeus) and Juno (Hera)
tricked the girl into begging Jupiter to show himself to her in the
full splendor of his godhead (as the other gods saw him). Semele was
consumed to ash by that radiance. (See Ovid, *Metamorphoses* III, 253
ff., and *Inferno* XXX, 1–2, note.)

13–15. *the Seventh Splendor:* The Seventh Heaven (Saturn). Once
again the arrival is instantaneous. For the reasons given, Beatrice
does not manifest the new bliss by smiling, but simply announces
that they have arrived. *the Lion:* The Constellation Leo. Dante de-
scribes Saturn as being in conjunction with Leo, as in fact it was in
parts of March and April of 1300. Thus the influence of Leo is mixed
with that of Saturn.

17. *this mirror:* The Sphere of Saturn. All the spheres are, in one
sense, crystalline reflectors of God's light. In another sense, of course,
they let the light through undiminished, but such differences are
of the mystery. Dante uses the same figure for the sun in *Purgatorio*
IV, 62.

19–24. A graciously turned devotion. The thought is complex
yet sweetly balanced. Sense: "Could the reader begin to imagine how
sweet it was to feast my eyes (like lambs in blessèd pasture) on the
beautitude of Beatrice's face, then he might understand how sweet
it was to obey even her command to turn away from such bliss to
find another."

25–27. *the crystal:* The Sphere of Saturn. It bears around the
world the name of Saturn, who was the world's king in the Golden
Age of man before sin had appeared among mankind.

28–42. THE VISION OF THE HEAVENLY LADDER. "And he
dreamed, and beheld a ladder set up on earth, and the top of it
reached to heaven: and behold the angels of God ascending and de-
scending on it." So *Genesis* xxvii, 12, describes Jacob's ladder. Here,
however, Dante adapts it to his own purposes, placing it within

the crystal of the Sphere of Saturn, describing it as being made of blazing gold (to signify the worth of the contemplative soul? as the height of the ladder signifies that soul's ascent to the top of heaven?).

The normal course of the contemplative soul would, of course, be to ascend rather than to descend the ladder. Love, however, remains a first principle, and to welcome Dante and Beatrice in purest love, these souls descend joyously, though forever rising again, to return to their natural height of bliss.

42–45. *a certain rung:* Dante offers no further specifications. The rung seems simply to fix a point below which these souls (whose natural impulse is to rise) choose not to descend at first, though one spirit does draw closer (as, later, all do). This first spirit indicates, by the increase of its radiance, the love it feels for Dante, and its readiness to offer him any service, though protesting that its love is no greater than that of any other soul of this host.

43. *And one:* St. Peter Damiano (1007–1072), as he will later identify himself. He was never officially canonized though he was venerated in Ravenna. He was, however, officially pronounced a Doctor of the Church. His many writings enjoin strict monastic rules and mortification of the flesh.

Born in Ravenna, he became a Benedictine and entered the Camaldolese house at Fonte Avellana in 1035, became Prior about 1043, and Cardinal-Bishop of Ostia in 1057 or 1058, accepting his elevation, as all reports agree, against his own inclination, and continuing in every high office a life of monastic severity.

46–51. Beatrice's allegorical role as Divine Revelation is especially relevant here. Looking into the vision of all-seeing God, she sees Dante's yearning and gives him permission to speak to the waiting soul.

52–60. DANTE'S QUESTIONS. With Beatrice's permission, Dante asks the spirit, first, why it was chosen to come closer than the others, and, second, why there is no heavenly harmony to be heard in this Sphere, since all the Spheres below ring with joyous singing. The second question, being the more important, is answered first (lines 61–63), and then the first (lines 64–72).

67–69. The reply may, perhaps, best be taken as an example of heavenly modesty. At the same time, however, it is partly a statement of fact: all souls in heaven are glorious with love (as the radiances about the poet make clear), and since Peter Damiano is not the foremost soul in Heaven, there are those whose souls will shine more brightly than does his.

70–72. These lines are, in effect, Dante's way of introducing the theme of predestination, which will be discussed later. If the language is difficult, the difficulty lies not in the language itself but in the fact that the concept is unusual and necessarily abstruse. Peter Damiano explains that he descended farther than the other souls because he was predestined to by the will of God. In so saying, he makes clear that every action of all these souls, as each goes up and down the ladder, is similarly predestined. Every heavenly soul, in the grace of love that is granted to it, is a glad servant of the Divine will that assigns the fate of each.

And here, certainly, is the extension of what Virgil foresaw dimly in *Purgatorio* XXVII, 140–143, in telling Dante he was free to follow his own inner impulse. "Here," Virgil says, "your will is upright, free, and whole." At the Paradisal level, however, glorified by revelation, Dante makes it clear that it is not a matter of the individual will but of joyous identification with the service for which God has predestined each soul. (Cf. III, 85: "In His will is our peace." See also XX, 130 ff.)

74. *this court:* The court of Heaven.

75. *Eternal Providence:* It may be well, in this discussion of predestination, to remind some readers that "providence" derives from Latin *pro,* before, and *videre,* to see. Note also that the heavenly souls need not be commanded to follow God's foreseeing and predestined will: this glad love suffices to move them in concord with God.

79–81. *Before I finished speaking:* Before the last three words of line 78. It is at the sound of the word "predestination" that the soul of Peter Damiano begins to spin for joy. Dante does not specifically say that it went on spinning as it talked, but he does describe the soul as beginning to spin, and he does not say that it stopped. The spinning seems an aptly Dantean way to indicate great joy. The soul, moreover, goes into a trance in which it has a direct vision of God; and the spinning might well serve as an established symbol of the trancelike state (cf. "whirling dervish"). There is also the thematic precedent of the grackles in whirling flight, whereby the act of spinning becomes a motif of this canto. Allegorically, too, it may be said that the contemplative soul revolves around its own center (which is, of course, love).

For all these reasons, I think the soul of Peter Damiano should be visualized as spinning on through the rest of the canto, whirled round and round in a glorious vision of God.

82–90. PETER DAMIANO'S VISION OF GOD. Speaking in a trance of bliss, spinning for joy in the rapture of its vision, yet moved by heavenly Love to share its joy with Dante, the soul explains that it is experiencing a vision of God, who focuses His ray into the ray in which the soul hides. (Dante says "in which I embowel myself," i.e., embody myself, and I have been unable to render this felicity.) As has been explained in XIV, 40–42, this is God's grant of grace, and the soul shines brighter to the extent that grace enables it to reflect God's ray.

96. *created vision:* The vision of which any created thing is capable. Only God's uncreated vision can plumb the mystery of predestination. And if the truth is beyond the highest soul in Heaven—as Peter Damiano goes on to say—how can the feeble mind of man think to reach to it? For this reason, he charges Dante, upon his return to the world, to warn men away from presuming to know the unknowable (for such a presumption would involve the sin of pride).

99. *to move his feet:* As a hunter does.

104–105. *so limited, was content:* The question of the soul's identity is not a trivial one. In due observance of fit proportion, however, it has to be recognized as a lesser matter than the abysmal mystery of predestination.

109. *Catria:* Lies between Gubbio and Pergola. Below it (the "holy hermitage") stands the monastery of Santa Croce di Fonte Avellana of the Camaldolese rule (established at Camaldoli about 1012 by St. Romualdo). This rule minimized the community orga-

nization of the monastery but established a particularly severe rule for the individual monks.

115–116. *lenten olive-food:* Olive oil being common in Italy, and butter and lard (like all animal products) being expensive, and therefore luxurious, lenten food (*"cibi di liquor di'ulivi"*) was prepared in nothing but olive oil. Here we should probably understand a diet of simple crusts dipped in olive oil. Even at that, Peter Damiano seems to be suggesting that he ate high on the ecclesiastical hog: Rohrbacher's "Ecclesiastical History" (cited by Scartazzini) gives the diet of the order as plain bread and water for four days of each week, with a few greens added on other days, and with such feasting regularly interrupted by days of fasting. *both heat and cold:* The rule required the monks to go barefoot.

120. *as . . . righteous punishment shall make clear:* As everyone in Heaven seems to do, Peter mourns for the good old days when Fonte Avellana sent whole harvests of monks to heaven (and particularly, one may infer, to Saturn, which is the kingdom of the contemplative). Now, however, the saintly rule has been corrupted, and since God's justice will not long tolerate such a state of affairs, that corruption shall be made manifest by the punishment God shall, soon now, send down upon it.

121–123. This tercet has been a scholar's battleground and reputations have fought and died over the question of its proper punctuation and of its relevance to the historical record, such as it is. Civilian readers need only know that Peter went by both names, adopting the second as an act of piety (he had adopted the first in gratitude to his brother, who had made possible his education), and that he went to Ravenna ("by the Adriatic") as a papal emissary. He lived there for two years in the monastery of Santa Maria Pomposa.

124. *little was left me of my mortal course:* Peter became a cardinal in 1057 or 1058. He died in 1072.

125–126. *the hat:* Of a cardinal. In passing from one wearer to another, it seems forever to go from a bad man to a worse—another lament for the corruption of the times.

127. *Cephas:* The name Christ gave to Simon, who became Peter. The word means "rock" in Hebrew, as *"pietra"* does in Italian,

"Pietro" being the masculine form of the word used as a man's name. Cf. "founded on a rock." *the great ark of the Holy Ghost:* St. Paul.

130. *pastors:* Can only mean "popes" here—those who fill the offices once held by the pastors Peter and Paul. The parish priests of Dante's time may have eaten better than did Peter Damiano, but they did not move about without a great retinue, a warder out in front to clear the way, servants and officials on either side to press back the throng, and a trainbearer following to carry the trailing skirts of their opulent robes.

136–138. *yearning . . . and grew more radiant:* So moved by their renewed joy in the justice of Peter Damiano's denunciation; for their love of what is good and their righteous indignation at what is evil are a conjoined impulse in them. They proceed to cry out like thunder against the evils Peter Damiano has condemned, their cry so loud that Dante's senses reel at the thunderous sound and are unable to make out the words of the cry. Heaven has no other voice in which to speak of evil. Such, on the Paradisal level, is righteous indignation. Cf. *Inferno* VIII, 43 and note.

CANTO XXII

The Seventh Sphere: Saturn—The Contemplative: St. Benedict

Ascent to the Sphere of the Fixed Stars

*The Eighth Sphere: The Fixed Stars—Dante Looks Back
at the Universe Below*

Dante's senses still reeling, he turns to Beatrice, who reassures him and prophesies that he will live to see *God's Vengeance Descend on the Corruptors of the Church*. She then calls his attention to the other souls of this sphere. Looking up, Dante sees *A Hundred Radiant Globes,* one of which draws near and identifies itself as the heavenly splendor that had been *St. Benedict*.

Benedict explains that the Golden Ladder, like the contemplative life, soars to the summit of God's glory, and he laments that so few of his Benedictine monks remain eager to put the world behind them and begin the ascent, for they are lost in the degeneracy of bad days. Yet God has worked greater wonders than would be required to restore the purity of the church.

So saying, Benedict is gathered into his heavenly choir of radiances, and the whole company ascends to the top of the sky and out of sight.

Beatrice then makes a sign and Dante feels himself making the *Ascent to the Eighth Sphere, The Sphere of the Fixed Stars*. But before the souls of that Sphere are revealed to him, Beatrice bids him look back to see how far she has raised him. Dante looks down through the Seven Spheres in their glory, seeing all the heavens at a glance, and the earth as an insignificant speck far below. Then turning from it as from a puny thing, he turns his eyes back to the eyes of Beatrice.

My senses reeled, and as a child in doubt
  runs always to the one it trusts the most,
  I turned to my guide, still shaken by that shout;   3

and she, like a mother, ever prompt to calm
  her pale and breathless son with kindly words,
    the sound of which is his accustomed balm,   6

said: "Do you not know you are in the skies
  of Heaven itself? that all is holy here?
    that all things spring from love in Paradise?   9

Their one cry shakes your sense: you can now see
  what would have happened to you had they sung,
    or had I smiled in my new ecstasy.   12

Had you understood the prayer within their cry
  you would know now what vengeance they called down,
    though you shall witness it before you die.   15

The sword of Heaven is not too soon dyed red,
  nor yet too late—except as its vengeance seems
    to those who wait for it in hope or dread.   18

But look now to the others. Turn as I say
  and you shall see among this company
    many great souls of the Eternal Ray."   21

I did as she commanded. Before my eyes
  a hundred shining globes entwined their beams,
    soul adding grace to soul in Paradise.   24

I stood there between longing and diffidence
  and fought my longing back, afraid to speak
    for fear my questioning might give offense.   27

And the largest and most glowing globe among
  the wreath of pearls came forward of its own prompting
    to grant the wish I had not given tongue.   30

These words came from within it: "Could you see,
  as I do, with what love our spirits burn
  to give you joy, your tongue would have been free.   33

To cause you no delay on the high track
  to the great goal, I shall address myself
  to none but the single question you hold back.   36

The summit of that mountain on whose side
  Cassino lies, once served an ill-inclined
  and misled people in their pagan pride.   39

And I am he who first bore to that slope
  the holy name of Him who came on earth
  to bring mankind the truth that is our hope.   42

Such grace shone down on me that men gave heed
  through all that countryside and were won over
  from the seductions of that impious creed.   45

These other souls were all contemplatives,
  fired by that warmth of soul that summons up
  the holy flowers and fruits of blessèd lives.   48

Here is Romualdus, and Maccarius, too.
  Here are my brothers who kept within the cloister
  and, never straying, kept hearts sound and true."   51

And I to him: "The love you have made clear
  in speaking as you have, and the good intent
  I see in all the glories of this sphere,   54

have opened all my confidence: it grows
  and spreads wide on your warmth, rejoicing in it
  as does, in the Sun's heat, a full-blown rose.   57

I therefore beg you, Father: can I rise
  to such a height of grace that I may see
  your unveiled image with my mortal eyes?"   60

And he then: "Brother, this shall be made known
  in the last sphere. Your wish will be answered there
  where every other is, including my own.   63

There, every wish is perfect, ripe, and whole.
  For there, and there alone, is every part
  where it has always been; for it has no pole,   66

not being in space. It is to that very height
  the golden ladder mounts; and thus you see
  why it outsoars the last reach of your sight.   69

The patriarch Jacob saw it, saw it mount
  to lean on that very sill, that time he dreamed it
  covered with angels beyond all mortal count.   72

To climb it now, however, none makes haste
  to lift his feet from earth. My rule lives on
  only to fill the parchments it lays waste.   75

The walls that were retreats in their good hour
  are dens for beasts now; what were holy cowls
  are gunny sacks stuffed full of evil flour.   78

But even compound usury strikes less
  against God's will and pleasure, than does that fruit
  whose poison fills the hearts of monks with madness. 81

For all the goods of the Church, tithes and donations,
  are for the poor of God, not to make fat
  the families of monks—and worse relations.   84

The flesh of mortals is so weak down there
  that a good beginning is not reason enough
  to think the seedling tree will live to bear.   87

Peter began with neither silver nor gold;
  I, with prayer and fasting. And Brother Francis
  in humble poverty gathered souls to his fold.   90

And if you look at the origins of each one,
  then look again at what it has become,
  you will see that what was white has changed to dun.   93

Yet Jordan flowing backward, and the sea
  parting as God willed, were more wondrous sights
  than God's help to His stricken church would be."   96

So did he speak; then faded from my eye
  into his company, which closed about him,
  and then, like a whirlwind, spun away on high.   99

And my sweet lady with a simple sign
  raised me along that ladder after them,
  conquering my nature with her power divine.   102

There never was known down here, where everything
  rises or falls as natural law determines,
  a speed to equal the motion of my wing.   105

Reader, so may I hope once more to stand
  in that holy Triumph, for which I weep my sins
  and beat my breast—you could not draw your hand   108

out of a tongue of flame and thrust it back
  sooner than I sighted and had entered
  the sign that follows Taurus on Heaven's track.   111

O glorious constellation! O lamp imbued
  with great powers, to whose influence I ascribe
  all my genius, however it may be viewed!   114

When I drew my first breath of Tuscan air
  the Sun, the father of all mortal life,
  was rising in your rays and setting there.   117

And then when I was granted Heaven's grace
  to enter the great wheel that gives you motion,
  I was led upward through your zone of space.   120

To you devoutly now my prayer is sped:
  make my soul worthy of the call it hears
  to the great passage that still lies ahead!   123

"You are so near the final health of man
  you will do well to go clear-eyed and keen
  into that good," my Beatrice began.   126

"Therefore, before you enter further here
  look down and see how vast a universe
  I have put beneath your feet, bright sphere on sphere. 129

Thus may you come in the fullness of delight
  to the Triumphant Court that comes in joy
  through the round ether to your mortal sight."   132

My eyes went back through the seven spheres below,
  and I saw this globe, so small, so lost in space,
  I had to smile at such a sorry show.   135

Who thinks it the least pebble in the skies
  I most approve. Only the mind that turns
  to other things may truly be called wise.   138

I saw Latona's daughter glowing there
  without that shadow that had once misled me
  to think her matter was part dense, part rare.   141

My eyes looked on your son, Hyperion,
  nor did they falter. And wheeling close around him,
  I saw the motion of Maia and Dione.   144

Next I saw how Jupiter mediates
  between his father and son, and I understood
  why the motion of one and the other vacillates.   147

And all the seven, in a single view,
  showed me their masses, their velocities,
  and the distances between each in its purlieu.   150

And turning there with the eternal Twins,
  I saw the dusty little threshing ground
  that makes us ravenous for our mad sins,   153

saw it from mountain crest to lowest shore.
  Then I turned my eyes to Beauty's eyes once more.

NOTES

13–15. *the prayer within their cry:* Dante heard the sound of the cry, but not the prayer within it (what the words said). We may now understand that these souls called on God to show His wrath at the corruption of the Church, and perhaps of the papacy in particular. What retribution Dante will witness before he dies is not specified. History suggests the capture of Boniface VIII at Alagna by the mercenaries of Philip the Fair under William de Nogaret as one possible vengeance (see *Purgatorio* XX, 85–93 and note). Or it may suggest Philip's maneuver in 1304 whereby Clement V was elected Pope and the papacy removed to Avignon (see *Purgatorio* XXXII, 158 and note). But neither event can be taken as a large-scale visitation of God's wrath, and neither, certainly, ended papal corruption. Beatrice's prophecy is best taken, I believe, as simply one more way of denouncing the corrupt. Dante would, of course, have welcomed such a visitation of God's wrath, but he clearly has no specific event in mind.

16–18. Beatrice is making the point that God's vengeance is always taken at the proper and inevitable moment, never too soon, and never too late, though to the wicked (who wait for it with dread) it seems always to come too soon, and to the pious (who wait for it with hope for the downfall of evil) it seems always to come too late.

19. *the others:* Dante's attention has been fixed on St. Peter Damiano. Now Beatrice directs his attention to the other great spirits of this sphere.

28–29. *the largest and most glowing globe:* Contains the spirit of St. Benedict (480–543). There is some historic uncertainty about his life, the recorded facts having been subject to pious increment. He was born at Nursia in Umbria and went to Rome for his education. There, appalled by the wickedness of the Romans, he left the world about the year 500 and lived in a cave on Mount Subiaco, his rigid asceticism and holiness drawing disciples to him, though he seems never to have been ordained. About 525 he moved with his followers to Monte Cassino and there, after destroying a temple to Apollo, founded the great central monastery of the Benedictine order on the rule he had already established for his followers on Subiaco. He died at Monte Cassino on March 21, his feast day, and was buried in the same grave with his sister, Ste. Scholastica.

33. *your tongue would have been free:* To ask the questions Dante held back from speaking.

34–36. St. Benedict's exact point in this passage will be clear if one recalls that many of the heavenly spirits have answered not only the questions Dante had spoken or framed in his mind, but others, too, though he had not yet thought to think them. To speed Dante on his way, St. Benedict will answer only the one question Dante has clearly in mind.

38. *once served:* By having upon its peak a temple of Apollo. Especially in the outlying districts, paganism survived well into the

Middle Ages. St. Benedict is saying that he was the first to bring Christianity to the mountain people on and around Cassino.

45. *that impious creed:* The cult of Apollo.

49. *Romualdus:* St. Romualdo (956–1027), founder of the Camaldolese Order (see note to XXI, 109). *Maccarius:* Probably St. Maccarius of Alexandria (died 404) a disciple of St. Anthony. He lived in the desert between the Nile and the Red Sea and was reputed to have been the leader of 5000 eremites. Dante may have had in mind Maccarius the Egyptian (circa 301–391) also a disciple of St. Anthony. Or Dante may have thought of the two as one person.

55–57. A literal rendering of these lines might read: "[These things] have caused my confidence to dilate just as the sun does a rose, which, when opened, becomes as great as it had the power to become."

60. *unveiled image:* The image in which the soul would appear were Dante's eyes not blinded by the radiance that veils it.

61. *Brother:* Dante has addressed him as "Father" out of respect, but all the souls in Heaven are brothers and sisters of the one Father, and above honorary titles.

62. *in the last sphere:* In the Empyrean. There (see XXXII, 35) St. Benedict does appear to Dante among the glories of the mystic rose.

63. *including my own:* My own wish to content you in your wish. St. Benedict does not imply that every wish finds fulfillment in the presence of God, but rather that "this good" and "every other" do.

64–69. Only the mystery of revelation will make clear, and only to the elected soul, these mysteries of God's love. In one sense, we may gather from the vocabulary of exaltation, all good is from God, and since no part of good has ever left Him, every part of every good wish, in being returned to God's presence, is back where it always has been. For God is also ubiquitous, His presence limited by no boundary, since it is not a dimension of space.

It is to the crown of that sublimity that exists beyond dimension that the Golden Ladder mounts, outsoaring the reach of any soul's (physical or spiritual) sight.

70–72. The vision of Jacob's ladder is described in *Genesis* xxviii, 12 ff.

73–75. Another sounding of the theme of latter-day degeneracy, St. Benedict's rule for the contemplative was designed to raise the soul toward Heaven (as if climbing the ladder). Now, however, none of his monks is in any hurry to forego the pleasures of the earth, and so the Benedictine rule lives on as a waste of the parchments on which it is copied, since none observe it.

78–84. Once the clerics sought God in prayer, meditation, and acts of charity. Then all the possessions of the church were held in trust for the poor, to be distributed to them at need. Now, however, the fruit of avarice has poisoned the hearts of clerics, and the wealth that should be used to help God's poor is used by the monks themselves to swell the purse and position of their families, or for worse relations (the latter probably signifying that corrupt monks kept mistresses and bad companions in luxurious establishments).

86–87. Dante says, literally: "A good beginning is not enough [to certify the interval] from the birth of the oak to the harvest of acorns."

91. *each one:* Of the three folds founded by the three great saints.

94–96. *Jordan . . . the sea parting:* Most commentators read these lines as a statement of hope: "The same will that caused the Jordan to flow backward and the Red Sea to divide, could will the lesser miracle of restoring purity to the church." Others read it in the opposite sense: "It would be more wondrous to see Jordan flow backward and the sea divide than to see the church restored to purity." Especially in view of the fact that Beatrice has promised Dante that he would live to see God's vengeance on the corruptors of the Church, the more hopeful interpretation seems to be the more likely.

98. *his company:* The other souls of the Contemplative. Their choir closes about him (an allegory of the unity of the souls of Heaven?) and instantly ascends to the top of the sky.

100–111. ASCENT FROM SATURN TO THE SPHERE OF THE FIXED STARS. Once again the ascent is instantaneous. Beatrice, by a simple sign, raises Dante to the next sphere, her power overcoming his nature. On one level his "nature" is his mortal weight, which is here uplifted despite the forces of gravity. On another, it is the human soul, gross and imperfect in itself, yet able by the power of Divine Revelation to soar toward God.

103. *down here:* On earth, and within the operations of earth's natural laws, from which Dante has escaped.

105. *my wing:* To signify "my flight." But note that Dante says "wing" rather than "wings." He may have intended an allegorical point. The soul, while still earthbound, may seek to soar with reason as one wing and with faith as the other. In Heaven, however, the ascent is accomplished by the single wing of faith, that power of the soul that brings it to the transcendent recognition of God.

108. *beat my breast:* In penitence.

108–109. *draw your hand . . . and thrust it back:* The sequence of this action is deliberately reversed in another hysteron-proteron. See note to II, 23–24.

111. *the sign that follows Taurus:* Gemini. *Heaven's track:* The Zodiac.

112–123. INVOCATION OF GEMINI. Dante's invocation is spoken not in the *persona* of the pilgrim en route, but in that of the poet at his desk, looking back to his great journey.

Gemini, Dante lets us know, is the zodiacal sign under which he was born (lines 115–117) and whose influence determined his poetic genius (lines 112–114). In 1265 the Sun entered the sign of Gemini on May 18 and passed from it on June 17. (The exact date of Dante's birth is not known, but these dates set firm limits for it.) It is allegorically felicitous certainly that Dante, in ascending to (being born into) the Sphere of the Fixed Stars, should pass through his natal constellation.

124. *the final health of man:* God.

134. *this globe:* The Earth.

139. *Latona's daughter:* The Moon (as Diana, sister of Apollo, the Sun, both children of Latona).

140–141. *without that shadow:* See II, 46 ff. Dante is looking now at the face of the moon we call the dark side and which is never visible from Earth. The sun that lights it, moreover, must be between it and Dante, probably to one side, though it would be nothing now for His Heaven-heightened vision to see through the sun. As the next tercet indicates, Dante was at least able to look directly into the sun.

142. *your son, Hyperion:* The Sun as the son of Hyperion, himself the son of Uranus and Terra.

144. *Maia and Dione:* Here stand for Mercury and Venus. Maia was one of the seven sisters of the Pleiades and the mother of Mercury. Dione was the mother of Venus. I do not know why Dante takes the mothers for the children here.

145–147. *Jupiter . . . his father and son:* Jupiter was the son of Saturn and the father of Mars. The temperate planet, Jupiter, lies between the excessively hot planet Mars and the excessively cold planet Saturn. Such are the terms of Dante's astrology. Dante does not explain how this theory of a temperate mean between fire and ice allows him to understand the eccentricities of the orbits of Mars and Saturn—perhaps he conceives Jupiter as a moderating force that attracts the planets on its either side. Whatever the theory, the observable fact is that these planets, as seen from Earth, do wander all over the star chart; their orbits swing sometimes close to the sun and sometimes away, and they rise sometimes before it and sometimes after it. But Dante's reference here is all the more confusing in that all the planets wander in this way.

150. *purlieu:* Dante uses the word *"riparo"* (the place to which one repairs) in the same sense that astrologers speak of "the house" of Mars or of some other planet. Hence Dante must mean the orbit of each considered as the place that is particularly its own.

151. *the eternal Twins:* Gemini.

152. *the dusty little threshing ground:* The Earth, so described as an insignificant and busy flat patch of dust as compared to the glory and serenity of the Heavens.

153. *Beauty's eyes:* The eyes of Beatrice, which are the eyes of Heaven.

CANTO XXIII

The Eighth Sphere: The Fixed Stars—The Triumph of
Christ · The Virgin Mary · The Apostles ·
The Angel Gabriel · St. Peter

Beatrice stares expectantly toward that part of the sky where the Sun is at its highest point, and Dante, moved by the joy of her expectation, follows her look. Almost at once there descends from the highest Heaven the radiant substance of the *Vision of Christ Triumphant* as it rays forth on the garden of all those souls who have been redeemed through Christ. The splendor too much for his senses, *Dante Swoons.* He is recalled to himself by Beatrice and discovers that, newly strengthened as he has been by the vision of Christ, he is able to look upon her smile of bliss.

Beatrice urges him to look at the Garden of Christ's Triumph, upon the Rose of the *Virgin Mary* and the Lilies of the *Apostles.* Christ, taking mercy on Dante's feeble powers, has withdrawn from direct view and now rays down from above.

Dante fixes his eyes on the brightest splendor (the Virgin Mary) and sees a crown of flame descend to summon her back to the Empyrean. It is the *Angel Gabriel.* So summoned, Mary ascends to where her son is, and the flames of the souls yearn higher toward her. There, among the souls that remain below, Dante identifies *St. Peter.*

As a bird in its sweet canopy of green
   covers the nest of its beloved young
   through all the night when nothing can be seen;   3

but eager for the loved, lit face of things,
   and to go hunting for its fledglings' food
   in toil so glad that, laboring, she sings;   6

anticipates the day on an open bough
   and in a fire of love awaits the sun,
   her eyes fixed eagerly on the pre-dawn glow—   9

just so my lady waited—erect, intense—
  all her attention toward that part of heaven
  beneath which the sun's daily pace relents: 12

and I, observing her blissful expectation,
  became like one who yearns for more than he has,
  feeding his hope with sweet anticipation.   15

But the interval between *when* and *when* was slight—
  the *when* of my waiting, I say, and the *when* of seeing
  the sky begin to swell with a new light.   18

And Beatrice said: "Before you now appears
  the militia of Christ's triumph, and all the fruit
  harvested from the turning of the spheres."   21

I saw her face before me, so imbued
  with holy fire, her eyes so bright with bliss
  that I pass on, leaving them unconstrued.   24

As Trivia in the full moon's sweet serene
  smiles on high among the eternal nymphs
  whose light paints every part of Heaven's scene;   27

I saw, above a thousand thousand lights,
  one Sun that lit them all, as our own Sun
  lights all the bodies we see in Heaven's heights;   30

and through that living light I saw revealed
  the Radiant Substance, blazing forth so bright
  my vision dazzled and my senses reeled.   33

Oh my Beatrice, sweet and loving guide!
  "What blinds you," she said to me, "is the very power
  nothing withstands, and from which none may hide.   36

This is the intellect and the sceptered might
  that opened the golden road, from Earth to Heaven,
  for which mankind had yearned in its long night."   39

Fire sometimes spreads so wide that it shoots forth
  from a cloud that can no longer hold it in,
  and against its nature, hurtles down to earth.   42

That feast of bliss had swollen my mind so
  that it broke its bounds and leapt out of itself.
  And what it then became, it does not know.   45

"Open your eyes and turn them full on me!
  You have seen things whose power has made you able
  to bear the bright smile of my ecstasy!"   48

As one whose senses have been stricken blind
  by a forgotten vision comes to himself
  and racks his wits to call it back to mind—   51

such was I at that summons, my spirit moved
  to a thankfulness that shall live on forever
  within the book where what is past is proved.   54

If there should sound now all the the tongues of song
  Polyhymnia with her eight sisters nourished,
  giving their sweetest milk to make them strong,   57

they could not help me, singing thus, to show
  a thousandth part of my lady's sacred smile,
  nor with what glory it made her features glow.   60

Just so, that Heaven may be figured forth,
  my consecrated poem must make a leap,
  as a traveler leaps a crevice there on earth.   63

My theme is massive, mortal shoulders frail
  for such a weight. What thoughtful man will blame me
  for trembling under it for fear I fail?   66

The seas my ardent prow is plowing here
  are no place for small craft, nor for a helmsman
  who will draw back from toil or cringe in fear.   69

"Why are you so enamored of my face
  you do not turn your eyes to see the garden
  that flowers there in the radiance of Christ's grace?   72

The Rose in which the Word became incarnate
  is there. There are the lilies by whose odor
  men found the road that evermore runs straight."   75

Thus Beatrice. And I, prompt to her guidance
  in fullest eagerness, raised my feeble lids
  once more to battle with that radiance.   78

At times when the sun, through broken clouds, has rayed
  one perfect beam, I have seen a field of flowers
  blazing in glory, my own eyes still in shade: 81

just so, I saw a host of hosts made bright
  by rays of splendor striking from above,
  but could not see the source of that pure light.   84

O Majesty that seals them in such glory!
  you raised yourself on high, withdrawing there
  in order that my feeble eyes might see!   87

The name of that Sweet Flower to which I pray
  morning and night, seized all my soul and moved it
  to fix my eyes upon the brightest ray;   90

And when both my eyes had been allowed to know
  the luster and magnitude of that chosen star
  that triumphs there as it triumphed here below,   93

from Heaven's height a torch of glory came,
  shaped like a ring or wreath, and spinning round her,
  it wound and crowned her in its living flame.   96

The sweetest strain that ever swelled aloud
  to draw the soul into itself down here,
  would be as thunder from a shattered cloud,   99

compared to the melody that then aspired
  from the bright lyre that crowned the purest gem
  by which the brightest heaven is ensapphired.   102

"I am the Angelic Love that wheels around
  the lofty ecstasy breathed from the womb
  in which the hostel of Our Wish was found;   105

so shall I wheel, Lady of Heaven, till
  you follow your great Son to the highest sphere
  and, by your presence, make it holier still."   108

Thus the encircling melody of that flame
  revealed itself; and all the other lamps
  within that garden rang out Mary's name.   111

The royal mantle whose folds are spread abroad
  round all the spheres, and that most burns and quickens
  being nearest to the breath and ways of God,   114

turned its inner shore at such a height
  above the point at which I then was standing
  that I could not yet bring it into sight.   117

I could not, therefore, with my mortal eyes
  follow the flight of that crowned flame that soared
  to join her son in the highest Paradise.   120

And as a newly suckled infant yearns
  after its mother with its upraised arms,
  expressing so the love with which it burns;   123

each of the splendors of that company
  extended its flame on high in such a way
  as made its love of Mary plain to me.   126

Then they remained there, still within my sight,
  singing *"Regina coeli"* in tones so sweet
  the memory still fills me with delight.   129

Oh what treasures cram and overflow
  those richest coffers of the eternal grace
  who sowed such good seed in the world below!   132

Here is true life and relish of the treasure
  their tears laid up in the Babylonian exile,
  in which Christ left man gold beyond all measure.   135

Here sits in triumph under the lofty Son
  of God and the Virgin Mary in His triumph,
  and in the company of everyone   138

crowned from the New or the Old Consistory,
  the soul that holds the great keys to such glory.

NOTES

1–15. THE EAGERNESS OF BEATRICE. Beatrice is awaiting
the vision of the Triumph of Christ. Dante does not know what ex-

pected delight has filled her with such bliss, but seeing her so tranced in expectation, he, too, begins to yearn for what has not yet been revealed.

The poet expresses this feeling of intense and joyous anticipation in a memorable long-tail simile of a mother bird that has spent the night covering its young, held there by love and by the night that keeps her from the joyous labors of hunting their food. Before the light of day, the mother bird is already out of the leaf-canopy, poised on an open bough to await the new dawn, and to begin her love's labors at the first possible instant.

Beatrice is compared to that mother bird. (Thematically, this expectation of a great new rebirth of the light must certainly be related to the fact that Dante is in Gemini, his zodiacal birth sign.) Dante, as if he were her fledgling, is fired by the contagion of Beatrice's blissful expectation.

This memorable figure marks the transition to the upper Heaven, for Dante and Beatrice are now beyond the planetary spheres, in the sphere of the Fixed Stars, and beyond them lies only the Empyrean itself, which is the total presence of God.

12. *the sun's daily pace relents:* At meridian the Sun seems to slow its pace. Beatrice is looking toward that part of heaven where the Sun (Divine Illumination) is at its noon height. It is all but inevitable that the vision of the Triumph of Christ should come from that portion of the sky.

16. *when:* Dante uses "when" *(quando)* as it is used in Scholastic terminology, meaning "time of" or "duration."

20–21. *all the fruit harvested from the turning of the spheres:* The first-created angels of Heaven did, of course, share in Christ's triumph, but they were not part of its harvest, which consisted of the redemption of the souls of men. Once the soul had entered into that triumph (mounted to Heaven), it would manifest itself in one of the spheres, though it was in essence in the choir of the Empyrean. Thus the militia of Christ must contain all the souls of glory whose manifestations populate the spheres of Heaven (including now the Sphere of the Fixed Stars).

In another sense "harvested from the turning of the spheres" intends the shaping influences of the spheres upon the souls of men, disposing them to the good that gains their triumph. And, of course, the phrase also intends "harvested from time" (i.e., distinct from the angels, who were never temporal).

24. *unconstrued:* In Scholastic terminology "to construe" meant "to express the true essense of a thing."

25–26. *Trivia:* Diana, the Moon, in her manifestation as a nymph. *eternal nymphs:* The stars. See *Purgatorio* XXXI, 106.

30. *lights all the bodies:* Lights all stars (which are supposed, as the moon does, to send forth only the reflection of the sun's light).

32. *the Radiant Substance:* Of Christ.

33. *my vision dazzled:* Only a moment ago (XXII, 142–143) Dante had looked straight into the Sun without discomfort. At the vision of the radiance of Christ, however, Dante's senses reel, and in a moment he will swoon. The art of juxtaposing details in a way that constantly gives scale to an all-containing system of values is one of the marvels of Dante's genius.

35. *the very power:* Of Christ.

40. *fire:* Lightning.

42. *against its nature:* The nature of fire is to ascend toward the Sphere of Fire (see I, 115, and *Purgatorio* XXXII, 109 ff.). Contrary to its nature (which is to rise to God), Dante's spirit swoons and falls.

43. *That feast of bliss:* The vision of the Triumph of Christ.

46–48. See XXI, 4 ff. and 62 ff. There Beatrice had to hold back her smile of ecstasy because it would have destroyed Dante, whose sense could not have contained it. Now, allegorically, having sustained the vision of the Triumph of Christ and looked upon His Radiant Substance, Dante's eyes have been prepared for the full glory of Beatrice (Divine Revelation).

56–57. *Polyhymnia:* The Muse of sacred songs. (Her name means "many-hymned.") She and her eight sisters were the fountainhead of all song and all poetry. *their sweetest milk:* The Muses gave suck to the poets, thereby transmitting to them the powers of song. How these virgin sisters maintained their milk supply is one more item to be filed among the sacred mysteries.

61. *Just so:* Just as it is impossible to describe to mortal sensibilities the glory of the smile of Beatrice (an allegory of revelation), so must the poem that would describe Heaven leap over such matters as human understanding cannot fathom.

67–69. Cf. the opening lines of Canto II.

73–75. *The Rose:* The Virgin Mary. *the Word:* Logos. *the lilies:* Primarily, perhaps, the Apostles, but also the total of all souls that share in the Triumph of Christ, their example forever showing the straight way to others. *whose odor:* Cf. the common pious phrase, "odor of sanctity."

77. *lids:* Rather than eyes. Dante has just swooned at the radiance of Christ. Now, obedient to the command of Beatrice, he turns to look again, but with his eyes lidded, his mortal senses bracing themselves to bear the ineffable radiance (cf., too, his admonition in line 69. Only the spirit that will risk all may dare the glories of Heaven).

79–87. The figure is based on the common phenomenon of seeing a ray of sun light a field of flowers while one is standing in the shadow of covering cloud. So the rays of Christ's glory strike down to illuminate the souls of the redeemed, Christ, of his infinite mercy, having withdrawn from Dante's sight, for it could not have borne the full glory of His shining. Lines 85–87 may certainly be pondered as a possible allegory of the resurrection of Christ.

85. *seals:* The seal here would be the ray; the flowers, the wax that takes the impress of the light and shines forth as marked by the light.

88 ff. THE VISION OF THE VIRGIN MARY. Beatrice (line 73) has told Dante that Mary was among the radiances he saw before him. When Dante finally manages to fix his eyes on the splendor before him (the radiance of Christ having withdrawn mercifully) he makes out the brightest star in that host of splendors. As he watches, a crown of flame descends from the Empyrean and encircles her. This new radiance is God's messenger, Gabriel, the Angel of the Annunciation. *Sweet Flower, brightest ray:* The Virgin Mary. *had been allowed to know:* As always in Paradise, it is not Dante's will that discerns the

vision (though he wills it utterly) but the souls that reveal themselves to him.

101–102. *gem . . . ensapphired:* The original is *zaffiro . . . s'inzaffira*. Dante must have chosen the sapphire as the gem of purest blue, the color of Heaven. *purest gem:* The Virgin Mary. *the bright lyre:* The Angel Gabriel. *the brightest heaven:* The Sphere of the Fixed Stars.

105. *Our Wish:* Christ. The womb of Mary was the hostel in which the Word found lodging in mortal flesh.

107. *the highest sphere:* The Empyrean.

110. *revealed itself:* Dante says literally, "impressed its seal," the equivalent of writing its signature, i.e., "identified itself."

112–114. *the royal mantle:* The Primum Mobile. *most burns:* With ardent joy. *and quickens:* Being the outer sphere whose revolutions control the turning of all those it encloses, it turns faster than any of the others.

115. *its inner shore:* The spheres of course, have depth. Could Dante's vision have reached to see the Primum Mobile it would have seen only its inner surface, here called a shore.

120. *to join her son:* As Gabriel had prayed her to do.

128. *Regina coeli:* Queen of Heaven.

133–135. Both the text and the interpretation of the original are disputed. I have settled for what seems to be the most direct rendering, taking "the Babylonian exile" to signify the soul's time on earth. Heaven, then, would be the longed-for Jerusalem. In their exile, in steadfast faith and holy tears, these souls laid up the heavenly treasure they now enjoy, as Christ left it to all men.

139. *Old and New Consistory:* The Old and the New Testament.

140. *the soul that holds the keys:* St. Peter.

CANTO XXIV

*The Eighth Sphere: The Fixed Stars—The Triumph of
Christ · St. Peter · The Examination of Faith*

Christ and Mary having ascended to the Empyrean, St. Peter re-
mains as the chief soul of the Garden of Christ's Triumph. Bea-
trice addresses the souls in Dante's behalf, and they, in their joy,
form into a dazzling *Vertical Wheel of Spinning Radiances.*

Beatrice then begs St. Peter to conduct an *Examination of
Dante's Faith.* St. Peter thereupon questions Dante on the *Nature
of Faith, The Possession of Faith, The Sources of Faith, The Proof of the
Truth of Faith, Man's Means of Knowing that the Miracles of Faith Ac-
tually Took Place,* and finally on *The Content of Christian Faith.*

Dante answers eagerly, as would a willing candidate being ex-
amined by his learned master. The examination concluded, St.
Peter shows his pleasure by dancing three times around Dante.

"O spirits of that chosen company
    that feeds on the Lamb of God, the flesh of which
    satisfies hunger to all eternity—   3

if by God's grace this man is given a foretaste
    of what falls from your table, before death
    takes him from time and lays his body waste,   6

consider the boundless thirst with which he burns;
    bedew him from your plenty. You drink forever
    the waters of that spring for which he yearns!"   9

So spoke Beatrice, and those blissful souls,
    flaming as bright as comets, formed themselves
    into a sphere revolving on fixed poles.   12

As the wheels within a clockwork synchronize
    so that the innermost, when looked at closely
    seems to be standing, while the outermost flies;   15

just so those rings of dancers whirled to show
   and let me understand their state of bliss,
      all joining in the round, some fast, some slow.   18

From one I saw, the loveliest of them all,
   there grew a radiance of such blessedness
      that it outshone the hosts of the celestial.   21

Three times it danced round Beatrice to a strain
   so heavenly that I have not the power
      so much as to imagine it again.   24

Therefore my pen leaps and I do not write;
   not words nor fantasy can paint the truth:
      the folds of heaven's draperies are too bright.   27

"O sacred sister whose prayer is so devout,
   the ardor of your love enters my bliss
      within that lovely sphere and calls me out."   30

—When it had come to rest, that Fire of Love
   directed its breath to my lady and spoke these words
      exactly as I have set them down above.   33

And she: "Eternal Light of the great priest
   to whom Our Lord brought down and gave the keys
      to the sublimities of this joyous feast;   36

at your own pleasure, whatever it may be,
   test this man on the greater and lesser points
      of the faith in which you once walked on the sea.   39

If love and hope and faith are truly his
   you will discover it, for your eyes are turned
      where you can see the image of all that is.   42

But since this realm is peopled from the seed
  of the true faith, he will the better praise it,
  could he discuss with you the perfect creed."   45

As a bachelor arms himself for disquisition
  in silence till the master sets the terms
  for defending, not deciding, the proposition;   48

so did I arm myself for the expression
  of every proof, preparing while she spoke
  for such an examiner, and such profession.   51

"Speak, good Christian, manifest your worth:
  what is faith?"—At which I raised my eyes
  to the light from which these words had been
                        breathed forth: 54

then turned to look at Beatrice, and she
  urged me with her eyes to let the waters
  of the spring that welled within my soul pour free.   57

"May the Grace that grants the grace of this confession
  to the captain of the first rank," I began,
  "grant that my thoughts may find worthy expression!"   60

Continuing: "Father, as it was set down
  by the pen of your dear brother, who, with you,
  set Rome on the road that leads to glory's crown,   63

faith is the *substance* of what we hope to see
  and the *argument* for what we have not seen.
  This is its *quiddity*, as it seems to me."   66

Next I heard: "This is, in fact, the essence.
  But do you understand why he classifies it
  first with substances, then with *argument*?"   69

And I in answer: "The profundities
  that here reveal themselves so liberally
  are so concealed, down there, from mortal eyes   72

they exist in belief alone. On belief the structure
  of high hope rises. It is *substant,* therefore,
  or 'standing under' by its very nature.   75

Starting with this belief, it is evident,
  we must reason without further visible proofs.
  And so it partakes, by nature, of *argument*."   78

I heard: "If all that mortal man may know
  through mortal teaching were as firmly grasped,
  sophists would find no listeners there below."   81

Such was the breath from that Love's Ecstasy,
  continuing then: "You have assayed this coinage,
  its weight and metal content, accurately;   84

now tell me if you have it in your possession."
  And I then: "Yes. I have. So bright, so round,
  usage has worn down none of its impression."   87

After these words the breath once more resounded
  from the light that shone before me: "This dear gem
  on which all good and power of good are founded—   90

whence comes it to you?" And I, "The shower of gold
  of the Holy Ghost, which pours down endlessly
  over the sacred Scrolls, both New and Old,   93

reasons it to such logical certainty
  that, by comparison, all other reasoning
  can only seem confused and dull to me."   96

And I heard: "These propositions, the Old and New
  that move you to this conclusion, for what reason
  do you accept them as divinely true?"   99

And I: "The proof that shows the truth to me
  is in the works that followed. Never has nature
  heated and forged such iron in its smithy."   102

And I was answered: "Tell me how you know
  there were such works. What seeks to prove itself—
  it only and nothing more—swears it was so."   105

"If the whole world became Christian without the aid
  of the miraculous, that is a miracle
  a hundred times greater than the rest," I said,   108

"for poor and hungry, by faith alone upborne,
  you entered the field and sowed there the good plant
  that was a vine once, and is now a thorn."   111

This said, that high and holy choir let ring
  "Te Deum laudamus!" sounding through the spheres
  such melody as the souls of heaven sing.   114

And that Baron, who, examining my belief
  from branch to branch, had drawn me out already
  to where we were approaching the last leaf,   117

began again: "The grace whose loving good
  had pledged itself to your mind, has moved your mouth,
  up to this point, to open as it should.   120

I approve what has emerged thus far, but now
  it is time you should explain *what* you believe,
  and from what source it comes to you, and how."   123

"O holy Father, spirit that now can see
  what faith once held so firmly that you were prompter
  than younger feet to the tomb in Galilee,"   126

my answer ran, "you wish me to expound
  the *form* of my own promptness to believe,
  and you ask what reasons for it I have found.   129

And I reply: I believe in one God, loved,
  desired by all creation, sole, eternal
  who moves the turning Heavens, Himself unmoved. 132

And for this faith I have the evidences
  not only of physics and of metaphysics,
  but of the truth that rains down on my senses   135

through Moses, the prophets, the psalms, through the
                                          Evangel,
  and through you and what you wrote when the
                                          Ardent Spirit
  made you the foster father of God's People.   138

And I believe in three Persons; this Trinity,
  an essence Triune and Single, in whose being
  is and *are* conjoin to eternity.   141

That this profound and sacred nature is real
  the teachings of the evangels, in many places,
  have stamped on the wax of my mind like a living
                                          seal.   144

This is the beginning, the spark shot free
  that gnaws and widens into living flame,
  and, like a star in Heaven, shines in me."   147

As a master who is pleased by what he hears
  embraces his servant as soon as he has spoken,
  rejoicing in the happy news he bears;   150

so, that glorious apostolic blaze
  at whose command I had spoken heard me out,
  and blessing me in a glad chant of praise,   153

danced three times round me there in the eighth great rim,
  such pleasure had my speaking given him.

NOTES

1–9. PRAYER OF BEATRICE TO THE TRIUMPHANT HOSTS. Now that Christ and Mary have returned to highest heaven, the triumphant spirits are gathered around St. Peter (an allegory of Peter's role as Christ's vicar following the Resurrection). As usual, Beatrice asks the spirits to grant Dante's still unspoken wish. The tone of her prayer is clear enough, but its ellipses and metaphoric shifts require some agility of the reader:

What Dante is burning for is, of course, the revelation on which these spirits feed, forever replete (the Feast of the Lamb of God). God's grace has given him a foretaste of that feast while he is yet in the flesh: not, so to speak, a seat at Heaven's table but some of the scraps from it.

In recognition of the immensity and worthiness of Dante's wish, therefore, Beatrice asks these spirits to bless his thirst to know ("bedew him from your plenty"). Dew as a blessing and a refreshment is a well-established metaphor. Beatrice carries it a step further (relating it to the scraps of Heaven's table) by pointing out that the elect drink forever (their thirst forever sated) the waters of that Font (the Presence of God) for which the man thirsts (who would be gratified by so much as a drop from the waters of that illimitable spring).

10–18. It is a little difficult to visualize the dance of the triumphant souls. Dante says they formed into a sphere with fixed poles and compares them to clockwork. But Dante often uses "sphere" and "wheel" interchangeably. It is reasonable, therefore, to visualize the souls as forming into a great wheel of substantial depth (perhaps another millstone) that revolves around a fixed axis ("fixed poles"). The image of clockwork suggests (and the action of the next two cantos verifies) that the wheel is above Dante and broadside to him.

Within that vertical wheel the souls dance in circles to express the joy they feel in being able to give joy to Dante and Beatrice. So rapidly do they spin their circles that they appear only as wheels of light. Like clockwork—i.e., many motions contained within one master motion—the individual wheels spin at various rates. Since the speed with which each soul circles indicates the degree of bliss it feels, and knowing Dante's inclination to set things forth in exact gradations, it seems well to think of each wheel as being produced by the circling of a single soul rather than by a group of souls dancing in a ring.

19. *one . . . the loveliest of them all:* The radiance of St. Peter.

22. *three times:* It would be all but impossible for Dante to use the number three without intending the Trinity.

23–24. *my imagination fails:* Dante is not only unable to express, but he cannot even reimagine the blessèd beauty of Peter's song.

25. *my pen leaps:* Cf. XXIII, 62.

27. *the folds of Heaven's draperies are too bright:* To indicate the folds of a drapery, a painter must shadow the recesses of the cloth while highlighting the raised surfaces. But the inner radiance of heavenly things is such that the folds shine as bright as the surfaces, or, perhaps, Dante means to say more brightly.

Or in another, or in a complementary sense: A painter can depict the folds of draperies only when subtleties of color are available to him, and human speech and human imagination are too gross to portray the subtleties of Heaven.

31. *that Fire of Love:* St. Peter. Note that he has already descended from the great wheel, so prompt are the souls of Heaven to give joy.

39. See *Matthew* xiv, 28 ff.

44. *he will the better praise it:* To men, on his return to Earth.

46. *bachelor:* As in "bachelor of arts," i.e., a candidate for a learned degree.

48. *for defending, not deciding:* The candidate marshals and evaluates the evidence which he submits to the master. Only the master decides. The relation is essentially that of lawyer and judge.

51. *such an examiner:* St. Peter. *and such a profession:* Of the Christian faith.

52–147. THE EXAMINATION OF FAITH. It may seem a spectacular action for Dante to be examined on his catechism by St. Peter himself (in the next two cantos he is further examined by St. James as the Apostle of Hope and by St. John as the Apostle of Love), yet, properly understood, the conception is a sublime one. For in a final sense every man of the faith must answer to nothing less than the Apostolic Creed, making himself worthy to be examined by the true source. As, allegorically, all values must be derived from the supreme test of values.

The examination is divided into six parts:

52–81. WHAT IS FAITH? The anonymous *Epistle to the Hebrews* (which Dante attributes to St. Paul) provides the source of the first answer (XI, 1) "Now faith is the substance of things hoped for, the evidence of things not seen."

substance: In Scholastic terminology "what exists in itself." But Aquinas had set forth that "No quality is a substance; but faith is a quality." Faith, therefore, could not be a substance. Dante circumvents this difficulty, perhaps more ingeniously than persuasively, by rendering the *"substantia"* of *Hebrews* as "that which stands under" *(sub* and *stare).*

argument: The means whereby the intellect reaches toward the inherent truth of things. It is necessary but limited, as reason is limited.

quiddity: See XX, 92. The companion term "quality" signifies the likeness of a thing to something else, "quiddity" signifying the way in which a thing is like itself.

59. *captain of the first rank:* St. Peter. Dante calls him *"l'alto primipilo,"* literally, "the chief fighter in the first rank" according to the classifications of the Roman army. Such is St. Peter's rank in the militia of Christ.

62. *of your dear brother:* St. Paul.

79–81. *through mortal teaching:* As distinct from Heavenly revelation. Could all men grasp that much as firmly as Dante has done, the fine spun arguments of the sophists would find no audience on earth, for none would pay attention to them.

82–87. THE POSSESSION OF FAITH. *Such was the breath of that love's ecstasy:* Below this height of Heaven Dante had been content with such phrases as "so spoke that radiance." But the conversations of high Heaven will not answer to the terms that describe human discourse. Dante is conversing not with a man but with a breath that issues from a radiance. *this coinage:* The golden coinage of faith by which man purchases Heaven. *weight:* Faith as argument. *content:* Faith as substance.

Peter then asks if Dante has faith: "Have you this coinage in your purse?" (I could find no rhyme for "purse" and had to settle for "in your possession.") Dante affirms that he does indeed have it, so bright (clear) and so round (not worn down by usage nor clipped or shaved by subterfuge) that he is left in no doubt of the mint impression (i.e., there is no uncertainty about his faith).

89–96. THE SOURCES OF FAITH. Dante affirms that his faith comes to him from the word of God as set forth in the Testaments ("the Sacred Scrolls, both New and Old"). *this dear gem:* Faith.

97–102. THE PROOF OF THE TRUTH OF FAITH. Dante affirms that he knows the divine truth of Scripture by the proof of the works (the miracles) that followed from them. *these propositions:* The Testaments. A metaphoric extension of the preceding terminology of logic. *works that followed:* Miracles. Nothing in nature (here conceived as a smithy) could bring such works into being.

103–114. HOW DO WE KNOW THE MIRACLES DESCRIBED IN THE OLD AND NEW TESTAMENTS ACTUALLY OC-CURRED? Scripture, says St. Peter, seeks to prove itself as the word of God by asserting the existence of miracles. But if one has not actually observed a miracle, he has only Scripture's own word for it. How then can he be sure of the truth of miracles?

With the sort of ingenuity that characterizes Scholastic argument at times, Dante delivers his final and (to him) most telling argument:

had the miracles reported by Scripture not taken place, one would have to assert an even greater miracle to explain how Christianity had spread through "the whole world" without divine intercession. St. Augustine had used the same argument as proof of the truth of Scripture.

At Dante's words the redeemed souls break into a hymn of praise.

what seeks to prove itself: Scripture. *field:* Battlefield. As God's Captain of the first rank Peter entered the field of pagan Rome and sowed there the good seed of faith. *that was a vine . . . now a thorn:* Another denunciation of papal corruption. Peter had planted the Lord's vineyard (the Church) but corruption has left only a barren thicket choked by thorns.

115–147. IN WHAT DOES A CHRISTIAN HAVE FAITH? "That Baron" (St. Peter) asks in *what* Dante believes and from what source he derives it and how he derives it. Dante affirms his belief in a single triune and everlasting God, and declares that he is persuaded to believe by physical, metaphysical, and scriptural proofs.

124–125. *now can see what faith once held so firmly:* The Triumph of Christ, a matter of faith during his mortal life, a fact forever before his eyes in Heaven.

125–126. *you were prompter than younger feet:* See John xx, 3–10. St. John was the first to approach the tomb of Christ, but Peter was the first to enter it and the first to believe in the resurrection. The greater promptness indicates the greater zeal, and thus the greater triumph of the heavenly soul.

128. *form:* In Scholastic terminology, the same as the Platonic Form, the idea of the thing, which is independent of particular instances, as, for example, the "form" of Justice would exist noumenally, if only in God's mind, even if no single instance of Justice could be found on earth. Contingency is that which comes into being as an instance of form, the form itself being eternal.

130–132. THE ATTRIBUTES OF GOD. *loved, desired:* See I, 77. *sole:* Not plural as believed by the pagans and by various heretical sects. *eternal:* Without beginning or end, contrary to the heresy that ascribed a beginning to God and, hence, duration. *moves . . . Himself unmoved:* against the heresy that God was moved (affected) by things,

Dante asserts his unchangeability, for God is perfect and any change (motion) in Him would have to be away from perfection.

136–138. *Moses, the prophets, the psalms:* i.e., the Old Testament, *the Evangel and through you:* The New Testament, commonly divided into the Evangelical and Apostolic books. *you:* The Italian is the plural form *"voi."* The reference, therefore, is to all the apostles. *people:* In mercy's heavenly name, the reader is requested to avert his eyes as he passes this rhyme.

143. *the teachings of the evangels in many places:* Among various New Testament passages that assert the Unity of the Trinity, see *Matthew* xxviii, 19, and *John* v, 19 ff.

154. *danced three times round me:* Dante implies no proud boast in being so honored by St. Peter. Peter would rejoice in the same way over any soul that has shone Dante's zeal and faith.

CANTO XXV

The Eighth Sphere: The Fixed Stars—St. James ·
The Examination of Hope · St. John the Apostle

Dante, blessed by St. John himself as a reward for his labors and
his hope, declares that if his poem may serve to soften his sen-
tence of exile from Florence, he will return to his baptismal font
at San Giovanni and there place on his own head the poet's lau-
rel wreath. Such is one of the great hopes of his poem, and on
that note *St. James,* the Apostle of Hope, shows himself.

Beatrice begs James to conduct the *Examination of Hope* and
she herself, in answer to the first question, testifies to Dante's *Pos-
session of Hope.* Dante then replies on *The Nature of Hope,* on the
Content of His Hope, and on the *Sources of Hope.*

The examination triumphantly concluded, a cry in praise of
the grace of hope rings through Paradise, and thereupon *St. John
the Apostle* appears. Dante stares into John's radiance hoping to see
the lineaments of his mortal body. The voice of John, the Apos-
tle of Love (*caritas*) calls to him that what he seeks is not there,
and when Dante looks away he discovers he has been *Blinded by
the Radiance of Love.*

If ever it comes to pass that the sacred song,
   to which both heaven and earth so set their hand
   that I grew lean with laboring years long,   3

wins over the cruelty that exiles me
   from the sweet sheepfold where I slept, a lamb,
   and to the raiding wolves an enemy;   6

with a changed voice and with my fleece full grown
   I shall return to my baptismal font,
   a poet, and there assume the laurel crown;   9

for there I entered the faith that lets us grow
  into God's recognition; and for that faith
  Peter, as I have said, circled my brow.   12

Thereafter another radiance came forth
  from the same sphere out of whose joy had come
  the first flower of Christ's vicarage on earth.   15

And my lady, filled with ecstasy and aglow,
  cried to me:"Look! Look there! It is the baron
  for whom men throng to Galicia there below!"   18

At times, on earth, I have seen a mating dove
  alight by another, and each turn to each,
  circling and murmuring to express their love;   21

exactly so, within the eighth great sphere,
  one glorious great lord greeted the other,
  praising the diet that regales them there.   24

Those glories, having greeted and been greeted,
  turned and stood before me, still and silent,
  so bright I turned my eyes away defeated.   27

And Beatrice said, smiling her blessedness:
  "Illustrious being in whose chronicle
  is written our celestial court's largesse,   30

let hope, I pray, be sounded at this height.
  How often you personified that grace
  when Jesus gave His chosen three more light!   33

"Lift up your head, look up and do not fear,
  for all that rises from the mortal world
  must ripen in our rays from sphere to sphere."   36

So spoke the second flame to comfort me;
  and I raised my eyes to the mountains that before
  had borne them down by their weight of majesty.   39

"Since of His grace Our Lord and Emperor calls
  and bids you come while still in mortal flesh
  among His counts in His most secret halls;   42

that you, the truth of this great court made clear,
  may make the stronger, in yourself and others,
  the hope that makes men love the good down there,   45

say what it is, what power helped you to climb,
  and how you bear its flowering in your mind."
  —So spoke the second flame a second time.   48

And that devout sweet spirit that had led
  the feathers of my wings in that high flight
  anticipated my reply, and said: 51

"Church Militant, as is written in the Sun
  whose ray lights all our hosts, does not possess
  a single child richer in hope—not one.   54

It was for that he was allowed to come
  from Egypt to behold Jerusalem
  before his warring years had reached their sum.   57

The other two points—raised not that you may know
  but that he may report how great a pleasure
  hope is to you, when he returns below—   60

I leave to him. They will not be difficult.
  Nor will the truth seem boastful. Let him answer
  and may God's grace appear in the result."   63

As a pupil who is eager to reply
  to his professor, knowing his subject well,
  and quick to show his excellence—such was I.   66

"Hope," I said, "is the certain expectation
  of future glory. It is the blessèd fruit
  of grace divine and the good a man has done.   69

From many stars this light descends to me,"
  but it was first distilled into my heart
  by the ultimate singer of Ultimate Majesty.   72

'Let them hope in Thee,' sang the God-praising poet,
  'whoso doeth know Thy name!' And who can feel
  a faith as firm as mine is and not know it?   75

And your epistle sent down once again
  a fresh dew on his dew, till I was full
  and overflowed to others your sweet rain."   78

While I was speaking thus a luminescence
  trembled within the bosom of that flame,
  sudden and bright as lightning's incandescence.   81

"Love that still burns in me," I heard it breathe,
  "for that grace that followed even to the palm,
  and till I left the field for happy death,   84

moves me to speak further: you know the true
  and lasting joy she brings: gladden me, therefore,
  by telling me what Hope holds forth to you."   87

And I: "From scripture, new and old, descends
  the symbol, and the symbol points me to it.
  All those whom God has chosen as His friends—   90

as Isaiah testifies—they shall be dressed
  in double raiment in their native land;
  and that land is this sweet life with the blest.   93

And your brother, where he writes so ardently
  of the white robes, sets forth this revelation
  in great detail for all of us to see."   96

As soon as I had spoken there rang clear
  from overhead, "Let them hope in Thee, O Lord!"
  and the response rang back from all that sphere.   99

At once within that choir there blazed a ray
  so bright that if the Crab had such a star
  one month of winter would be a single day.   102

And as a joyous maid will rise and go
  to join the dance, in honor of the bride
  and not for any reasons of vain show,   105

so did that radiant splendor, there above,
  go to the two who danced a joyous reel
  in fit expression of their burning love.   108

It joined them in the words and melody;
  and like a bride, immovable and silent,
  my lady kept her eyes fixed on their glory.   111

"This is he who lies upon the breast
  of Our Pelican; and this is He elected
  from off the cross to make the great behest."   114

So spoke my lady, nor, her pose unbroken,
  did she once let her rapt attention stray,
  either before or after she had spoken.   117

As one who stares, squinting against the light,
  to see the sun enter a partial eclipse,
  and in the act of looking loses his sight—   120

so did I stare at the last flame from that sphere
  until a voice said, "Why do you blind yourself
  trying to see what has no true place here?   123

My body is earth in earth where it shall be
  one with the rest until our numbers grow
  to fill the quota of eternity.   126

Only the Two Lamps that are most aglow
  rose to their blessèd cloister doubly clad.
  Explain this to your world when you go below."   129

And when these words were said the flaming wreath
  broke off the dancing and the sweet accord
  in which it had combined its three-part breath,   132

as oars that have been striking through the sea
  pause all together when a whistle sounds
  to signal rest or some emergency.   135

Ah, what a surge of feeling swept my mind
  when I turned away an instant from such splendor
  to look at Beatrice, only to find   138

I could not see her with my dazzled eyes,
  though I stood near her and in Paradise!

NOTES

1–12. DANTE'S HOPE. Dante has just been examined on his Faith,
the first of the Christian Graces. Now he will be examined on Hope,

the second. As a first sounding of the theme of Hope, perhaps to demonstrate that hope is ever green within him, he declares his dream of returning to Florence and of being crowned with a laurel wreath (baptized as a poet) at the font of "his beautiful San Giovanni" at which he was baptized into the faith, for the possession of which St. Peter so honored him at the end of the last canto.

3. *that I grew lean:* With the labor of writing his great poem.

5–6. *the sweet sheepfold:* Florence, *the wolves:* The leaders of Florentine politics.

7. *with a changed voice:* He will return not as a singer of love songs, as he began, but as the master singer of God's universal scheme. And not as a baby but as a man. *and with my fleece full grown:* Continues the lamb image of line 5.

13. *Thereafter:* After St. Peter had three times circled Dante's brow.

14. *the same sphere:* Not from the Sphere of the Fixed Stars, the Eighth Heaven, in which Dante, Beatrice, and these souls are, but from the sphere of light the souls had formed for joy when Beatrice uttered her prayer (XXIV, 12).

17–18. *the baron . . . Galicia:* The second of the barons of Christ is St. James. His tomb is in Santiago di Compostela in Galicia, Spain, and was a shrine to which many pilgrimages were made in the Middle Ages.

23. *one glorious great lord:* St. Peter. *the other:* St. James.

24. *the diet that regales them there:* The love of others, *caritas.*

29–33. *in whose chronicle . . . largesse:* i.e., "whose writings tell of the generosity and benevolence of the court of Heaven." See *Epistle of James* i, 5, 17. Dante seems to have confused two St. Jameses into one. The *Epistle of James* is generally attributed to the James called "the Lord's brother" in *Galatians* i, 19 (see also *Acts* xv, 13) not to James the Apostle whose shrine is in Compostela. *let hope be sounded at this height:* St. James was particularly associated with the grace of hope. In Heaven, however, there is nothing to hope for, all having been achieved. *his chosen three: Matthew* (xvii, 1 ff.), *Mark* (ix, 2), and *Luke* (viii, 51, and ix, 28) all cite the special trust Jesus placed in Peter, James, and John ("gave his chosen three more light"). Medieval commentators on Scripture cited them as the three pillars of the church and had them representing the Christian Graces, Peter representing Faith; James, Hope; and John, Charity (*caritas*).

34–36. *do not fear:* Dante is afraid the splendor will blind him. St. James, as a first example of hope, perhaps, reassures him; these rays do not destroy but strengthen, preparing Dante's developing soul for the vision of God. "Sphere to sphere" is a rhyme-forced addition, not in the text but implicit.

37. *second flame:* St. James.

38. *mountains:* Peter and James. So called to indicate their stature among the blessèd. (See *Psalms* lxxxvi, 1, cxx, 1, and *Matthew* v, 14.).

48. *So spoke:* This, of course, is Dante's way of saying that St. James had spoken lines 34–36, that Dante had obeyed him (lines 37–39), and that St. James had then continued (lines 40–47).

49. *that devout sweet spirit:* Beatrice.

49–63. THE EXAMINATION OF HOPE. In lines 46–47, St. James has put three questions to Dante, the last of which asks if Dante possesses the Grace of Hope. Before Dante can speak, Beatrice answers for him that no man in the church possesses more, for how else could he have ascended to Heaven itself? Were Dante to speak the greatness of his hope, however, his words might seem immodest. It is for this reason that she (Divine Revelation) speaks for him.

The other two questions are "What is Hope?" and "What are its sources?" On these points she will let Dante speak, not that James (who already knows) needs his reply, but to let Dante say it out in order that he may return to Earth with a full accounting in terms mortal reason can grasp.

52. *the Sun:* God. Dante's hope is known to God, therefore, to all the blessèd.

56–57. *Egypt:* The mortal life, earthly bondage. *Jerusalem:* Heaven, deliverance. *warring years:* Dante's mortal years in the church militant.

58. *not that you may know:* Since he knows already, informed by the ray of God.

59–60. *how great a pleasure hope is to you:* As the special patron of the grace he himself no longer needs.

67–69. THE NATURE OF HOPE. These lines are Dante's answer to "say what it is" (line 45).

70–78. THE SOURCES OF HOPE. Dante offers no physical or metaphysical proofs. Hope arises in man as a direct revelation, its light coming "from many stars" (many sacred writings), the first of them, for him, being the Psalms and the second St. James' own epistle. *ultimate singer of Ultimate Majesty . . . the God-praising poet:* David. *"Let them hope in thee . . .": Psalms* ix, 11.

83–84. *that grace:* Hope, *the palm:* Martydom. *left the field:* Abandoned the warfare of the church militant for the bliss of the church triumphant, i.e., heaven.

86. *her:* Hope.

88–96. THE PROMISE (OR OBJECT) OF HOPE. The one hope that matters is, of course, the hope of Heaven. *the symbol:* Of the blessings to which hope leads. *it:* Hope. Sense: The scriptures show the good that awaits those who hope in God, and the good so symbolized points me to hope.

91–92. *Isaiah testifies:* See *Isaiah* lxi, 7. *double raiment:* The glory in which Dante sees the souls clad plus the glory of the resurrected flesh after the Day of Judgment.

94–96. *your brother:* St. John. *where he writes . . . white robes: Apocalypse* vii.

97–102. Dante has affirmed the promise of hope offered by the revelations of Scripture, particularly of Isaiah in the Old Testament and of John in the New. As soon as he has spoken, the words of the Ninth Psalm ring out from far above and all the whirling spheres chorus the response. Then, from among them, there grows a splendor that outshines all others there. It is the soul of St. John, the apostle of love, and brightest of the chosen three as Love (*caritas*) is the greatest of the Christian Graces.

100. *a ray:* St. John.

101–102. *so bright:* That if the Crab (the constellation which is the zodiacal sign for December and January) contained a star as bright, that winter month would be one long day, the light of such a star replacing the light of the sun during the night hours.

113. *Our Pelican:* One of the medieval epithets for Christ. The pelican was believed to nourish its young by striking its breast until it bled and then giving them its blood. Another legend ran that the pelican performed in this way when it found its young dead, reviving them with its blood.

113–114. *chosen from off the cross:* Chosen by Christ while He was on the cross to remain behind and be a son to Mary (*John* xix, 26–27).

118–135. THE LEGEND OF ST. JOHN. *John* xxi, 20–23, provided the basis for the medieval legend that St. John had been translated to heaven body and soul. Here, Dante sets out to correct that misinterpretation of scripture.

He starts with a long-tail simile of a man who has heard there will be a partial eclipse of the sun and who, therefore, allows himself to look directly at it and becomes blind in trying to see what he cannot bear. The eclipse here would, of course, be the darkening of the soul's radiance when the physical body moves in front of it.

As Dante is staring, the voice of St. John asks why he is blinding himself in the useless effort to see what is not there (see *I Corinthians* xv, 50). St. John's mortal body, as he tells Dante, is in the earth. Only Jesus and Mary ascended to heaven in their physical bodies. (Some readers will recall that Enoch and Elijah were translated to heaven in their physical bodies, but Dante is obviously following the legend that they were borne only as high as the Terrestrial Paradise.)

125. *one with the rest:* One among all other mortal bodies left in the earth and indistinguishable from them until the resurrection.

125–126. *until our number . . . quota of eternity:* Clearly, Dante believes that God has ordained salvation for some exact number of souls and that the Judgment will follow when the last elected soul has been gathered to Heaven.

127–128. *the Two Lamps that are most aglow:* Christ and Mary. *doubly clad:* In body and soul.

130–135. In the usual order of his long-tail similes, Dante puts the likeness first and then compares to it the thing that is like it. Here he reverses that usual order, first describing the action, and then comparing it.

136. DANTE SUFFERS TEMPORARY BLINDNESS. Turning from the splendors before him to speak to Beatrice, Dante discovers that he cannot see her! I take St. John's remarks at the beginning of the next canto as the key to this allegory on the progress of the soul. God is beyond our mortal senses. The true vision can come, therefore, only when the senses are enlarged, having been shattered in the blaze of revelation and replaced by a new perception. As St. John says in line 12 of the next canto, Beatrice (Divine Revelation) has the power to heal. Not only will she remove Dante's blindness but he will see the better for it.

CANTO XXVI

*The Eighth Sphere: The Fixed Stars—Examination of Love
(Caritas) · Adam*

John assures Dante that Beatrice will restore his sight. Dante expresses his willingness to await her will since he knows her to be Love. John, thereupon, begins the *Examination of Love,* asking Dante to explain how he came into the *Possession of Love,* and what drove him to seek it. He then asks Dante to describe the *Intensity of Love* and to discuss the *Sources of Love.*

Dante concludes with a praise of God as the source of Love. At his words all Heaven responds with a paean, and immediately *Dante's Vision Is Restored.*

There appears before him a fourth great splendor which Beatrice identifies as the soul of *Adam.* Dante begs Adam to speak, and learns from him the *Date of Adam's Creation, How Long Adam Remained in Eden, The Cause of God's Wrath,* and *What Language Adam Spoke in His Time on Earth.*

While I stood thus confounded, my light shed,
   out of the dazzling flame that had consumed it
   I heard a breath that called to me, and said: 3

"Until your eyes once more regain their sense
   of the sight you lost in me, it will be well
   for discourse to provide a recompense.   6

Speak, therefore, starting with the thing that most
   summons your soul to it, and be assured
   your sight is only dazzled and not lost;   9

for she who guides you through this holy land
   has, in a single turning of her eyes,
   the power that lay in Ananias' hand."   12

"As she wills, late or soon, let remedy
  come to my eyes," I said, "the gate through which
  she brought the fire that ever burns in me.   15

The Good that is this cloister's happiness
  is the Alpha and Omega of the scripture
  love reads to me with light and heavy stress."   18

The same voice that had soothed my fear away
  when I found suddenly that I could not see
  called me back to the question. I heard it say: 21

"Surely a finer sieve must sift this through.
  You must explain what made you draw your bow
  at this exalted target—what and who."   24

And I: "By the arguments of philosophy
  and by authority that descends from here
  such Love has clearly stamped its seal upon me.   27

For the Good, to the extent imperfect sense
  grasp its goodness, kindles love; the brighter
  the more we understand its excellence.   30

To the Essence then in which lies such perfection
  that every good thing not immediate to It
  is nothing more than Its own ray's reflection—   33

to It, above all else, the mind must move
  once it has seen the truth that is the proof
  and argument that so compels man's love.   36

That truth he first made evident to me
  whose proofs set forth the First Cause and First Love
  of every sempiternal entity.   39

It was proved by the True Maker's voice sent forth
  to Moses when It said, meaning Itself,
  'I shall cause you to see a vision of all worth.'   42

And proved by you in the high proclamation
  that cries to earth the secrets of this heaven
  more clearly than any other revelation."   45

And I heard: "As human reason and Holy Writ
  in harmony have urged you, keep for God
  the first, most sovereign passion of your spirit.   48

But tell me if you feel yet other ties
  bind you to Him. Say with how many teeth
  this love consumes you." So in Paradise   51

Christ's Eagle spoke his sacred purpose whole,
  concealing nothing; rather, urging me
  to make a full profession of my soul.   54

I therefore: "All those teeth with power enough
  to turn the heart of any man to God
  have joined in my heart, turning it to Love.   57

The existence of the world, and my own, too;
  the death He took on Himself that I might live;
  and what all believers hope for as I do—   60

these and the living knowledge mentioned before
  have saved me from the ocean of false love
  and place me by the true, safe on the shore.   63

The leaves that green the Eternal Garden's grove
  I love to the degree that each receives
  the dew and ray of His all flowering love."   66

The instant I fell still, my love professed,
  all Heaven rang with "Holy! Holy! Holy!"
  my lady joining with the other blest.   69

As bright light shatters sleep, the man being bid
  to waken by the visual spirit running
  to meet the radiance piercing lid by lid,   72

and the man so roused does not know what he sees,
  his wits confounded by the sudden waking,
  till he once more regains his faculties;   75

so from my eyes, my lady's eyes, whose ray
  was visible from a thousand miles and more,
  drove every last impediment away;   78

in consequence of which I found my sight
  was clearer than before, and half astonished,
  I questioned her about a fourth great light   81

near us, and she: "In that ray's Paradise
  the first soul from the hand of the First Power
  turns ever to its maker its glad eyes."   84

As a bough that bends its crown to the wind's course,
  and then, after the blow, rises again
  uplifted by its own internal force;   87

so did I as she spoke, all tremulous;
  then calmed again, assured by a desire
  to speak that burned in me, beginning thus: 90

"O first and only fruit earth ever saw
  spring forth full ripe; O primal sire, to whom
  all brides are equally daughters and daughters-in-law; 93

speak, I beg, devoutly as I may.
 You know my wish. To hear you speak the sooner
 I leave unsaid what there is no need to say."   96

An animal, were it covered with a shawl
 and moved beneath it, would reveal its motion
 by the way in which the cloth would rise and fall;   99

in the same way, that first soul let me see
 through the motion of its covering, with what joy
 it moved in Heaven to bring joy to me.   102

Then breathed forth: "Without any need to hear
 what you would say, I know your wish more surely
 than you know what you take to be most clear.   105

I see it in the True Mirror, Itself the perfect
 reflector of all things in Its creation,
 which nothing in creation can reflect.   108

You wish to know how many years it is
 since God created me in the high garden
 where she prepared you for these stairs to bliss;   111

and how long my eyes enjoyed the good they prized;
 and the true reason for the great rejection;
 and the tongue I spoke, which I myself devised.   114

Know, my son, that eating from the tree
 was not itself the cause of such long exile,
 but only the violation of God's decree.   117

Longing to join this company, my shade
 counted four thousand three hundred and two suns
 where your lady summoned Virgil to your aid.   120

And circling all its signs, I saw it go
  nine hundred and thirty times around its track
  during the time I was a man below.   123

The tongue I spoke had vanished utterly
  long before Nimrod's people turned their hands
  to the work beyond their capability,   126

for nothing of the mind is beyond change:
  man's inclination answers to the stars
  and ranges as the starry courses range.   129

That man should speak is nature's own behest;
  but that you speak in this way or in that
  nature lets you decide as you think best.   132

Till I went down to the agony of Hell
  the Supreme Good whose rays send down the joy
  that wraps me here was known on earth as *EL;*   135

and then was known as *JAH;* and it must be so,
  for the usage of mankind is like a leaf
  that falls from the branch to let another grow. 138

On the peak that rises highest, my total stay,
  in innocence and later in disgrace,
  was from the first bright hour of my first day, 141

to the hour after the sixth, at which the sun
  changed quadrant, being then at meridian."

NOTES

12. *the power . . . Ananias' hand:* Ananias cured the blindness of
St. Paul by the laying on of hands. *Acts* ix, 10 ff.

16–18. The gist of this passage is that the love of Beatrice (Revelation) is identical with the love of God. Beyond that gist, almost every commentator has his own interpretation. "The Good" is clearly God, the joy of heaven's cloister, and the Alpha and Omega of all scripture. But is scripture to be taken as specifically Holy Scripture, as all that Christian Love has been able to read of God's intent, or as both together? And is "light and heavy stress" to be taken poetically to signify "both accented and unaccented feet" (i.e., reading every last syllable), or to signify "both the more and the less important messages," or (again) some combination of the two?

19–66. THE EXAMINATION OF LOVE. In lines 4–9 St. John had called on Dante to discourse on love (the love of God, Christian love, *caritas*) assuring him in lines 10–12 that Beatrice (Divine Revelation) would restore his sight. Dante replies that he will await her pleasure since it was through his eyes that she first brought him the fire of love with which he burns. He then adds the generalized and elusive comment of lines 16–18. Now St. John calls Dante to a more searching examination and a more detailed answer. So to the first question of the examination proper: by whose hand (by what means) was the bow of his intention aimed at such a target as love?

25. *from here:* Heaven. The authority from Heaven is Scripture.

26–63. THE SOURCES OF LOVE. Dante answers that the knowledge of God's goodness inevitably leads to love and that the sources of that knowledge are, jointly, human reason and divine revelation. St. John, however, presses Dante to speak of the intensity of love and of his other promptings to it. So pressed, Dante cites the existence of the world as the creation of Divine Love, his own existence, the death Jesus took upon Himself, and the hope that is common to all faith.

37. *That truth:* That God is the Supreme Good and Supreme Love. *he:* Possibly Plato. "The Symposium" identifies love as the first of all the eternal essences. But more likely Aristotle who argued a single God of Love as the first principle of creation, the "unmoved mover" of "The Metaphysics" which is "the object of desire."

40–42. *See Exodus* xxxiii, 19.

43–45. "I am Alpha and Omega, the beginning and the ending, saith the Lord which is, and which was, and which is to come, the Almighty" (*Revelation* i, 8).

50–57. *teeth:* Urgings, promptings. It is not by accident that the Apostle of Love uses such a figure and that Dante repeats it. A softer figure would detract from the ardor necessary to the love of God, about which there can be nothing bland.

52. *Christ's Eagle:* St. John.

61. *the living knowledge mentioned before:* That God is the Supreme Good.

63. *by the true:* By the sea of true love. Cf. *Inferno* I, 91 ff.

64–66. The Eternal Gardener is, of course, God; His grove, the world; its leaves, mankind. Heretofore Dante has discussed only Love of God. Here he adds Love of Others. Men are worthy of love to the extent each is loved by God. (Cf. *Inferno* XX, 26–30, where Virgil scolds Dante for the impiety of pitying those whom God has justly damned.)

70–72. In simplest gloss: "As a bright light wakes a sleeping man." But how does the light reach the man's consciousness when he is asleep? Dante follows medieval authorities, Albertus Magnus among them, who posited a "visual spirit," an essence of man's nervous system which rises to respond to the light penetrating the layers of the eyelid and eye. Albertus Magnus theorized that this visual spirit rose from the vapors of certain delicate foods.

78. *drove every last impediment away:* The power of Beatrice's thousand-mile ray having penetrated the lids (of blindness) that covered Dante's eyes after the dazzling vision of St. John, rouses Dante's visual spirit and he is able to see again, more clearly than before. The figure will seem strange to present-day physiologists but the moral is clear: only as one loses his mortal senses can he endure the enlargement of revelation.

83. *the first soul:* Adam.

91. *only:* Eve might be thought to be such a fruit but Dante must have thought of her as part of Adam. *Genesis* ii, 22–24 would have given him ample scriptural authority for such a view.

97–102. Not Dante's most felicitous figure. It hardly honors the First Father to be compared to an animal under a cloth, the cloth representing his enshrouding radiance. Adam, moreover, is *in* not *under* the radiance. Yet the figure does convey a sense of how things are perceived in Heaven.

109–114. Dante's first wish is to know the date of Adam's creation. (*the exalted garden:* The Terrestrial Paradise. *she:* Beatrice.) His second is to know how long Adam remained there. His third, to know the exact cause of God's wrath. His fourth, to know what language Adam invented for himself.

Adam answers not in the order in which he finds these questions in Dante's mind, but in the order of their importance (a fine subtlety in portraying the heavenly souls) beginning with Original Sin.

118–120. *this company:* Of elected souls. *suns:* Annual, not daily. Were daily suns intended the time would amount to less than twelve years. And any possible ambiguity is resolved in line 121 where Adam speaks of the sun turning through all the signs of the zodiac. *where your lady summoned Virgil:* Limbo.

121–123. *all its signs:* Of the Zodiac. *nine hundred and thirty:* Adam's age at death is so given in *Genesis* v, 5. *below:* on earth.

124–132. In *De vulgari eloquentia*, I, 6, Dante had claimed that Adam's original language was used by all of mankind up to the time Nimrod and his people were stricken at the Tower of Babel; and that it was still spoken thereafter by the Hebrews. As a mortal theorist, Dante was speculating there, as he is here. As the master builder of his own great metaphor, however, this touch in which revelation cancels the earlier error of human reason, is a superb detail. *answer to the stars:* To the influence of the stars. What we call the stars do not vary notably in their courses, but the moon and the planets (stars to Dante) wander all over the face of the heavens causing ever shifting conjunctions.

133–138. *EL . . . JAH:* Dante has Adam speak these syllables as *"J"* and *"EL,"* the *"J"* being a form of *"Y."* in that order, *"Y"* or *"Yeah"* or *"Jah"* followed by *"EL"* may suggest some primitive form of JAHVEH or JAHVEL. Such an interpretation is conjectural, however, and I have transposed the two syllables for rhyme purposes.

139–143. Adam declares that his whole sojourn in the Terrestrial Paradise was six hours (and perhaps part of the seventh). His time was from the dawn on the day of his creation, to the hour that follows the sixth. The total circuit of the sun is 360°, which divides into four quadrants of 90° or six hours. Assuming the time of Adam's creation to be at the vernal equinox, when day and night are each twelve hours long, the first hour of light would be from six to seven A.M., the end of the sixth would be at noon, and the hour after the sixth would be from noon to one P.M. Adam says "from the first hour . . . to the hour after the sixth." He does not say how far into that hour he remained, but it would be native to Dante's mind and style to intend Adam's expulsion to fall exactly at high noon. Half an allegorical day is about as long as any man can stay innocent.

CANTO XXVII

The Eighth Sphere: The Fixed Stars—
Denunciation of Papal Corruption

Ascent to the Primum Mobile

St. Peter grows red with righteous indignation and utters a *Denunciation of Papal Corruption.* All Heaven darkens at the thought of such evil. Peter's charge, of course, is that the papacy has become acquisitive, political, and therefore bloody. Having so catalogued the crimes of the bad popes, Peter specifically charges Dante to repeat among mankind the wrath that was spoken in Heaven.

The triumphant court soars away and Dante is left with Beatrice who tells him to look down. Dante finds he is standing above a point midway between Jerusalem and Spain, and having seen earth (and all its vaunted pomps) as an insignificant mote in space, Dante once more turns his thoughts upward as Beatrice leads him in the *Ascent to the Primum Mobile,* discoursing en route on the *Nature of Time* (which has its source in the Primum Mobile). The *Time of Earth's Corruption,* Beatrice tells Dante, is drawing to a close.

"Glory to the Father, the Son, and the Holy Ghost"—
   a strain so sweet that I grew drunk with it
   rang from the full choir of the heavenly host.   3

I seemed to see the universe alight
   with a single smile; and thus my drunkenness
   came on me through my hearing and my sight.   6

O joy! O blessedness no tongue can speak!
   O life conjoint of perfect love and peace!
   O sure wealth that has nothing more to seek!   9

The four great torches were still burning there,
   and the one that had descended to me first
   began to outshine all else in that sphere.   12

As Jupiter might appear if it and Mars
  were birds and could exchange their glowing plumes—
  such it became among the other stars.   15

The Providence that assigns to Heaven's band
  the offices and services of each,
  had imposed silence there on every hand   18

when I heard: "You need not wonder that I change hue,
  for as I utter what I have to say
  you shall see all these beings change theirs, too.   21

The usurper of the throne given to me,
  to me, to me, there on the earth that now
  before the Son of God stands vacant, he   24

has made a sewer of my sepulcher, a flow
  of blood and stink at which the treacherous one
  who fell from here may chuckle there below."   27

With the same color I have seen clouds turn
  when opposite the rising or setting sun,
  I saw the sweet face of all heaven burn.   30

And as a modest lady whose pure bearing
  is self-secure, may blush at another's failings,
  though they be only mentioned in her hearing;   33

so Beatrice changed complexion at a breath,
  and such eclipse came over heaven then
  as when Supreme Might suffered mankind's death.   36

Then he continued speaking as before,
  his voice so changed, so charged with indignation
  that his appearance could not darken more: 39

"The bride of Christ was not suckled of old
  on blood of mine, of Linus, and of Cletus
  to be reared as an instrument for grabbing gold.   42

It was to win this life of blessedness
  Sixtus, and Pius, and Calixtus, and Urban
  let flow the blood and tears of their distress.   45

We never meant that men of Christian life
  should sit part on the right, part on the left
  of our successors, steeled for bloody strife.   48

Nor that the keys consigned into my hand
  should fly as emblems from a flag unfurled
  against the baptized in a Christian land.   51

Nor that my head should, in a later age,
  seal privilege sold to liars. The very thought
  has often made me burn with holy rage!   54

From here in every pasture, fold, and hill
  we see wolves dressed as shepherds. O hand of God,
  mankind's defender, why do you yet lie still?   57

Gascons and Cahorsines are crouched to drink
  our very blood. Oh excellent beginning,
  to what foulest conclusion will you sink?   60

Yet the high Providence that stood with Rome
  and Scipio for the glory of the world
  will once again, and soon, be seen to come.   63

You, son, who must yet bear around earth's track
  your mortal weight, open your mouth down there:
  do not hold back what I have not held back!"   66

Just as the frozen vaporings sift down
  out of our earthly atmosphere when the horn
  of heaven's Goat is burnished by the Sun;   69

Just so, up there, I saw the ether glow
  with a rising snow of the triumphant vapors
  who had remained a while with us below.   72

My eyes followed their traces toward the height,
  followed until the airy medium
  closed its vast distance on my upward sight;   75

at which my lady, seeing me absolved
  from service to the height, said: "Now look down
  and see how far the heavens have revolved."   78

I looked down once again. Since the last time,
  I had been borne, I saw, a length of arc
  equal to half the span of the first clime;   81

so that I saw past Cadiz the mad route
  Ulysses took; and almost to the shore
  from which Europa rode the godly brute.   84

And yet more of this little threshing floor
  would have been visible but, below my foot,
  the sun was ahead of me by a sign and more.   87

My mind, which ever found its Paradise
  in thinking of my lady, now more than ever
  burned with desire to look into her eyes.   90

If nature or art ever contrived a lure
  to catch the eye and thus possess the mind,
  whether in living flesh or portraiture,   93

all charms united could not move a pace
  toward the divine delight with which I glowed
  when I looked once more on her smiling face.   96

In one look then I felt my spirit given
  a power that plucked it out of Leda's nest
  and sent it soaring to the swiftest heaven.   99

From its upper and lower limits to its center
  it is so uniform, I cannot say
  what point my lady chose for me to enter.   102

But she, knowing what yearning burned in me,
  began thus—with so rapturous a smile
  God seemed to shine forth from her ecstasy: 105

"The order of the universe, whose nature
  holds firm the center and spins all else around it,
  takes from this heaven its first point of departure.   108

This heaven does not exist in any place
  but in God's mind, where burns the love that turns it
  and the power that rains to it from all of space.   111

Light and Love contain it in one band
  as it does all the rest; and such containment
  only the Cunctitenant can understand.   114

Its own motion unfactored, all things derive
  their motions from this heaven as precisely
  as ten is factored into two and five.   117

So may you understand how time's taproot
  is hidden in this sphere's urn, while in the others
  we see its spreading foliage and its fruit.   120

O Greed that has drawn down all Adam's blood
  so deep into its dark that none has strength
  to raise his eyes above its evil flood!   123

The will of man comes well to its first flower,
  but then the rain that sets in endlessly
  blights the good fruit and leaves it green and sour.   126

Faith and innocence are found nowhere
  except in little children; and both have fled
  before their cheeks have sprouted a first hair.   129

Still young enough to lisp, one fasts and prays;
  then, his tongue freed, devours all sorts of food
  even in Lent, even on fasting days.   132

Another will love his mother and behave
  while yet a lisper, who, with his freed speech
  will be impatient to see her in her grave.   135

So the fair daughter of Him who leaves us night
  and brings us morning, changes her complexion,
  and her white skin turns black in Heaven's sight.   138

Consider, if you marvel at what I say,
  how there is none to govern on the earth,
  whereby the human family goes astray.   141

But before January falls in spring
  because of that odd day in each hundred years
  that all neglect down there, these spheres shall ring   144

so loud with portents of a season's turn
  that the long awaited storm will sweep the fleet,
  blowing the bows around to dead astern   147

and set the true course straight. Then all shall see
first blossom turn to good fruit on the tree."

NOTES

10–11. *the four great torches:* Peter, James, John, and Adam. *the one that had descended to me first:* Peter.

13–15. Jupiter (white) and Mars (red) are conceived here as two firebirds who partially exchange their glowing plumage. The point is that the aura of St. Peter, without losing its essential white brilliance, begins to glow with a redder (more martial) light. The change indicates a change of mood: a fiercer St. Peter is about to denounce the corruption of the Papacy by his evil successors.

17. *offices:* Empowering appointments. Cf. "office of the mass." *services:* The times each is called upon to perform his offices. Since all is preordained by God, each slightest action is from God's will.

21. *change theirs:* Change their hues.

22. *the usurper:* Boniface VIII.

25. *my sepulcher:* Rome as the seat of papal authority. According to tradition, Peter was buried there.

26. *the treacherous one:* Satan.

35–36. "Now from the sixth hour there was darkness over all the land until the ninth hour." *Matthew* xxvii, 45. See also *Mark* xv, 33, and *Luke* xxiii, 44–45. The apostles report the eclipse as darkness and Dante treats it as a reddening. It seems unlikely it was so dark a red as to suggest night shadow. Perhaps Dante saw that flush of righteous indignation as showing like night on earth, but blush-red as seen from heaven's height.

37–39. The quality of the reaction invites a speculation: men work themselves into moods and are carried away by them at times, but heavenly beings express instant recognition and total justice; they register instantly, therefore, the exactly right reaction to things.

41–44. All these here named were early bishops of Rome, Peter's first successor being traditionally believed to be Linus, and his successor, Cletus (Anacletus). The others followed at various intervals: Sixtus 117–circa 127, Pius 142–circa 149, Calixtus 217–222, and

Urban 222–230. Not all were martyred, as line 45 would seem to suggest, but all suffered in the flesh and in the spirit for the sins of mankind.

47–48. *part on the right, part on the left:* To indicate any warring parties of Christians, the bloody divisions of Dante's time being first the Guelphs and Ghibellines, and then the Black and the White Guelphs, those divisions often incited or abetted by the corrupt Popes for purposes of their own politics.

49–51. *keys:* The papal keys, emblems of the Pope's authority were used on the banner of the Vatican States, which had often been carried into battle against Christians—a bloody perversion, in Dante's view, of the papal mission.

52–53. *my head . . . a seal:* The papal seal, stamped on many documents whose intent was venial, bore the purported likeness of St. Peter.

58. *Gascons and Cahorsines:* Clement V was from Gascony; John XXII from Cahors. Both filled the Papal Court with greedy favorites from their native lands. And both, of course, were guilty of the further sin of being French in Italy.

61–63. God's foreseeing provision, as Dante would have understood it, must have helped Scipio overthrow Hannibal, else Rome would not have remained the glory of the world and could not have become the proper seat of holy church.

64–66. This charge, laid upon him by St. Peter himself, is, of course, Dante's ultimate license to denounce papal corruption. Effectively enough, the very charge is itself the ultimate denunciation.

67–75. All the souls who remained below when Mary ascended now rise to the Empyrean like a reverse snowfall. The figure Dante chooses for their ascent is not his most felicitous in that the snow image cannot suggest either the radiance of the souls or the necessary speed of their ascent. *when the horn of heaven's Goat is burnished by the Sun:* The sun is in Capricorn (heaven's Goat) at about mid-January, hence at the time when "frozen vaporings" come down as snow.

79 ff. The last (and first) time Dante looked down was as he entered the Sphere of the Fixed Stars (XXII, 127 ff.). Now, as he is

about to leave this Sphere, he looks down again and sees he has revolved through 90°. He has, therefore, been in this heaven six hours, one quarter of a daily turn. 90° is the amount of arc equal to half the span of the first clime. Geographers of Dante's time divided the northern hemisphere into seven habitable "climes" or "climates" running parallel to the equator. The southern hemisphere, of course, was taken to be water, the Mount of Purgatory excepted, and the northern landmass was taken to spread 180° from Spain to India.

The earthly point above which Dante is passing is about midway between Jerusalem and Spain. He can see the eastern shore of the Mediterranean and westward beyond Spain into the Atlantic. It would be allegorically pleasant to be able to say he was over Rome at this moment before ascending into the last sphere, and Dante may well have had that thought in mind, but nothing in the text permits more than a guess.

82–84. *past Cadiz:* The Atlantic. *the mad route Ulysses took:* See *Inferno* XXVI, 90 ff. *the shore from which Europa:* Phoenicia on the eastern coast of the Mediterranean. Zeus appeared to Europa there as a bull and, taking her on his back, bore her to Crete. "Godly brute" is rhyme-forced: Dante says, literally, "the shore on which Europa became a sweet burden."

85–87. *threshing floor:* The Earth. (See XXII, 127 ff.) *more . . . would have been visible:* Dante's view is cut off by darkness because the Sun is ahead of him in Aries. He is in Gemini. The sign of Taurus lies between. A zodiacal sign covers 30°. The sun, therefore, is something more than two hours ahead of him and perhaps as much as four (if it is in the middle of Aries and he in the middle of Gemini). Part of the world below Dante must, therefore, lie in shadow.

98. *Leda's nest:* Gemini, the sign of the twins, Castor and Pollux. Zeus appeared to Leda as a swan and, according to the most common legend, she bore him Castor and Pollux. "Nest" is a *jeu d'esprit* derived from Zeus's traveling costume when he called on Leda.

100–102. ENTRANCE INTO THE PRIMUM MOBILE. Dante knew he entered the Eighth Sphere at the point of heaven marked by Gemini (XXII, 152). The Ninth Sphere, however, is so uniform that he can make out no point of reference. Beatrice, of course, knows his confusion and hastens to explain to him the nature of the Ninth Sphere.

103. *what yearning:* To understand the nature of the new sphere.

106–108. The firmly held center is the Earth. In the nature of the Ptolemaic universe, whose originating motion is the Primum Mobile, all else is made to revolve around that center.

114. *the Cunctitenant:* God, the all-containing. He contains the Primum Mobile as it contains all else.

115–117. Ten is precisely determined as the product of the factors two and five. The Primum Mobile, itself unfactorable (i.e., defined and limited by nothing), imparts the factors that determine every other motion, setting the speed, regularity, and deviation of every other heavenly motion.

118–120. Time is measured by the motion of the heavenly bodies, but the source of time, like the root of a tree, is hidden in the urn (flowerpot) of the Primum Mobile, while the heavenly bodies show forth in the other spheres as the foliage and fruit of the hidden cause. *So may you understand:* By what I say.

131. *his tongue freed:* When he has grown out of his childish lisp.

132. I have translated what I take to be Dante's intent rather than his words. Dante says simply "in whatever moon," meaning both "in whatever month" (including Lent) and "at whatever time of the month" (including Fridays and other stated days of fasting).

136–138. Few of Dante's tercets are open to so many interpretations. I follow Scartazzini-Vandelli in reading the passage as a denunciation of the corruption of the church, the fair daughter of the Sun (it being always, in Dante, a symbol of God). The Sun, arriving, brings morning and, departing, leaves night. The fair daughter, once immaculately white (the color of innocence) and still apparently so in mortal manifestation shows black (corrupt and evil) in the sight of Heaven.

140. *none to govern:* The Church being corrupt and the Emperor having abandoned Italy.

143. *that odd day in each hundred years:* The calendar as reformed under Julius Caesar fixed the year at 365 days and 6 hours, intro-

ducing an error of about 13 minutes, approximately one hundredth of a day. In each century, therefore, the calendar would move the months a day forward into the advancing season. In a millennium, January would have moved ten days nearer the spring. In 1582, the Gregorian calendar (developed under Pope Gregory XIII) substantially corrected this error.

CANTO XXVIII

The Ninth Sphere: The Primum Mobile—The Angel Hierarchy

Dante turns from Beatrice and beholds a vision of *God as a Non-Dimensional Point of Light* ringed by *Nine Glowing Spheres* representing the *Angel Hierarchy.*

    Dante is puzzled because the vision seems to reverse the order of the Universe, the highest rank of the angels being at the center and represented by the smallest sphere. Beatrice explains the mystery to Dante's satisfaction, if not to the reader's, and goes on to catalogue the *Orders of the Angels.*

When she whose powers imparadise my mind
  had so denounced and laid bare the whole truth
  of the present state of miserable mankind;   3

just as a man before a glass can see
  a torch that burns behind him, and know it is there
  before he has seen or thought of it directly;   6

and turns to see if what the glass has shown
  is really there; and finds, as closely matched
  as words to music, the fact to its reflection;   9

just so, as I recall, did I first stare
  into the heaven of those precious eyes
  in which, to trap me, Love had set his snare;   12

then turned, and turning felt my senses reel
  as my own were struck by what shines in that heaven
  when we look closely at its turning wheel.   15

I saw a Point that radiated light
  of such intensity that the eye it strikes
  must close or ever after lose its sight.   18

The star that seems the smallest, seen from here,
  would seem a moon, were it placed next to this,
  as often we see star by star appear.   21

And at about the distance that a halo
  surrounds a heavenly radiance that paints it
  on the densest mist that will yet let it show;   24

so close around the Point, a ring of fire
  spun faster than the fastest of the spheres
  circles creation in its endless gyre.   27

Another surrounded this, and was surrounded
  by a third, the third by a fourth, the fourth
  by a fifth, and by a sixth the fifth, in turn, was bounded. 30

The seventh followed, already spread so wide
  that were Juno's messenger to be made complete
  she could not stretch her arc from side to side.   33

And so the eighth and the ninth, and each ring spun
  with an ever slower motion as its number
  placed it the further out from the first one,   36

which gave forth the most brilliant incandescence
  because, I think, being nearest the Scintilla,
  it drew the fullest share of the true essence.   39

I was on tenterhooks, as my lady saw.
  To ease my mind she said: "From that one Point
  are hung the heavens and all nature's law.   42

Look at the closest ring: I would have you know
  it spins so fast by virtue of Love's fire,
  the ray of which pierces it through and through."   45

And I to her: "Were the ordering we find
  in the universe like that of these bright wheels,
  what I have seen would satisfy my mind.   48

But in the sensible universe one can see
  the motions of the spheres become more godlike
  the nearer they are to the periphery.   51

If there is food for my soul's appetite
  in this most glorious and angelic temple
  whose only boundaries are love and light,   54

you must explain why it has been so planned
  that the form and the exemplum are at odds;
  for by myself I cannot understand."   57

"It is small wonder such a knot defies
  your fingers, for since none has ever tried it,
  the coils have set together like a vise."   60

So spoke my lady, going on to say:
  "If you would understand, grasp what I tell you,
  and around it give your mind's best powers full play.   63

The physical spheres are graduated in size
  according to the power that infuses each
  and fixes it to its station in the skies.   66

The greater good intends a greater grace.
  A greater body can hold more of good
  if all its parts are perfect, as in this case.   69

This sphere, then, that spins with it as it goes
  all of the universe, must correspond
  to the angel sphere that most loves and most knows.   72

If you will measure not by what appears
  but by the power inherent in these beings
  that manifest themselves to you as spheres,   75

you will observe a marvelous correspondence
  of greater power to larger, and lesser to smaller,
  between each Heaven and its Intelligence."   78

As the airy hemisphere serenes and glows,
  cloudless and blue into its furthest reach,
  when from his gentler cheek Boreas blows,   81

purging and dissolving with that breeze
  the turbulent vapors, so that heaven smiles
  with the beauty of its every diocese;   84

so was it in my mind, once I was given
  my lady's clear reply; and I saw the truth
  shining before me like a star in heaven.   87

And at her last word every angel sphere
  began to sparkle as iron, when it is melted
  in a crucible, is seen to do down here.   90

And every spark spun with its spinning ring:
  and they were numberless as the sum of grain
  on the last square of the chessboard of the king.   93

From choir to choir their hymn of praise rang free
  to the Fixed Point that holds them in fixed place,
  as ever was, as evermore shall be.   96

And she who felt uncertainty bedim
  my dazzled mind explained: "The first two circles
  have shown you the Seraphim and Cherubim.   99

Being led, they chase the reins in their eagerness
  to resemble the Point the more, and they can the more
  the more they look upon Its blessedness.   102

The beings in the next bright wheel you see
  are titled Thrones of the Eternal Aspect;
  and they complete the first great trinity.   105

And know that all these raptures are fulfilled
  to the degree that each can penetrate
  the Truth in which all questioning is stilled.   108

Hence one may see that the most blest condition
  is based on the act of seeing, not of love,
  love being the act that follows recognition.   111

They see as they are worthy. They are made
  to their degrees by grace and their own good will.
  And so their ranks proceed from grade to grade.   114

The second trinity that blossoms here
  in this eternal springtime of delight
  whose leaves nocturnal Aries does not sear,   117

warble 'Hosannah!' everlastingly,
  and their three melodies sound the three degrees
  of blessedness that form this trinity.   120

These are the divinities therein found:
  Dominations first, then Virtues, then, in order,
  the ranks of Powers within the widest round.   123

In the next two dances of this exaltation
  whirl Principalities first, then the Archangels.
  The last contains the Angelic jubilation.   126

All fix their eyes on high and as their sight
  ascends their power descends to all below.
  So are all drawn, as all draw, to God's height.   129

Dionysius gave himself to contemplation
  of these same orders with such holy zeal
  that he named and ranked them just as I have done. 132

Gregory, later, differed with his conclusions.
  But hardly had he wakened in this heaven
  then he was moved to laugh at his own delusions.   135

And if a truth so hidden was made clear
  by one still in the weight of mortal dust,
  you need not wonder: one who saw it here   138

returned and told him this: this and much more
  of the bright truth these circles hold in store."

NOTES

1–21. The figure is based on *Psalms* xix, 1: "The heavens are telling the glory of God and the firmament proclaims his handiwork." Wherever we look in the Primum Mobile, Dante tells us in lines 13–15, we see the glory of God.

He proceeds to describe this glory as a vision of God and the Hierarchies of the Angels. (What David saw dimly from Earth, Dante sees in detail at heaven's height.)

But first the image is approached by seeing it reflected in the heaven of Beatrice's eyes (Revelation) to which Dante's soul is ever drawn by love. From the revelation of Love (a heaven in itself), Dante turns to the glory itself, to find the fact in exact accord with the reflection.

It is an elaborate and sublimely conceived figure, and will certainly do as an example of Dante's fully let out paradisal style, of the high range of his rhetoric as opposed to some of the deliberate coarsening of style he found necessary in treating the Inferno.

6. *directly:* Not reflected.

14. *my own:* His own eyes. *that heaven:* The Primum Mobile.

16. *a Point:* The term is used in its strict mathematical sense to symbolize God as an immaterial and non-spatial essence.

19. *from here:* From Earth.

26. *the fastest of the spheres:* The Primum Mobile.

32. *Juno's messenger:* Iris, the rainbow. As Juno's messenger, the rainbow is conceived as descending from heaven to earth; at most, therefore, as a quarter of a circle. Were the rainbow to be extended to a full 180° across the sky, the distance it could span at its greatest spread could not equal the circumference of the seventh ring.

21–36. THE HEIRARCHY OF ANGELS. They surround God as the heavenly spheres surround the Earth, but their motions, contrary to those of the heavenly spheres, are greater as they lie closer to the center. Opposition (paradox) is a natural part of the language of mysticism. These spheres seem at first to be a sort of counter-universe. But note that the principle of both "universes" remains the same, for in either system, the spheres have greater motion and greater "virtue" as their placement draws nearer to God. In lines 52–57 below, Dante begs Beatrice to explain the mystery of this seeming paradox and in 58–78 Beatrice resolves Dante's uncertainties, going on then (97–129) to set forth the nine orders of the angelic beings grouped in three trinities: First Trinity: Seraphim, Cherubim, Thrones; Second Trinity; Dominations, Virtues, Powers; Third Trinity: Principalities, Archangels, Angels.

36. *the first one:* The first ring. Not to be confused with The Point.

37. *which:* The first ring.

38. *the Scintilla:* God. The Point.

50. *more godlike:* Possessed of greater powers as indicated by greater speed and greater brilliance.

56. *the form:* Platonic form, the essential, unchanging noumenal concept of which any exemplum is an instance.

59. *since none has tried it:* Small wonder. Since Dante is the first to have reached this height of Heaven and to have returned from it, Dante is the first to state the problem.

58–60. BEATRICE'S REPLY. The gist of Beatrice's reply is that Dante is to observe a marvelous correspondence between each of the physical spheres and its assigned Angel Intelligence. Yet the juxtaposition of these two, so to speak, mirror images, speaks a masterful conception. God conceived as the center of the Angel Hierarchy and God conceived as the circumference of the physical universe, are not two but one, twin manifestations of one creative force; and the interplay of these two images is powerfully relevant to Dante's belief that physical and spiritual law co-exist and interplay as twin manifestations of one will. God is the radiating center of all spiritual energy and He is simultaneously the all-containing bound and limit of physical creation.

Yet, aside from the magnificence of Dante's conception here, there remain problems of interpretation in Beatrice's reply. If the largest physical sphere corresponds to the smallest angelic sphere, what then of the assertion that a larger body contains more good than a smaller one, if both are perfect? Dante, even as a pilgrim awaiting instruction, most have grasped that the greater power results from closer proximity to God: the whole journey of the *Comedy* is scaled to that proximity. It is odd that Beatrice, having mentioned so much else, does not mention proximity to God as the essence of the mystery.

In accepting the beauty of Beatrice's revelation, Dante certainly implies that we must ponder these points. Perhaps the central clue is in lines 73–75: Dante does not see the Angel Hierarchy as it is but as it manifests itself to him in the form of nine spheres. Seen from all lower levels, these spheres are contained in God and surrounded by Him, for God is Allness. Seen in this nonphysical manifestation at the height of Heaven, the spheres surround Him, for God is nondimensional essence.

65. *the power:* The "virtue" of each, its power to influence the course of what lies below it. The power, of course, descends to each as a ray from God, more powerfully to the nearer spheres, but in each

the amount of power is infused through all parts of the sphere equally.

70. *this sphere:* The Primum Mobile, the source of all motion in the physical universe. As the most powerful of the spheres and as the one closest to God, it corresponds to the inner ring of the Angel Hierarchy, the Seraphim.

78. *Intelligence:* The Angel Intelligence of each sphere.

82. *Boreas:* The North Wind. When he blows straight out of his mouth the wind is from the north, which in Italy is from the Alps. Italians call that wind "*il tramontano,*" and think of it as the stormy source of bitter winter cold. When Boreas blows from his left cheek, the resultant northeaster ("*il grecale*") is thought of as a source of storms and of cloudy skies. But when he blows from the right (the gentler) cheek, Italians experience "*il maestrale,*" the sky-clearing wind from the northwest.

84. *every angel sphere:* The rings of the Angel Hierarchy. They react to the perfection of Beatrice's answer with a sparkling shower of joy.

91. *is worked:* Dante says only "iron that boils." But molten iron does not shoot sparks in the quantity Dante suggests unless it is hammered or poured. *spun with its spinning ring:* On earth, sparks tend to fly away from their sources. Here they stay in place, keeping pace with the rotation of the heavenly ring. The sparks may be taken as the individual angel intelligences within each ring; the added brightness of each, as evidence of the increase of its joy.

92–93. *the chessboard of the king:* The legend is still common and variously told. In one form, the inventor of chess offered the game to the king, who was so pleased with it that he ordered the inventor to name his own reward. The inventor asked that a single grain of wheat be placed on the first square of the board, two on the second, four on the third, and so on until the 64th increment was reached. The king, no mathematician, agreed gladly. It must have been at about the twelfth square (1,080,576 grains, if my figuring is sound) that the king began to learn the power of mathematics and that the number of grains would mount by the 64th square to something more than 18,000,000,000,000,000,000.

99. *have shown you:* As ever in Heaven, Dante does not see through the power of his own senses; rather, visions are manifested to him out of *caritas.* These symbolic visions cannot be taken as the thing itself, for the mystery of heavenly being is beyond Dante; as, in one sense, it is beyond all but God. Dante is offered symbolic representations at a level he can begin to grasp with the aid of Beatrice (Revelation).

100–102. *Being led, they chase the reins:* The figure should become clear if one thinks of the opposite condition of drawing back from the reins. The Angel Intelligences are all eagerness to pursue what leads them ever faster. *to resemble the Point, etc.:* To make themselves more godlike. Pride, the first of sins, it must be noted, springs from man's desire to be himself God. The Angel Intelligences yearn toward God in love (as it is man's charge to make himself over in God's image), not in rebellion, as Satan was moved.

102–105. Dante, ever a symbolic numerologist, divides the nine ranks into three trinities. Each rank, likely, expresses an aspect of God. The first two ranks of the first trinity may well be taken as being entirely beyond human understanding. Of the Thrones he has already spoken in IX, 61–62: "On high are mirrors (you say 'Thrones') and these reflect God's judgment to us." Thus the Thrones would seem to be God's aspect as Supreme Justice.

106. *all these raptures:* All the angelic beings of all the nine ranks, not simply those of the first trinity.

108. *the Truth in which all questioning is stilled:* God.

116–117. *springtime . . . nocturnal Aries:* In spring the sun is in Aries and its stars are not visible in the day sky. In autumn the sun has moved to the opposite sign (Libra) and the stars of Aries are visible at night. Thus nocturnal Aries may be said to be the sign under which the plants that blossomed in spring turn to seared leaves.

118. *warble:* The idea of "warbling" Hosannah may seem odd and yet it is native to the language Dante has invented for his *Paradiso.* The angel beings sing their praises with an ecstasy akin to the nisus of birds. The word Dante uses is *"sverna"* (*svernare*—literally, "to unwinter," and by extension, "to sound the glad spring song of birds").

121–123. *therein:* Within the second trinity. *the widest round:* The third of the second trinity.

124. *dancers:* Ranks, orders. Called dances to denote exaltation.

130. *Dionysius:* St. Dionysius, the Areopagite. A Greek mystic of the first century A.D. His conversion by St. Paul is recorded in *Acts* xvii, 34. To him was attributed the thesis *De coelesti hierarchia,* from which Dante draws the details for his Angel Hierarchy.

133. *Gregory:* St. Gregory (circa 540–604), called "the Great." Pope from 590. Among many other writings he revised Dionysius' treatise on the angel hierarchies. As Beatrice tells it, he had hardly awakened in heaven before he saw how wrong he had been, whereupon he was moved to laugh at his own delusions. His error, to be sure, was a harmless mistake; not a heresy, nor in any way sinful.

138. *one who saw it here:* St. Paul (*II Corinthians* xii, 2 ff.) tells of his ascent to the third heaven "whether in the body or out of the body I do not know." Dante's presumption here is that Paul told Dionysius what he had seen in heaven, and thus the accuracy of Dionysius' description (though if he were merely reporting what he had been told by Paul, he need hardly have given himself to such zealous contemplation as Beatrice ascribes to him in 130–132).

140. *hold in store:* A rhyme-forced addition. Dante says simply "of the truth of those circles." Since that truth is the revelation that awaits the pious soul, I hope I may argue that "hold in store" is implicit.

CANTO XXIX

The Ninth Sphere: Primum Mobile—The Angel Hierarchy

Beatrice, gazing on God, sees Dante's unspoken questions and explains to him *God's Intent in Willing the Creation, The Eternity of God,* and the *Simultaneity of Creation.*

    She proceeds then to explain the *Time from the Creation to the Revolt of the Angels, How the Loving Angels Began Their Blissful Art,* and that *Grace Is Received According to the Ardor of Love.*

    She then *Denounces Foolish Teachings,* and concludes by pointing out *The Infinity and The Distinction of the Angels.*

When Latona's twins, one setting in the sign
  of Aries and the other rising in Libra,
  are belted by the same horizon's line;   3

as long then as the zenith's fulcrum bears
  their perfect balance, still one and the other leave
  their common belt and change their hemispheres,   6

so long did Beatrice, smiling her delight,
  stay silent, her eyes fixed on the Fixed Point
  whose power had overcome me at first sight.   9

Then she began: "I do not ask, I say
  what you most wish to hear, for I have seen it
  where time and space are focused in one ray.   12

Not to increase Its good—no mil nor dram
  can add to true perfection, but that reflections
  of his reflection might declare 'I am'—   15

in His eternity, beyond time, above
  all other comprehension, as it pleased Him,
  new loves were born of the Eternal Love.   18

Nor did He lie asleep before the Word
  sounded above these waters; 'before' and 'after'
  did not exist until His voice was heard.   21

Pure essence, and pure matter, and the two
  joined into one were shot forth without flaw,
  like three bright arrows from a three-string bow.   24

And as in glass, in amber, or in crystal
  a ray shines so that nothing intervenes
  between its coming and being, which is total;   27

so the threefold effect rayed from its Sire
  into created being, without beginning
  and without interval, instantly entire.   30

Order was the co-created fact
  of every essence; and at the peak of all,
  these angel loves created as pure act.   33

Pure potential held the lowest ground;
  between, potential-and-act were tied together
  so tight they nevermore shall be unbound.   36

Hieronymus wrote to you of the long span
  of centuries in which such beings existed
  before the other world was made for man;   39

but the Scribes of the Holy Ghost clearly declare
  the true account in many passages,
  as you will see if you will read with care.   42

It can, in part, be grasped by intellection,
  which cannot grant such powers could long exist
  apart from the functioning of their perfection.   45

This much will answer where, and when, and how
  the angels were created; and so are quenched
  the first three flames of your desire to know.   48

Nor could you count to ten and ten before
  some of those angels fell from Heaven to roil
  the bedrock of the elemental core.   51

The rest remained here and around their Cause
  began the art you see, moved by such bliss
  that their glad revolutions never pause.   54

It was accursèd pride for which they fell,
  the pride of that dark principal you saw
  crushed by the world's whole weight in deepest Hell. 57

These you see here were humble, undemanding,
  and prompt in their acknowledgment of the Good
  that made them capable of such understanding;   60

whereby their vision was exalted higher
  by illuminating grace and their own merit,
  in which their wills are changeless and entire.   63

Now hear this and, beyond all doubt, believe it:
  the good of grace is in exact proportion
  to the ardor of love that opens to receive it.   66

And now, if you have heeded what I said,
  you should be able to observe this college
  and gather much more without further aid.   69

But since your earthly schoolmen argue still
  that the angelic nature is composed
  of understanding, memory, and will,   72

I will say this much more to help you see
  the truth that is confounded there below
  by the equivocations of sophistry: 75

these beings, since their first bliss in the sight
  of God's face, in which all things are revealed,
  have never turned their eyes from their delight.   78

No angel's eye, it follows, can be caught
  by a new object; hence, they have no need
  of memory, as does divided thought.   81

So men, awake but dreaming, dare to claim,
  believing it or not, they speak the truth—
  though the hypocrite's is the greater sin and shame.   84

You mortals do not walk a single way
  in your philosophies, but let the thought
  of being acclaimed as wise lead you astray.   87

Yet heaven bears even this with less offense
  than it must feel when it sees Holy Writ
  neglected, or perverted of all sense.   90

They do not count what blood and agony
  planted it in the world, nor Heaven's pleasure
  in those who search it in humility.   93

Each man, to show off, strains at some absurd
  invented truth; and it is these the preachers
  make sermons of; and the Gospel is not heard.   96

One says the moon reversed its course to throw
  a shadow on the sun during Christ's passion
  so that its light might not shine down below;   99

others say that the sun itself withdrew
  and, therefore, that the Indian and the Spaniard
  shared the eclipse in common with the Jew.   102

These fables pour from pulpits in such torrents,
  spewing to right and left, that in a year
  they outnumber the Lapi and Bindi in all Florence.   105

Therefore the ignorant sheep turn home at night
  from having fed on wind. Nor does the fact
  that the pastor sees no harm done set things right.   108

Christ did not say to His first congregation:
  'Go and preach twaddle to the waiting world.'
  He gave them, rather, holy truth's foundation.   111

That, and that only, was the truth revealed
  by those who fought and died to plant the faith.
  They made the Gospel both their sword and shield.   114

Now preachers make the congregation roar
  with quips and quirks and so it laugh enough,
  their hoods swell, and they ask for nothing more.   117

But in their tippets there nests such a bird
  that the people, could they see it, would soon know
  what faith to place in pardons thus conferred.   120

Because of these such folly fills the earth
  that, asking neither proof nor testimonials,
  men chase whatever promise is held forth.   123

On such St. Anthony's pig feeds on, unstinted,
  and others yet more swinish feast and guzzle
  and pay their way with money never minted.   126

But we have strayed. Therefore before we climb
    turn your attention back to the straight path
    that we may fit our journey to our time.   129

So many beings are ranked within this nature
    that the number of their hosts cannot be said
    nor even imagined by a mortal creature.   132

Read well what Daniel saw at heaven's height.
    You will soon see that when he speaks of 'thousands'
    every finite number is lost from sight.   135

To all, the Primal Light sends down Its ray.
    And every splendor into which it enters
    receives that radiance in its own way.   138

Therefore, since the act of loving grows
    from the act of recognition, the bliss of love
    blazes in some of these, and in some it glows.   141

Consider then how lofty and how wide
    is the excellence of the Eternal Worth
    which in so many mirrors can divide   144

its power and majesty forevermore,
    Itself remaining One, as It was before."

NOTES

1–9. Latona (or Leto) was, according to early legend, the wife of Zeus before he married Hera. Later legend has her as his mistress. In any case she bore him Apollo (the Sun) and Diana, or Artemis (the Moon).

At the vernal equinox the sun sets in Aries as the moon rises in the opposite sign of Libra. For a moment, with the zenith as the fulcrum of these sky-wide scales, they are perfectly balanced and wear the line of the horizon as a common belt. Then, each changing hemisphere—one dropping below the horizon, the other rising above it—the balance is broken.

The language of astronomy, legend, and the zodiac is not as immediate to us as it was to Dante and the figure may seem strained, yet it does describe Beatrice's brief pause with tonal embellishments sweetly appropriate to the Paradisal elevation.

Gist of this passage: "Beatrice looked up a moment in silence."

12. *where time and space focus into one ray:* God, ubiquitous and eternal.

13–15. A much disputed passage. (Where I have used "reflected" Dante used "*splendore,*" but Dante always used the verb "*splendare*" or the noun "*splendore*" to mean reflected rather than direct light.) God, being perfect, cannot add to His own good, already having all. It was not for self-increase that He created other beings, but that His ray of love, reflected to His created beings, might permit those reflections to say "I am," i.e., to share in the joy of existence.

18. *new loves:* The angels.

19–21. The question would be: "Where was God and what did He do before the Creation?" The answer: "He was Himself, sufficient, perfect, and eternal." *Before* and *after* are conditions of time, and God, as stated in line 16, is beyond time.

21–24. THE SIMULTANEITY OF CREATION. All created things came into being in the same instant, projected perfectly from God's perfect will.

There were, in fact, three-string crossbows in Dante's time. The figure, therefore, has precedent, but the numerological significances of trinity are always apt and may be read into the figure at will.

Pure essence: Immaterial intelligences. The angels. *pure matter:* The physical materials of the universe and the lower animals. *the two joined into one:* Creatures composed of both soul and physical matter. Mankind.

31–36. The Creation is an act of love imposed upon formless chaos. It was, therefore, inherently orderly. All the essences of that instant creation emerged in fixed ranks within the order of creation. The angels rank highest because (see XXVIII, 127–129) they have the power to influence what lies below them, having been created as pure act. At the bottom rank stands man, the material intelligence that exists as pure potential, as the receiver of divine influences he cannot influence. In between, the heavens were created as both act and potential, subject to influences from above, and able to influence what lies below.

37. *Hieronymus:* St. Hieronymus, also known as St. Jerome (circa 342–420), was one of the first great biblical scholars. *wrote to you:* "To you," of course, is the equivalent of "to mankind." In one of his epistles he asserted the pre-creation of the angels, a doctrine opposed to the one Beatrice is expounding.

40. *the Scribes of the Holy Ghost:* The writers of scripture. All of them were said to have been "entered" (i.e., inspired by) the Holy Ghost.

42–45. Dante must not be understood to imply that the angels, whose pure act or function is to move toward God, would cease to exist if they were denied the exercise of their perfection. Rather, they are eternal, which is to say they cannot cease to exist; and, as even man's intellect may understand, for such perfect action and existence to be expended on nothing would be chaos and a denial of the orderliness of creation. Since that order cannot be denied, the angels cannot be denied their perfect function.

51. *the elemental core:* Earth. Its elements are earth, air, fire, and water. Earth is, of course, the bedrock of the material universe; its core, Hell; and Hell's core, Satan. Beatrice informs Dante that Satan and his rebellious crew plunged to Earth (roiling the elemental core in the splash that raised the Mount of Purgatory, and roiling it since by their very existence) within a twenty-count of the Creation. The inherent orderliness of creation—a force for setting things instantly in their right ranking—could not tolerate the presence of perverted angels in Heaven for more than an instant.

At the end of Canto XXVI, Adam told Dante that his stay in the Terrestrial Paradise was less than seven hours. Beatrice has already asserted the simultaneity of the Creation. Since Satan was in the Garden and tempting Eve for some time before the Fall, he could not, in any case, have remained long in Heaven.

53. *this art:* Of circling around God, their cause. The art of the angels is to receive God's ray from above and to spread its influence below.

56. *that dark Principal:* Satan.

61–66. Dante intends a distinction here between illuminating grace and consuming grace. He is following Aquinas (*Summa theologica* I, 62, 4). Illuminating grace is God's gift to the soul, which may then, through zealous love, earn the consuming grace of the direct vision of God. The power of illuminating grace is, in fact, directly measurable by the ardor of love with which the soul receives it.

67–69. Beatrice tells Dante he is now prepared to look about this heaven and to observe its nature without further help from her. Characteristically, however (was Dante indulging a gentle and tender humor on the narrative level?), she talks on to the end of the canto.

81. *divided thought:* Human intelligence, lacking absolute content and concentration, must categorize, dividing its attention, which is to say, putting some things out of mind at times to be summoned back later by memory. The intelligence of angels, on the contrary, is eternally aware of all knowledge and memory, therefore, is irrelevant to it.

83. *believing it or not:* None has the truth, but some are only deluded, whereas others, ambitious for reputation and gifts, preach as truth what they do not themselves believe. These latter, as hypocrites and falsifiers, are clearly more sinful than those who are merely misled.

97–102. An eclipse of the sun by the moon would throw only a limited cone of shadow, whereas were the sun itself to withdraw, the whole earth (from Spain to India) would be dark. Recent commentators have disputed the text of this passage. As I have done throughout, I follow the reading established by Scartazzini-Vandelli.

104. *spewed to right and left:* In the manner of demagogic oratory.

105. *the Lapi and Bindi:* Lapo and Bindo were, and are, common

Florentine surnames. An equivalent reading in American terms might be: "they outnumber the Joneses and Smiths in the phonebook."

111. *holy truth's foundation:* "For no other foundation can one lay than that which is laid, which is Jesus Christ." *I Corinthians* iii, 11.

117. *their hoods swell:* With pride in their clownish performances. "Hoods" here for "heads."

118. *in their tippets:* The tippet is the long hanging point of a monk's hood or sleeves. Mendicant friars stuffed their tippets with all sorts of dubious religious articles and trade goods to be sold to pious simpletons along with unauthorized indulgences. Thus did they do the devil's work, and so the bird that nests in their tippets is the devil himself.

122. *testimonials:* Documents bearing papal or episcopal seals as authority to sell indulgences. Genuine documents of this sort did exist, but false documents seemed to work equally well upon the gullible.

124–126. St. Anthony the Eremite (251–356) was usually depicted with a pig (representing the devil) rooting at his feet. In Florence, pigs belonging to the various monastery herds were called St. Anthony's pigs and enjoyed the status of sacred cows, rooting in gardens, and even in houses, with no interference from the superstitious and pious folk. On such credulity, St. Anthony's pigs (these swinish mountebank monks) feed, and with them others yet (concubines, cronies, relatives) who eat and drink their fill, paying with fantastic and worthless promises (money never minted).

127–129. To digress from a subject is, metaphorically, to wander from the straight path. The straight path of this sphere is toward the study of the angelic nature. Having strayed from it, Beatrice and Dante must now hurry if they are to complete their set course in the time remaining to them before they ascend to the Empyrean.

130. *this nature:* The angelic nature.

CANTO XXX

Ascent to the Empyrean

*The Empyrean—Praise of Beatrice's Beauty · The River of
Light · The Mystic Rose · The Throne of Henry VII ·
Denunciation of Evil Popes*

The great theme is drawing to a close. Here in the Empyrean,
Beatrice is at last at home, her beauty made perfect, and Dante
utters a lofty *Praise of Beatrice*.

Beatrice promises Dante a *Vision of Both Hosts of Paradise*. He
is blinded by a new radiance, hears a voice announce that he shall
be given new powers, and immediately he sees a *Vision of a River
of Light*. As in the Terrestrial Paradise, he is commanded to drink.
No sooner is his face submerged in the water than the vision
grows circular and re-forms as a *Vision of the Mystic Rose*.

When, as may be, the sun's noon heat is shed
  six thousand miles away, while, where we are,
  earth's shadow makes an almost level bed;   3

when, at our zenith, the sky begins to show
  such changes that a star or two begins
  to face from the eyes of watchers here below;   6

and as the sun's most radiant serving maid
  comes nearer yet, and heaven puts out its lamps
  one by one, till the loveliest, too, must fade—   9

just so that Triumph that forever races
  around the blinding ray of the fixed Point
  that seems embraced by what Itself embraces,   12

faded from sight, degree by slow degree;
  at which I turned my eyes from the lost vision
  to Beatrice, as love commanded me.   15

If all that I have said of her below
  were gathered now into a single paean,
  that would be scant praise of her beauty now.   18

The beauty I saw there transcends all measure
  of mortal minds. I think only her Maker
  can wholly comprehend so great a treasure.   21

Here I concede defeat. No poet known,
  comic or tragic, challenged by his theme
  to show his power, was ever more outdone.   24

As feeblest eyes, struck by the sun, go blind,
  so the remembrance of my lady's smile
  strikes every recognition from my mind.   27

From the first day I looked upon her face
  in this life, to this present sight of her,
  my song has followed her to sing her praise.   30

But here I must no longer even try
  to walk behind her beauty. Every artist,
  his utmost done, must put his brushes by.   33

So do I leave her to a clarion
  of greater note than mine, which starts to draw
  its long and arduous theme to a conclusion.   36

She, like a guide who has his goal in sight
  began to speak again: "We have ascended
  from the greatest sphere to the heaven of pure light.   39

Light of the intellect, which is love unending;
  love of the true good, which is wholly bliss;
  bliss beyond bliss, all other joys transcending;   42

here shall you see both hosts of Paradise,
  one of them in the aspect you shall see
  when you return the day all bodies rise."   45

As a flash of lightning striking on our sight
  destroys our visual spirits, so that the eye
  cannot make out even a brighter light;   48

just so, an aureole burst all about me,
  swathing me so completely in its veil
  that I was closed in light and could not see.   51

"The Love that keeps this Heaven ever the same
  greets all who enter with such salutation,
  and thus prepares the candle for His flame."   54

No sooner had these few words penetrated
  my hearing than I felt my powers increase
  beyond themselves; transcendant and elated,   57

my eyes were lit with such new-given sight
  that they were fit to look without distress
  on any radiance, however bright.   60

I saw a light that was a river flowing
  light within light between enameled banks
  painted with blossoms of miraculous spring;   63

and from the river as it glowed and rolled
  live sparks shot forth to settle on the flowers.
  They seemed like rubies set in bands of gold;   66

and then, as if the fragrance overthrew
  their senses, they dove back into the river;
  and as one dove in there, out another flew.   69

"The flame of high desire that makes you yearn
  for greater knowledge of these things you see
  pleases me more the more I see it burn.   72

But only this same water satisfies
  such thirst as yours. You must bend down and drink."
  —So spoke the sun and pole-star of my eyes.   75

And added: "The river and the jewels you see
  dart in and out of it, and the smiling flowers
  are dim foretastes of their reality.   78

Not that these fruits are in their natures tart
  and unformed, but that you still lack the vision
  of such high things. The defect is on your part."   81

No babe in arms that ever wakened hungry
  from having slept too long could turn its face
  to its dear mother's milk more eagerly   84

than I bent down to drink in Paradise
  of the sweet stream that flows its grace to us,
  so to make better mirrors of our eyes.   87

No sooner were my eyes' eaves sweetly drowned
  in that bright stream to drink, than it appeared
  to widen and change form till it was round.   90

I have seen masqueraders here below
  shed the disguises that had hidden them
  and show their true appearances. Just so,   93

the sparks and spring flowers changed before my eyes
  into a greater festival, and I saw
  the vision of both courts of Paradise.   96

O splendor of God eternal through which I saw
  the supreme triumph of the one true kingdom,
  grant me the power to speak forth what I saw!   99

There in Heaven, a lamp shines in whose light
  the Creator is made visible to His creature,
  whose one peace lies in having Him in sight.   102

That lamp forms an enormous circle, such
  that its circumference, fitted to the Sun
  as a bright belt, would be too large by much.   105

It is made up entirely of the reflection
  of rays that strike the top of the first-moved sphere,
  imparting to it all its power and motion.   108

And as a slope shines in the looking glass
  of a lake below it, as if to see itself
  in its time of brightest flower and greenest grass;   111

so, tier on tier, mounting within that light,
  there glowed, reflected in more than a thousand circles,
  all those who had won return to Heaven's height.   114

And if so vast a nimbus can be bound
  within its lowest tier, what then must be
  the measure of this rose at its topmost round?   117

Nor were my eyes confounded by that sea
  and altitude of space, but took in all,
  both number and quality, of that ecstasy.   120

There, far and near cause neither loss nor gain,
  for where God rules directly, without agents,
  the laws that govern nature do not pertain.   123

Into the gold of the rose that blooms eternal,
  rank on rank, in incenses of praise
  it sends up to the Sun forever vernal—   126

I, yearning to speak and silent—Beatrice drew me,
  and said: "Now see how many are in the convent
  of the white robes. Behold our far-flung city.   129

And see the benches—every one a throne—
  how every rank of them is filled so full
  that few are wanted before all is done.   132

That great throne with the crown already set
  above it draws your eyes. To it shall come—
  before your own call to this nuptial banquet—   135

the soul, already anointed, of Henry the Great,
  who will come to Italy to bring law and order
  before the time is ripe to set things straight.   138

Tranced in blind greed, your ever deepening curse,
  you have become as mindless as an infant
  who screams with hunger, yet pushes away his nurse. 141

The prefect of the holy court will be
  a man who will profess his cause in public
  while working to defeat it secretly.   144

But after that God will not long permit
  his simony, he shall be stuffed away
  where Simon Magus, headfirst in the pit,   147

pays for his guilt. There, paying for his own,
  he shall force the guilt of Alagna further down."

NOTES

1–15. ASCENT TO THE EMPYREAN. Heretofore the glories of the heavens have shone like stars in glorious night. In the Empyrean, God (the Sun) shines forever in the fullness of His glorious day, obscuring all other heavenly bodies except as they reflect His light. The ascent into the Empyrean, therefore, is a dawning, and Dante's figure for it is based on an earthly dawn.

When the sun is at its noon height over India (about 6000 miles away) dawn is just beginning in Italy and the Earth's shadow is almost a level line (level bed) out into space (i.e., nearly perpendicular to a line dropped from the zenith). Then the stars directly overhead begin to fade, the dimmest first, then the brighter. Then as dawn (Aurora, the serving maid of Apollo, the Sun) draws nearer, all the stars go out, even the loveliest and brightest.

Just so nine rings of the three trinities of Angelic beings fade as Dante and Beatrice ascend into the first dawning of the direct vision of God. Obviously the dimmer outer rings would fade first, then the others in order.

12. *embraced by what Itself embraces:* The Angel Rings seem to contain God within their rounds, whereas it is God who contains them and all else.

22–23. THE BEAUTY OF BEATRICE. As Dante ascended each new heaven and became more able to perceive, Beatrice grew more beautiful (was able to reveal more of herself to his senses). Now fully disclosed in the direct light of the Empyrean she surpasses conception: only God can realize her full beauty.

On another level it is only natural that Dante stand inarticulate before the full beauty of Divine Revelation. What religious man could think himself equal to describing the entire beauty of Revelation? (Such inarticulateness is all the more effective when it overtakes a man who boasted of his powers in *Inferno* IV, 100–102, XXV, 91–99, XXXII, 7–9, and in *Paradiso* II, 1–18.)

35–36. *to a clarion of greater note than mine:* Does Dante mean that a greater poet will follow to sing the full beauty of Beatrice? He has just said that only God can fully realize her beauty.

I think it is no accident that Dante says "clarion" rather than "lyre." The Day of Judgment will be announced by a clarion call, and on that day the souls of all mortals may look upon Beatrice in her full beauty. Dante's "clarion" must occupy itself with drawing its long and arduous theme to a conclusion.

39. *the greatest sphere:* The Primum Mobile. *heaven of pure light:* The Empyrean.

43. *both hosts of Paradise:* The Angels and the Blessèd.

44. *one of them:* The Blessèd. Those who once wore mortal bodies which shall be returned to them on Judgment Day. Within the Mystic Rose Dante does see the radiances of the Blessèd with their lineaments etched upon them. He is offered this sight as a special dispensation in a climactic act of *caritas*.

47. *visual spirits:* See XXVI, 70–72.

52. *The Love:* God. *that keeps his Heaven ever the same:* All the other heavens rotate in constant change. The Empyrean, reflecting God's unchanging and unchangeable perfection, is always the same.

54. *and thus prepares the candle for His flame:* Dante has several times been blinded by the light that prepared him for better vision. Here the candle of his soul is put out by the splendor of the Empyrean to be relit by the light of God Himself.

60–66. As Dante makes clear in line 95 below, the sparks are Angels and the flowers, the Blessèd. The river may be taken as the endless flowering of God's grace. Some religious commentators suggest that the two banks represent the Church. As verified by lines 76–78 below, the rubies of line 66 should be taken to be Angels and the bands of gold as the Blessèd.

77. *jewels:* Dante says "topazes" and the topaz was believed to have the power of reflecting things without distortion, certainly a relevant suggestion in context, though "topazes" here does not accord with "rubies" in line 66.

82 ff. *no babe in arms:* "Except ye be converted and become as little children, ye shall not enter into the kingdom of heaven" (*Matthew* xviii, 3).

87. *better mirrors:* The better to reflect God.

88–89. *my eyes' eaves:* His eyelashes. Dante has, of course, plunged his face into the river. It may seem odd to say that he drank with his eyes, but note that this is a river of light, and that it is to wash the last mortal weakness from his eyes that Dante is drinking. See also the common idiom: "My eyes drank in the sight of it."

95–97–99. *I saw:* Now and then in the *Paradiso* Dante says "I saw." More often he uses some such phrase as "there appeared to me" or "it manifested itself." Such phrasing is deliberate. "I saw" implies an action of the speaker's own powers. Heaven, however, is a gift of grace: Dante does not see it through his own powers; rather it manifests itself to him as an act of love, and does so not in its true essence but in manifestations graspable by Dante's mortal mind.

Here, however, Dante uses "I saw" as one of his rare triple rhymings on the same word. In Dante an unusual device always indicates unusual stress. It occurs, moreover, at one of the great climaxes of the poem.

For Dante has just experienced the first direct revelation of God. Until he drank from the stream he could not see things with the spontaneous intuition of heavenly souls, who partake directly of the mind of God. Now he, too, has achieved the beginnings of Paradisal power. This is the true rebirth, the spiritual enlargement to which the entire journey has been directed. And soon now, as Virgil left him below, Beatrice will leave him to take her throne among the hosts of the Blessèd, though in a larger sense she will be with him forever, both her soul and Dante's being contained in God.

108. *power:* Virtue. The ability to influence what lies below it. *motion:* Its own rapid revolution.

112 ff. THE MYSTIC ROSE. As ever in Paradise, the heavenly beings manifest themselves to Dante at the highest level he is capable of grasping at each point of his development. At every stage they have sent their manifestations down to him as an act of love. They themselves remain forever in the direct presence of God.

Now, his vision at last approaching perfection, Dante sees them in their supreme heavenly state, ranked tier on tier in a huge stadium that gives forth the appearance of an enormous white rose basking in the eternal springtime of the direct light of God. Note, however, that he sees the rose not directly (even at this point he is not yet ready) but as a vision reflected in the sea of God's light.

For purposes of placing Dante in relation to it, the Rose may be thought of as an immense, truncated, inverted, floating cone marked off in many tiers. The tier first reflected to Dante from that sea of light is the bottom one, the upper tiers being only partially visible at this point. The nimbus of the bottom tier (lines 115–116) is far greater than the circumference of the Sun (lines 104–105).

114. *those who had won return:* The loyal angels, having never left, would not have won return.

116–117. *what then must be its measure:* There are more than a thousand tiers. If the lowest is greater by far than the circumference of the Sun, what must be the dimensions of its upper ring, a thousand steps up from such magnitude?

118–123. On earth we see near things in detail and far things indistinctly. The laws of nature, however, are God's agencies and have no force where God rules without intermediaries. So, despite the galactic dimensions of the rose, Dante sees all in minute detail, not only each being in that multitude, but the quality of each one's ecstasy.

124 ff. *Into the gold of the rose:* The central corona of the rose, from which the petals grow, is always golden, or so it was in Dante's time, though some modern hybrids no longer have a golden center. *Beatrice drew me:* If the Mystic Rose is conceived as a vast circular stadium Dante and Beatrice are now in the center of the arena looking up at the tiers.

132. *few are wanted before all is done:* As with so many other revelationists, Dante believes God will not long endure the evils of mankind and that the trump of Judgment will soon sound.

136. *Henry:* Henry VII of Luxemburg, Emperor 1308–1313. He was not, strictly speaking, referred to as Henry the Great, but I have been forced to call him that for purposes of rhyme. See *Purgatorio* VII, 96, note, and for the background of Henry's attempt at order in Italy see *Purgatorio* VI, 100, note. In the *Purgatorio* Dante says Henry came too late. Here he says he came before the time was ripe. In either case the result was the same and Dante attributes Henry's fail-

ure to the evil designs of the bad popes Beatrice now goes on to denounce before the full court of Heaven. It is certainly relevant, here, to note that Dante placed his one hope of returning to Florence on the outcome of Henry's efforts to settle the hatreds of Italian politics.

138. *already anointed:* As Holy Roman Emperor.

140. *you:* You Italians.

142. *The prefect:* The pope. *The holy court:* Rome, the Vatican. Here Dante intends Clement V, who worked to defeat Henry's policy, though he professed to support it.

143–144. I have found it necessary to translate the intent rather than the phrasing of Dante's lines here. Literally rendered, they would read: "Who will not walk with him the same road openly and covertly," a strange figure that has Clement walking beside Henry on two separate roads at the same time.

145. *God will not long permit:* Clement died eight months after Henry, on April 20, 1314.

147. *where Simon Magus, headfirst in the pit:* With the Simoniacs in the Third Bolgia of the Eighth Circle (*Inferno* XIX). There the sinners are stuffed head-first into a tubelike baptismal font, their feet kicking the air, their soles aflame. As each replaces his successor in selling holy office, the earlier tenant is shoved down into some undescribed lower pit, sealed from the eyes of all.

149. *the guilt of Alagna:* Boniface VIII. He was born at Alagna (or, variantly, Anagna).

CANTO XXXI

The Empyrean—The Mystic Rose · The Angel Host ·
Beatrice Leaves Dante · St. Bernard

The second soldiery of the Church Triumphant is the *Angel Host*
and Dante now receives a vision of them as a *Swarm of Bees* in
eternal transit between God and the Rose.

Dante turns from that rapturous vision to speak to Beatrice
and finds in her place a reverend elder. It is *St. Bernard,* who will
serve as Dante's guide to the ultimate vision of God. Bernard
shows Dante his *Last Vision of Beatrice,* who has resumed her
throne among the blessèd. Across the vastness of Paradise, Dante
sends his soul's prayer of thanks to her. *Beatrice Smiles* down at
Dante a last time, then turns her eyes forever to the Eternal
Fountain of God.

Bernard, the most faithful of the worshippers of the Virgin,
promises Dante the final vision of God through the Virgin's in-
tercession. Accordingly, he instructs Dante to raise his eyes to her
throne. Dante obeys and burns with bliss at the vision of her
splendor.

Then, in the form of a white rose, the host
   of the sacred soldiery appeared to me,
   all those whom Christ in his own blood espoused.   3

But the other host (who soar, singing and seeing
   His glory, who to will them to his love
   made them so many in such blissful being,   6

like a swarm of bees who in one motion dive
   into the flowers, and in the next return
   the sweetness of their labors to the hive)   9

flew ceaselessly to the many-petaled rose
   and ceaselessly returned into that light
   in which their ceaseless love has its repose.   12

Like living flame their faces seemed to glow.
  Their wings were gold. And all their bodies shone
  more dazzling white than any earthly snow.   15

On entering the great flower they spread about them,
  from tier to tier, the ardor and the peace
  they had acquired in flying close to Him.   18

Nor did so great a multitude in flight
  between the white rose and what lies above it
  block in the least the glory of that light;   21

for throughout all the universe God's ray
  enters all things according to their merit,
  and nothing has the power to block its way.   24

This realm of ancient bliss shone, soul on soul,
  with new and ancient beings, and every eye
  and every love was fixed upon one goal.   27

O Threefold Light which, blazoned in one star,
  can so content their vision with your shining,
  look down upon us in the storm we are!   30

If the barbarians (coming from that zone
  above which Helice travels every day
  wheeling in heaven with her belovèd son)   33

looking at Rome, were stupefied to see
  her works in those days when the Lateran
  outshone all else built by humanity;   36

what did I feel on reaching such a goal
  from human to blest, from time to eternity,
  from Florence to a people just and whole—   39

by what amazement was I overcome?
  Between my stupor and my new-found joy
  my bliss was to hear nothing and be dumb.   42

And as a pilgrim at the shrine of his vow
  stares, feels himself reborn, and thinks already
  how he may later describe it—just so now   45

I stood and let my eyes go wandering out
  into that radiance from rank to rank,
  now up, now down, now sweeping round about.   48

I saw faces that compelled love's charity
  lit by Another's lamp and their own smiles,
  and gestures graced by every dignity.   51

Without having fixed on any part, my eyes
  already had taken in and understood
  the form and general plan of Paradise: 54

and—my desire rekindled—I wheeled about
  to question my sweet lady on certain matters
  concerning which my mind was still in doubt.   57

One thing I expected; another greeted me:
  I thought to find Beatrice there; I found instead
  an elder in the robes of those in glory.   60

His eyes and cheeks were bathed in the holy glow
  of loving bliss; his gestures, pious grace.
  He seemed a tender father standing so.   63

"She—where is she?" I cried in sudden dread.
  "To lead you to the goal of all your wish
  Beatrice called me from my place," he said;   66

"And if you raise your eyes you still may find her
  in the third circle down from the highest rank
  upon the throne her merit has assigned her."   69

Without reply I looked up to that height
  and saw her draw an aureole round herself
  as she reflected the Eternal Light.   72

No mortal eye, though plunged to the last bounds
  of the deepest sea, has ever been so far
  from the topmost heaven to which the thunder sounds 75

as I was then from Beatrice; but there
  the distance did not matter, for her image
  reached me unblurred by any atmosphere.   78

"O lady in whom my hope shall ever soar
  and who for my salvation suffered even
  to set your feet upon Hell's broken floor;   81

through your power and your excellence alone
  have I recognized the goodness and the grace
  inherent in the things I have been shown.   84

You have led me from my bondage and set me free
  by all those roads, by all those loving means
  that lay within your power and charity.   87

Grant me your magnificence that my soul,
  which you have healed, may please you when it slips
  the bonds of flesh and rises to its goal."   90

Such was my prayer, and she—far up a mountain,
  as it appeared to me—looked down and smiled.
  Then she turned back to the Eternal Fountain.   93

And the holy Elder said: "I have been sent
  by prayer and sacred love to help you reach
  the perfect consummation of your ascent.   96

Look round this garden, therefore, that you may
  by gazing at its radiance, be prepared
  to lift your eyes up to the Trinal Ray.   99

The Queen of Heaven, for whom in whole devotion
  I burn with love, will grant us every grace
  because I am Bernard, her faithful one."   102

As a stranger from afar—a Croat, if you will—
  comes to see our Vernonica, and awed
  by its ancient fame, can never look his fill,   105

but says to himself as long as it is displayed:
  "My Lord, Jesus Christ, true God, and is this then
  the likeness of thy living flesh portrayed?"—   108

just so did I gaze on the living love
  of him who in this world, through contemplation,
  tasted the peace which ever dwells above.   111

"Dear son of Grace," he said, "you cannot know
  this state of bliss while you yet keep your eyes
  fixed only on those things that lie below;   114

rather, let your eyes mount to the last round
  where you shall see the Queen to whom this realm
  is subject and devoted, throned and crowned."   117

I looked up: by as much as the horizon
  to eastward in the glory of full dawn
  outshines the point at which the sun went down;   120

by so much did one region on the height
  to which I raised my eyes out of the valley
  outshine the rays of every other light.   123

And as the sky is brightest in that region
  where we on earth expect to see the shaft
  of the chariot so badly steered by Phaeton,   126

while to one side and the other it grows dim—
  just so that peaceful oriflamme lit the center
  and faded equally along either rim.   129

And in the center, great wings spread apart,
  more than a thousand festive angels shone,
  each one distinct in radiance and in art.   132

I saw there, smiling at this song and sport,
  her whose beauty entered like a bliss
  into the eyes of all that sainted court.   135

And even could my speech match my conception,
  yet I would not dare make the least attempt
  to draw her delectation and perfection.   138

Bernard, seeing my eyes so fixed and burning
  with passion on his passion, turned his own
  up to that height with so much love and yearning   141

that the example of his ardor sent
  new fire through me, making my gaze more ardent.

NOTES

1–2. In XXX, 43, Beatrice promised that Dante would see both
hosts of Paradise. The first host is of the sacred soldiery, those who

were once mortal and who were redeemed by Christ. They are seated upon the thrones of the Mystic Rose in which are gathered eternally the essences of all those heavenly souls that manifested themselves to Dante in the various spheres below, moved by *caritas* to reveal themselves to Dante at the various levels of his developing understanding. How these souls could be eternally within the Rose while yet manifesting themselves to Dante in the various spheres is, of course, one of the mysteries to be grasped only by Revelation. The essential point is that as Dante becomes better able to see; the vision of Heaven unfolds to him ever more clearly and ever more profoundly.

The second soldiery is of the angels who never left heaven. They soar above the Rose like Heavenly bees, in constant motion between the Rose and the radiance of God. Unlike earthly bees, however, it is from God, the mystical hive of grace, that they bring the sweetness to the flower, bearing back to God, of course, the bliss of the souls of Heaven. (See lines 16–18).

The first host is more emphatically centered on the aspect of God as the Son; the second, on the aspect of God as the Father.

13. See the vision of God and Heaven in *Ezekiel* i, 14 ff.

14. See the similar vision in *Daniel* x, 4 ff.

22–24. God illuminates all things in the exact degree that each is worthy of illumination (which is to say, able to receive it), and nothing may block from any other thing the light it is in condition to receive. No soul, that is to say, can receive less of God than it is able to contain at any given stage of its development.

27. *one goal:* God.

32. *Helice:* The nymph Helice (I am afraid the reader will have to Anglicize her name as HEL-ees) attracted Zeus and was turned into a bear by jealous Hera. Zeus translated his nymph to heaven as Ursa Major, the constellation of the Great Bear which contains the Big Dipper. Arcas, her son by Zeus, was translated to Ursa Minor, within which he forms the Little Dipper.

The two dippers, being near the pole, are always above the horizon in the northland, the zone from which the barbarians came.

35. *the Lateran:* The Lateran is today a section of old Rome. Here Dante uses it to signify Rome in general.

39. *from Florence to a people just and whole:* This is Dante's last mention of Florence. Note that Florence has not improved but that on the universal scale it has become too insignificant for the sort of denunciation he once heaped upon it.

42. *my bliss was to hear nothing and be dumb:* At such a moment of ecstasy Dante wants neither to speak nor to hear others speak, but only to stand rapt before the glory of such revelation.

Note that Dante believes he is standing next to Beatrice. "To hear nothing" must mean he does not even wish to hear her speak. On the personal level, such a feeling might seem an affront to his lady; yet there is no affront: even she, as she herself would insist, must be silent before the greater vision. The figure of Beatrice is a complex symbol. To simplify matters for the beginning reader of Dante, I have taken her allegorically in simplest terms as Divine Revelation. So taking her, Dante's seeming rejection of her blends harmoniously with the total of his vision, for if Beatrice is Divine Revelation (an agent of God), Dante is now near God Himself (that which Revelation is meant to reveal).

43. *shrine of his vow:* It was a custom of the pious, as thanks for an answered prayer, to win forgiveness of sins, or as a testimony of faith, to vow a journey to a stated shrine or temple. Such pilgrimages were often dangerous. Travel was rare in the Middle Ages, and the pilgrim returned from far shrines was much sought after for the hopefully miraculous, and in any case rare, news he brought back. How could Dante, having traveled to the Infinite Summit, fail to think ahead to the way he would speak his vision to mankind?

58. *One thing I expected; another greeted me:* Dante expected to see Beatrice. He sees instead St. Bernard. As Virgil, his service done, vanished at the top of Purgatory, so now Beatrice has left Dante, though not to vanish but to resume her throne among the blessèd. In the next passage Dante will look up and see her there.

60. *an elder:* St. Bernard (1090–1153), the famous Abbot of Clairvaux, a contemplative mystic and author. Under him the Cistercian Order (a branch of the Benedictines with a stricter rule than the original order) flourished and spread. All Cistercian monasteries

are especially dedicated to the Virgin, and St. Bernard is particularly identified with her worship.

66. *Beatrice called me from my place:* In succeeding Beatrice, Bernard clearly becomes the allegorical figure of Contemplation, and so a progress of the soul: From Human Reason or Aesthetic Wisdom the soul mounts to Revelation at which time the final bliss becomes Contemplation of God as He reveals Himself.

Bernard, himself one of the most famous contemplatives of the church, has a second function. The ultimate revelation must come as a special grace and grace can be granted in answer to the prayers of the worthy. The worthiest being in the Mystic Rose is the Virgin and Bernard as her special servitor will pray to her that she pray God to grant Dante's most ardent wish.

68. *the third circle down:* In the Mystic Rose Mary sits in the topmost tier, Eve directly below her, Rachel (the Contemplative Life) below Eve. Beatrice sits to the right of Rachel. In Dante, of course, every mention of three must suggest trinity, but the reader is left to decide for himself the significance of the Mary-Eve-Rachel trinity.

73–75. To what altitude the sound of thunder reaches through the atmosphere and how far that would be from the bottom of the deepest sea are questions a scientist might perhaps determine. For Dante the upper height would be the top of the atmosphere and he would have understood that upper limit as being close to the moon. Whatever the specifications, the poetic force of the passage powerfully suggests vast dimensions.

81. *to set your feet upon Hell's broken floor:* As she did when she descended to Limbo (as, of course, a manifestation) to summon Virgil.

103. *a Croat:* Probably used here in a generic sense to signify the native of any far off Christian land, but Croatia, aside from lying at one of the outer limits of Christianity, was also known for the ardor of its religious belief.

104. *our Veronica:* From *vera icon,* the true image. Certainly the most famous relic in St. Peter's, the Veronica was the handkerchief of the faithful follower ever after known as St. Veronica. She gave it to Jesus to wipe the blood from his face on the road to Calvary, and

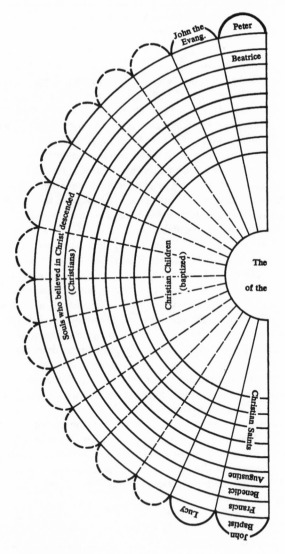

Labels within the figure:
- Peter
- John the Evang.
- Beatrice
- Souls who believed in Christ descended (Christians)
- Christian Children (baptized)
- The
- of the
- Christian Saints
- Augustine
- Benedict
- Francis
- Lucy
- John Baptist

THE MYSTIC ROSE (after Gardner)
No specific number of petals or of tiers should be understood. The

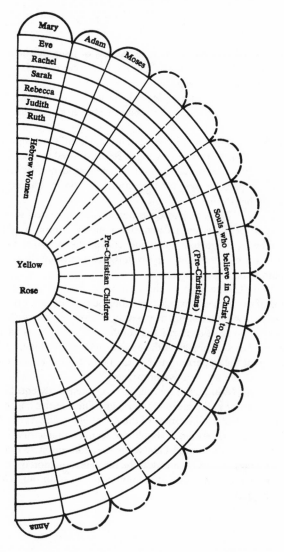

dotted lines indicate the parts of the rose which Dante does
not describe in detail.

what was believed to be the true likeness of Jesus was believed to have appeared on what was believed to be the cloth in what was believed to be His own blood.

110–111. According to legend, Bernard was rewarded for his holiness by being permitted a vision of Heaven's blessedness while he was yet on earth.

112–117. The way to perfect consummation is ever upward toward God. Dante has been staring at Bernard, awed by that vision of holiness. In modesty and as an act of loving guidance, Bernard tells him to prepare his eyes for the ultimate vision by looking up to Mary on her throne.

118–123. The comparison is not, as careless readers sometimes take it to be, between a dawn and a sunset (whose brightnesses would be approximately equal) but between the eastern and western horizons at dawn. Bright as Heaven is, Mary outshines it as the east outshines the west at daybreak.

124–129. The shaft of the chariot of the Sun would project ahead of the horses. It would, therefore, be the first point of light of the new dawn, that moment when light glows on the eastern rim while the horizon to north and south is still dark. Thus Mary not only outshines all heaven as the east at daybreak outshines the west, but even at the uppermost tier of the blessèd, those radiances at either side of her are dim by comparison.

132. *art:* Motion. No two angel beings are exactly equal in their brightness, nor in the speed of their flight. These festive angels are, of course, another manifestation of the Angel Hierarchy. At this height of heaven and revelation, it should not seem contradictory for them to revolve forever around God while they forever circle Mary. The two circlings are clearly meant to be one. Heaven, moreover, reveals itself in one manifestation after another of the truth only God can entirely grasp.

CANTO XXXII

The Empyrean—St. Bernard · The Virgin Mary ·
The Thrones of the Blessèd

His eyes fixed blissfully on the vision of the Virgin Mary, Bernard
recites the orders of the Mystic Rose, identifying the thrones of
the most blessèd.

Mary's Throne is on the topmost tier of the Heavenly Stadium.
Directly across from it rises the *Throne of John the Baptist.* From
her throne to the central arena (The Yellow of the Rose) de-
scends a *Line of Christian Saints.* These two radii form a diameter
that divides the stadium. On one side are throned *Those Who Be-
lieve in Christ to Come;* on the other, *Those Who Believed in Christ
Descended.* The lower half of the Rose contains, on one side, the
Pre-Christian Children Saved by Love, and on the other, the *Chris-
tian Children Saved by Baptism.*

Through all these explanations, Bernard has kept his eyes
fixed in adoration upon the Virgin. Having finished his prelimi-
nary instruction of Dante, Bernard now calls on him to join in a
Prayer to the Virgin.

Still rapt in contemplation, the sainted seer
  assumed the vacant office of instruction,
  beginning with these words I still can hear: 3

"The wound that Mary healed with balm so sweet
  was first dealt and then deepened by that being
  who sits in such great beauty at her feet.   6

Below her, in the circle sanctified
  by the third rank of loves, Rachel is throned
  with Beatrice, as you see, there at her side.   9

Sarah and Rebecca and Judith and she
  who was the great-grandmother of the singer
  who for his sins cried, 'Lord, have mercy on me!'—   12

as I go down the great ranks tier by tier,
  naming them for you in descending order,
  petal by petal, you shall see them clear.   15

And down from the seventh, continuing from those
  in the first six tiers, a line of Hebrew women
  forms a part in the tresses of the rose.   18

Arranged to form a wall thus, they divide
  all ranks according to the view of Christ
  that marked the faith of those on either side.   21

On this side, where the flower is in full bloom
  to its last petal, are arranged all those
  whose faith was founded upon Christ to Come;   24

on that, where the half circles show the unblended
  gaps of empty seats, are seated those
  whose living faith was fixed on Christ Descended.   27

And as, on this side, the resplendent throne
  of Heaven's Lady, with the thrones below it,
  establishes the line of that division;   30

so, facing hers, does the throned blessedness
  of the Great John who, ever holy, bore
  the desert, martyrdom, and Hell's distress;   33

and under him, forming that line are found
  Francis, Benedict, Augustine, and others
  descending to this center round by round.   36

Now marvel at all-foreseeing profundity:
  this garden shall be complete when the two aspects
  of the one faith have filled it equally.   39

And know that below that tier that cuts the two
  dividing walls at their centerpoint, no being
  has won his seat of glory by his own virtue,   42

but by another's, under strict condition;
  for all of these were spirits loosed from flesh
  before they had matured to true volition.   45

You can yourself make out their infant graces:
  you need no more than listen to their treble
  and look attentively into their faces.   48

You do not speak now: many doubts confound you.
  Therefore, to set you free I shall untie
  the cords in which your subtle thoughts have
                             bound you.   51

Infinite order rules in this domain.
  Mere accidence can no more enter in
  than hunger can, or thirst, or grief, or pain.   54

All you see here is fixed by the decree
  of the eternal law, and is so made
  that the ring goes on the finger perfectly.   57

These, it follows, who had so short a pause
  in the lower life are not ranked higher or lower
  among themselves without sufficient cause.   60

The king in whom this realm abides unchanging
  in so much love and bliss that none dares will
  increase of joy, creating and arranging   63

the minds of all in the glad Paradise
  of His own sight, grants them degrees of grace
  as He sees fit. Here let the effect suffice.   66

Holy Scripture clearly and expressly
  notes this effect upon those twins who fought
  while still within their mother. So we see   69

how the Supreme light fittingly makes fair
  its aureole by granting them their graces
  according to the color of their hair.   72

Thus through no merit of their works and days
  they are assigned their varying degrees
  by variance only in original grace.   75

In the first centuries of man's creation
  their innocence and the true faith of their parents
  was all they needed to achieve salvation.   78

When the first age of man had run its course,
  then circumcision was required of males,
  to give their innocent wings sufficient force.   81

But when the age of grace came to mankind
  then, unless perfectly baptized in Christ,
  such innocents went down among the blind.   84

Look now on her who most resembles Christ,
  for only the great glory of her shining
  can purify your eyes to look on Christ."   87

I saw such joy rain down upon that face—
  borne to it by those blest Intelligences
  created thus to span those heights of space—   90

that through all else on the long road I trod
  nothing had held my soul so fixed in awe,
  nor shown me such resemblances to God.   93

The self-same Love that to her first descended
  singing "*Ave Maria, gratia plena*"
  stood before her with its wings extended.   96

Thus rang the holy chant to Heaven's Queen
  and all the blessèd court joined in the song,
  and singing, every face grew more serene.   99

"O holy Father who endures for me
  the loss of being far from the sweet place
  where fate has raised your throne eternally,   102

who is that angel who with such desire
  gazes into the eyes of our sweet Queen,
  so rapt in love he seems to be afire?"   105

Thus did I seek instruction from that Great One
  who drew the beauty of his light from Mary
  as the morning star drew beauty from the sun.   108

And he:"As much as angel or soul can know
  of exultation, gallantry, and poise
  there is in him; and we would have it so,   111

for it was he who brought the victory
  to Mary when the Son of God had willed
  to bear the weight of human misery.   114

But let your eyes go where my words point out
  among this court, and note the mighty peers
  of the empire of the just and the devout.   117

Those two whose bliss it is to sit so close
  to the radiance of the Empress of All Joy
  are the two eternal roots of this our rose: 120

The one just to the left of her blessedness
  is the father whose unruly appetite
  left man the taste for so much bitterness; 123

and on her right, that ancient one you see
  is the father of Holy Church to whom Christ gave
  the twin keys to this flower of timeless beauty. 126

And that one who in his prophetic sight
  foretold the evil days of the Sweet Bride
  won by the spear and nails, sits on his right. 129

While by the other father and first man
  sits the great leader to whom manna fell
  to feed an ingrate and rebellious clan. 132

Across the circle from Peter, behold Anna.
  She feels such bliss in looking at her daughter
  she does not move her eyes to sing 'Hosanna!' 135

And opposite the father of us all
  sits Lucy, who first urged your lady to you
  when you were blindly bent toward your own fall. 138

But the time allowed for this dream vision flies.
  As a tailor must cut the gown from what cloth is given,
  just so must we move on, turning our eyes 141

to the Primal Love, that as your powers advance
  with looking toward him, you may penetrate
  as deep as may be through His radiance. 144

But lest you should fall backward when you flare
  your mortal wings, intending to mount higher,
  remember grace must be acquired through prayer. 147

Therefore I will pray that blessèd one
   who has the power to aid you in your need.
   See that you follow me with such devotion   150

your heart adheres to every word I say."
   And with those words the saint began to pray.

NOTES

1–3. *Still rapt in contemplation:* Of the Virgin. His eyes have not
left her. Nor do they turn again to Dante. Following his own preach-
ment in XXXI, 112–117, he keeps his eyes on high. The text per-
mits the assumption that Bernard turns his eyes from the Virgin to
look at the various parts of the Mystic Rose as he identifies them,
later, for Dante. Certainly, however, Bernard could identify every de-
tail of the Rose without having to look at it, and every quality of
Dante's mind and style would be better honored by thinking of
Bernard as staring adoringly on the Virgin throughout. *the vacant of-
fice of instruction:* Formerly held by Beatrice. *I still can hear:* A rhyme-
forced addition, not in Dante's text.

4–6. Mary, Mother of God, sits in the uppermost tier. At her feet
in the second tier sits Eve, Mother of Man. *the wound:* Original sin.
balm so sweet: Jesus. *opened:* The first fault, Eve's disobedience. *driven
deeper:* Her seduction of Adam, thus spreading sin to all mankind. *in
such great beauty:* Eve, having been created directly by God, was per-
fect in her beauty.

8–9. *Rachel . . . Beatrice at her side:* See *Inferno* II, 102: "Where I
was sitting with the ancient Rachel." Rachel, the younger wife of
Jacob, symbolizes the contemplative life, as her sister Leah, also
Jacob's wife, symbolizes the active life. In relation to Bernard she may
be taken allegorically to be Contemplation and he to be the Con-
templative Soul.

10–12. *Sarah:* Wife of Abraham. *Hebrews* xi, 11–14, cites her as
the mother (by miraculous fertility in her old age) of the Jews who
foresaw Christ's coming and believed in him. *Rebecca:* Wife of Isaac.
Judith: She killed Holofernes and freed the Jews. *and she:* Ruth,

great-grandmother of David. *that singer:* David. *who for his sins:* His lust for Bathsheba, wife of Uriah. In order to marry Bathsheba, David sent Uriah to his death in the first line of battle. David's lament is in *Psalm l.*

Thus, the first descending rank, down tier by tier from Mary, is made up of Hebrew women, mothers of the children of God.

18. *part . . . tresses:* As if the rose were a head of hair and that vertical row of Hebrew women formed a part in it. In the next line the part becomes a wall.

22. *in full bloom:* That half of the rose-stadium that holds the pre-Christian believers would naturally be completely filled. On the other side there are thrones waiting for those who have yet to win salvation through Christ Descended. Dante, in fact, is laboring to earn one of them for himself. The Day of Judgment will be upon mankind when the last throne is filled, for Heaven will then be complete.

32–33. *the Great John:* The Baptist. He denounced Herod Antipos and was beheaded two years before the Crucifixion. He had to wait in Limbo for two years, therefore, till Christ came for him at the Resurrection. For the Harrowing of Hell, see *Inferno* IV, 53, note.

40 ff. *below that tier:* The lower half of the rose-stadium contains the blessèd infants, the souls of those who died before they had achieved the true volition of reason and faith. They could not, therefore, win salvation by their own merit. *but by another's, under strict condition:* The necessary qualification for election is belief in Christ. These souls were too young at death to have formed their faith. Salvation is granted them not directly through belief in Christ but through the faith and prayers of their parents, relatives, and others of the faithful who interceded for them.

49. *many doubts:* The infants are ranked in tiers that indicate degrees of heavenly merit. But if they were saved through no merit of their own, how can one be more worthy than the other? Such is Dante's doubt, which Bernard goes on to set at rest by telling him, in essence, that God knows what He is doing.

58–59. *These . . . who had so short a pause:* The infants paused only briefly in the mortal life.

62. *dares:* I have no explanation of Dante's word choice here. "Not to dare" cannot fail to suggest intimidation. But in Paradise there can be no daring: every soul is in bliss exactly to the degree it is capable of bliss, and its capacity keeps increasing as it looks upon God. To dare (*ausare,* or in modern Italian, *osare*) must be taken as an impurity from the mortal vocabulary (in the sense of "even to think of") and not strictly of the heavenly tongue.

66. *the effect:* The cause is buried in God's mind. The effect must speak for itself.

67–72. The reference here is to Jacob and Esau. According to Genesis xxv, 21 ff., they were at odds while still in their mother's womb. (Cf. the legend of Polyneices and Eteocles, twin sons of Oedipus and Jocasta.) Dante follows St. Paul (*Romans* ix, 11–13) in interpreting the division between Jacob and Esau as a working of God's unfathomable will. "Even as it is written. Jacob I loved, but Esau I hated." Man can note the will of God in such matters ("the effect") but cannot plumb its causes. *according to the color of their hair:* For what may seem to be superficial reasons. Esau (*Genesis* xxv, 25) was red-headed.

81. *sufficient force:* To mount to Heaven.

84. *among the blind:* Among the souls of Hell. Such infants were assigned to Limbo.

85. *on her who most resembles Christ:* The Virgin Mary.

88–99. THE GLORY OF THE VIRGIN. As Bernard directs, Dante fixes his attention on Mary and beholds her blazing in a splendor that rains down upon her in a host of angel beings. These fly from God to the Rose and back again like bees between the hive and the flower, with the difference that these bees bring the rain of light to the flower and are themselves the glorious rain.

88. *that face:* Mary's.

94. *the same Love:* The archangel Gabriel, the Angel of the Annunciation. Dante seems to conceive of Gabriel suspended in air before her, repeating the blissful chant of the Annunciation as he had first hymned it in Nazareth.

112. *the victory:* (Dante says "the palm.") Of God's election. Some commentators gloss it as Mary's triumph over all other Jewish

women, all of whom would have been eager to bear the promised Messiah; and possibly so, but to be chosen by God would be triumph enough itself, and any thought of outshining the ladies of the neighborhood would be trivial by comparison.

118–126. *Those two:* Adam and St. Peter. Adam as Father of Mankind, Peter as Father of the Church. Note that Peter has the place of honor on the right.

127. *that one:* St. John the Evangelist. His *Apocalypse* was received as the prophetic book in which the entire history of the Church is foretold. He sits on Peter's right.

131. *that leader:* Moses. As the second great figure of the Old Testament he sits to the left of Adam.

133–135. *Anna:* Ste. Anna, Ste. Anne, mother of the Virgin. Her position directly across the circle from Peter's puts her to the right of John the Baptist. *does not move her eyes to sing 'Hosanna!':* Like all the other heavenly beings, she constantly sings the praise of God. All others, naturally enough, look up as they sing. She, however, is so filled with bliss by the sight of Mary that she does not turn her eyes from her blessèd daughter. She praises God while looking at Mary. This detail can be interpreted in many ways, but all of them, of course, must center on the special position of Mary in Catholic doctrine and feeling.

136–138. *Lucy:* See *Inferno* II, 97–100. It was she who first sent Beatrice to rescue Dante from the Dark Wood of Error. She sits opposite Adam. She would, accordingly, be to the left of John the Baptist.

139–141. The time granted for Dante's vision is limited. As a tailor must cut the gown from what cloth he is given, so Dante must get on with it, making what he can of his experience in the time allotted him.

142–144. In the act of looking at God man is given the power to see Him. Such is the gift of grace, and to the extent that grace is given, a man may see more or less deeply into God's glory.

148. *that blessed one:* Mary.

CANTO XXXIII

The Empyrean—St. Bernard · Prayer to the Virgin ·
The Vision of God

St. Bernard offers a lofty *Prayer to the Virgin,* asking her to inter-
cede in Dante's behalf, and in answer Dante feels his soul swell
with new power and grow calm in rapture as his eyes are per-
mitted the *Direct Vision of God.*

There can be no measure of how long the vision endures. It
passes, and Dante is once more mortal and fallible. Raised by
God's presence, he had looked into the Mystery and had begun
to understand its power and majesty. Returned to himself, there
is no power in him capable of speaking the truth of what he saw.
Yet the impress of the truth is stamped upon his soul, which he
now knows will return to be one with God's Love.

"Virgin Mother, daughter of thy son;
  humble beyond all creatures and more exalted;
  predestined turning point of God's intention;   3

thy merit so ennobled human nature
  that its divine Creator did not scorn
  to make Himself the creature of His creature.   6

The Love that was rekindled in Thy womb
  sends forth the warmth of the eternal peace
  within whose ray this flower has come to bloom.   9

Here, to us, thou art the noon and scope
  of Love revealed; and among mortal men,
  the living fountain of eternal hope.   12

Lady, thou art so near God's reckonings
  that who seeks grace and does not first seek thee
  would have his wish fly upward without wings.   15

Not only does thy sweet benignity
  flow out to all who beg, but oftentimes
  thy charity arrives before the plea.   18

In thee is pity, in thee munificence,
  in thee the tenderest heart, in thee unites
  all that creation knows of excellence!   21

Now comes this man who from the final pit
  of the universe up to this height has seen,
  one by one, the three lives of the spirit.   24

He prays to thee in fervent supplication
  for grace and strength, that he may raise his eyes
  to the all-healing final revelation.   27

And I, who never more desired to see
  the vision myself than I do that he may see It,
  add my own prayer, and pray that it may be   30

enough to move you to dispel the trace
  of every mortal shadow by thy prayers
  and let him see revealed the Sum of Grace.   33

I pray thee further, all-persuading Queen,
  keep whole the natural bent of his affections
  and of his powers after his eyes have seen.   36

Protect him from the stirrings of man's clay;
  see how Beatrice and the blessèd host
  clasp reverent hands to join me as I pray."   39

The eyes that God reveres and loves the best
  glowed on the speaker, making clear the joy
  with which true prayer is heard by the most blest. 42

Those eyes turned then to the Eternal Ray,
  through which, we must indeed believe, the eyes
  of others do not find such ready way.   45

And I, who neared the goal of all my nature,
  felt my soul, at the climax of its yearning,
  suddenly, as it ought, grow calm with rapture.   48

Bernard then, smiling sweetly, gestured to me
  to look up, but I had already become
  within myself all he would have me be.   51

Little by little as my vision grew
  it penetrated further through the aura
  of the high lamp which in Itself is true.   54

What then I saw is more than tongue can say.
  Our human speech is dark before the vision.
  The ravished memory swoons and falls away.   57

As one who sees in dreams and wakes to find
  the emotional impression of his vision
  still powerful while its parts fade from his mind—   60

just such am I, having lost nearly all
  the vision itself, while in my heart I feel
  the sweetness of it yet distill and fall.   63

So, in the sun, the footprints fade from snow.
  On the wild wind that bore the tumbling leaves
  the Sybil's oracles were scattered so.   66

O Light Supreme who doth Thyself withdraw
  so far above man's mortal understanding,
  lend me again some glimpse of what I saw;   69

make Thou my tongue so eloquent it may
  of all Thy glory speak a single clue
  to those who follow me in the world's day;   72

for by returning to my memory
  somewhat, and somewhat sounding in these verses,
  Thou shalt show man more of Thy victory.   75

So dazzling was the splendor of that Ray,
  that I must certainly have lost my senses
  had I, but for an instant, turned away.   78

And so it was, as I recall, I could
  the better bear to look, until at last
  my vision made one with the Eternal Good.   81

Oh grace abounding that had made me fit
  to fix my eyes on the eternal light
  until my vision was consumed in it!   84

I saw within Its depth how It conceives
  all things in a single volume bound by Love,
  of which the universe is the scattered leaves;   87

substance, accident, and their relation
  so fused that all I say could do no more
  than yield a glimpse of that bright revelation.   90

I think I saw the universal form
  that binds these things, for as I speak these words
  I feel my joy swell and my spirits warm.   93

Twenty-five centuries since Neptune saw
  the Argo's keel have not moved all mankind,
  recalling that adventure, to such awe   96

as I felt in an instant. My tranced being
　stared fixed and motionless upon that vision,
　ever more fervent to see in the act of seeing.　　99

Experiencing that Radiance, the spirit
　is so indrawn it is impossible
　even to think of ever turning from It.　　102

For the good which is the will's ultimate object
　is all subsumed in It; and, being removed,
　all is defective which in It is perfect.　　105

Now in my recollection of the rest
　I have less power to speak than any infant
　wetting its tongue yet at its mother's breast;　　108

and not because that Living Radiance bore
　more than one semblance, for It is unchanging
　and is forever as it was before;　　111

rather, as I grew worthier to see,
　the more I looked, the more unchanging semblance
　appeared to change with every change in me.　　114

Within the depthless deep and clear existence
　of that abyss of light three circles shown—
　three in color, one in circumference:　　117

the second from the first, rainbow from rainbow;
　the third, an exhalation of pure fire
　equally breathed forth by the other two.　　120

But oh how much my words miss my conception,
　which is itself so far from what I saw
　that to call it feeble would be rank deception!　　123

O Light Eternal fixed in Itself alone,
  by Itself alone understood, which from Itself
  loves and glows, self-knowing and self-known;   126

that second aureole which shone forth in Thee,
  conceived as a reflection of the first—
  or which appeared so to my scrutiny—   129

seemed in Itself of Its own coloration
  to be painted with man's image. I fixed my eyes
  on that alone in rapturous contemplation.   132

Like a geometer wholly dedicated
  to squaring the circle, but who cannot find,
  think as he may, the principle indicated—   135

so did I study the supernal face.
  I yearned to know just how our image merges
  into that circle, and how it there finds place;   138

but mine were not the wings for such a flight.
  Yet, as I wished, the truth I wished for came
  cleaving my mind in a great flash of light.   141

Here my powers rest from their high fantasy,
  but already I could feel my being turned—
  instinct and intellect balanced equally   144

as in a wheel whose motion nothing jars—
  by the Love that moves the Sun and the other stars.

NOTES

1–39. ST. BERNARD'S PRAYER TO THE VIRGIN MARY.
No reader who has come this far will need a lengthy gloss of

Bernard's prayer. It can certainly be taken as a summarizing state-
ment of the special place of Mary in Catholic faith. For the rest only
a few turns of phrase need underlining. 3. *predestined turning point of
God's intention:* All-foreseeing God built his whole scheme for
mankind with Mary as its pivot, for through her He would become
man. 7. *The Love that was rekindled in thy womb:* God. In a sense he
withdrew from man when Adam and Eve sinned. In Mary He re-
turned and Himself became man. 35. *keep whole the natural bent of his
affections:* Bernard is asking Mary to protect Dante lest the intensity
of the vision overpower his faculties. 37. *Protect him from the stirrings
of man's clay:* Protect him from the stirrings of base human impulse,
especially from pride, for Dante is about to receive a grace never be-
fore granted to any man and the thought of such glory might well
move a mere mortal to a hubris that would turn glory to sinfullness.

40. *the eyes:* Of Mary.

50. *but I had already become:* i.e., "But I had already fixed my en-
tire attention upon the vision of God." But if so, how could Dante
have seen Bernard's smile and gesture? Eager students like to believe
they catch Dante in a contradiction here. Let them bear in mind that
Dante is looking directly at God, as do the souls of Heaven, who
thereby acquire—insofar as they are able to contain it—God's own
knowledge. As a first stirring of that heavenly power, therefore,
Dante is sharing God's knowledge of St. Bernard.

54. *which in Itself is true:* The light of God is the one light whose
source is Itself. All others are a reflection of this.

65–66. *tumbling leaves . . . oracles:* The Cumean Sybil (Virgil de-
scribes her in *Aeneid* III, 441 ff.) wrote her oracles on leaves, one let-
ter to a leaf, then sent her message scattering on the wind.
Presumably, the truth was all contained in that strew, could one only
gather all the leaves and put the letters in the right order.

76–81. How can a light be so dazzling that the beholder would
swoon if he looked away for an instant? Would it not be, rather, in
looking at, not away from, the overpowering vision that the viewer's
senses would be overcome? So it would be on earth. But now Dante,
with the help of all heaven's prayers, is in the presence of God and
strengthened by all he sees. It is by being so strengthened that he can

see yet more. So the passage becomes a parable of grace. Stylistically it once more illustrates Dante's genius: even at this height of concept, the poet can still summon and invent new perceptions, subtlety exfoliating from subtlety.

The simultaneous metaphoric statement, of course, is that no man can lose his good in the vision of God, but only in looking away from it.

85–87. The idea here is Platonic: the essence of all things (form) exists in the mind of God. All other things exist as example.

88. *substance:* Matter, all that exists in itself. *accident:* All that exists as a phase of matter.

92. *these things:* Substance and accident.

109–114. In the presence of God the soul grows ever more capable of perceiving God. Thus, the worthy soul's experience of God is a constant expansion of awareness. God appears to change as He is better seen. Being perfect, He is changeless within himself, for any change would be away from perfection.

130–144. The central metaphor of the entire *Comedy* is the image of God and the final triumphant inGodding of the elected soul returning to its Maker. On the mystery of that image, the metaphoric symphony of the *Comedy* comes to rest.

In the second aspect of Trinal-unity, in the circle reflected from the first, Dante thinks he sees the image of mankind woven into the very substance and coloration of God. He turns the entire attention of his soul to that mystery, as a geometer might seek to shut out every other thought and dedicate himself to squaring the circle. In *Il Convivio* II, 14, Dante asserted that the circle could not be squared, but that impossibility had not yet been firmly demonstrated in Dante's time and mathematicians still worked at the problem. Note, however, that Dante assumes the impossibility of squaring the circle as a weak mortal example of mortal impossibility. How much more impossible, he implies, to resolve the mystery of God, study as man will.

The mystery remains beyond Dante's mortal power. Yet, there in Heaven, in a moment of grace, God revealed the truth to him in a flash of light—revealed it, that is, to the God-enlarged power of

Dante's emparadised soul. On Dante's return to the mortal life, the details of that revelation vanished from his mind but the force of the revelation survives in its power on Dante's feelings.

So ends the vision of the *Comedy,* and yet the vision endures, for ever since that revelation, Dante tells us, he feels his soul turning ever as one with the perfect motion of God's love.

A Note on the Type

The principal text of this Modern Library edition
was set in a digitized version of Bembo, a typeface
based on an old-style Roman face that was used
for Cardinal Bembo's tract *De Aetna* in 1495.
Bembo was cut by Francisco Griffo in the early
sixteenth century. The Lanston Monotype
Machine Company of Philadelphia brought
the well-proportioned letter forms of
Bembo to the United States
in the 1930s.